Microsoft® Excel 97 Illustrated Basic

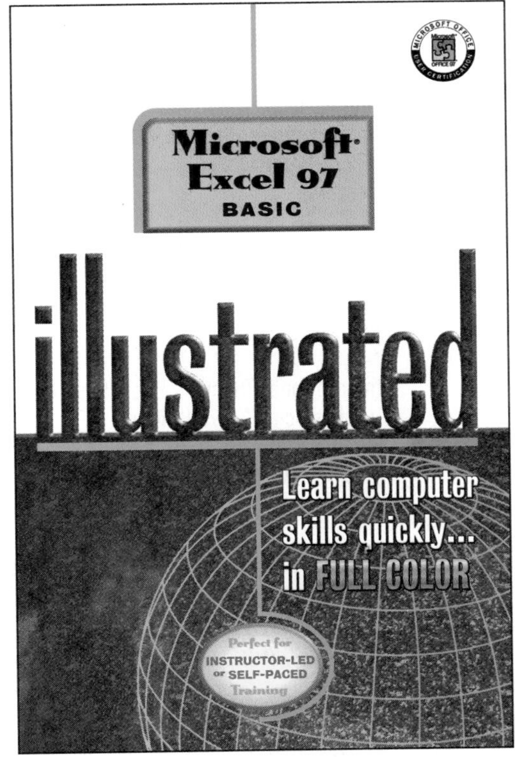

Elizabeth Eisner Reding
Tara Lynn O'Keefe

COURSE TECHNOLOGY
ONE MAIN STREET, CAMBRIDGE, MA 02142

an International Thomson Publishing company I(T)P®

Cambridge • Albany • Bonn • Boston • Cincinnati • London • Madrid • Melbourne • Mexico City
New York • Paris • San Francisco • Singapore • Tokyo • Toronto • Washington

Microsoft Excel 97—Illustrated Basic is published by Course Technology

Managing Editor: Nicole Jones Pinard
Product Manager: Kim T. M. Crowley
Production Editor: Christine Spillett
Developmental Editor: Meta Chaya Hirschi
Composition House: GEX, Inc.
QA Manuscript Reviewers: Chris Hall, John McCarthy, Brian McCooey
Text Designer: Joseph Lee
Cover Designer: Ulrike Balke—AdRules Art & Design—Heather Reid & Associates

For more information contact:

Course Technology
One Main Street
Cambridge, MA 02142
1-800-648-7450

International Thomson Publishing Europe
Berkshire House 168-173
High Holborn
London WC1V 7AA
England

Thomas Nelson Australia
102 Dodds Street
South Melbourne, 3205
Victoria, Australia

Nelson Canada
1120 Birchmount Road
Scarborough, Ontario
Canada M1K 5G4

International Thomson Editores
Campos Eliseos 385, Piso 7
Col. Polanco
11560 Mexico D.F. Mexico

International Thomson Publishing GmbH
Konigswinterer Strasse 418
53277 Bonn
Germany

International Thomson Publishing Asia
211 Henderson Road
#05-10 Henderson Building
Singapore 0315

International Thomson Publishing Japan
Hirakawacho Kyowa Building, 3F
2-2-1 Hirakawacho
Chiyoda-ku, Tokyo 102
Japan

ISBN 0-7600-5819-9

Printed in the United States of America

10 9 8 7 6

From the Illustrated Series™ Team

At Course Technology we believe that technology will transform the way that people teach and learn. We are setting a new standard for learning materials that are both practical and exciting to use. Our goal is to revolutionize training in the workplace by providing affordable and interesting tools that maximize technology.

► The Development Process

Our development process is unparalleled in the corporate education industry. Every product we create goes through an exacting process of design, development, review, and testing.

Reviewers give us direction and insight that shape our materials and bring them up to the latest standards. Every manual is quality tested. Our Quality Assurance (QA) testers work through every keystroke, carefully checking for clarity and pointing out errors in logic and sequence. Together with our own technical reviewers, these testers help us ensure that everything that carries our name is as error-free and easy to use as possible.

► The Products

Illustrated manuals work twice as hard, because they are the only manuals that work in instructor-led *or* self-paced study environments. Illustrated manuals are also the *only* full-color training offering available—and at a reasonable price.

Our time-tested, step-by-step instructions provide unparalleled clarity. Examples and applications are chosen and crafted to motivate learners and get them up and running quickly.

In order to provide training on just the right content, our Illustrated manuals come in three levels. Illustrated Basic manuals contain only the basic skills for working with a single program. Illustrated Intermediate manuals assume a basic understanding of the program and progress through more-complex skills from there. Illustrated Advanced manuals pick up where Intermediate manuals leave off, giving you the most advanced skills coverage.

The back cover of this manual lists the applications for which Illustrated manuals are available and also provides a handy task reference for the most commonly performed Excel 97 skills.

Preface

Welcome to *Microsoft Excel 97 — Illustrated Basic!* This book in our highly visual design offers new users a hands-on introduction to Microsoft Excel 97 and also serves as an excellent reference for future use. This book is part of an integrated learning system consisting of three manuals providing progressive training in Microsoft Excel 97. If you would like additional coverage of Microsoft Excel 97, we also offer *Microsoft Excel 97 — Illustrated Intermediate* and *Microsoft Excel 97 — Illustrated Advanced,* logical continuations of the Basic edition. These three manuals, when used in conjunction with one another, can serve as courseware for the Certified Microsoft Office User (CMOU) program. After completing the units in these books, you will be prepared to take the Proficient level CMOU exam for Microsoft Excel 97. By passing the certification exam, you demonstrate to employers your proficiency in Excel 97. CMOU exams are offered at participating test centers, participating corporations, and participating employment agencies. For more information about certification, visit the CMOU program World Wide Web site at http://www.microsoft.com/office/train_cert/.

▶ Organization and Coverage

This text contains five units that cover basic Excel skills. In these units students learn how to design, create, edit, and enhance Excel worksheets, and how to create charts to illustrate worksheet data.

▶ About This Approach

The Illustrated approach is designed to help make your workers more productive. It also works to help them to retain useful information. The skills your workers learn from these manuals can be immediately applied to their daily tasks. The manuals are ideal reference tools for after the training is completed, and, when used as such, can lower the demands on your internal technical support staff.

What makes the Illustrated approach so effective at teaching software skills? It's quite simple. Each skill is presented on two facing pages, with the step-by-step instructions on the left page, and large screen illustrations on the right. Learners can focus on a single skill without having to turn the page. The manual's hands-on approach makes it ideal for both self-paced or instructor-led classes. Its unique

Each two-page spread focuses on a single skill.

Concise text that introduces the basic principles in the lesson and integrates a brief case study.

Excel 97

Changing Attributes and Alignment of Labels

Attributes are font styling features such as bold, italics, and underlining. You can apply bold, italics, and underlining from the Formatting toolbar or from the Font tab in the Format Cells dialog box. You can also change the alignment of text in cells. Left, right, or center alignment can be applied from the Formatting toolbar, or from the Alignment tab in the Format Cells dialog box. See Table C-2 for a description of the available attribute and alignment buttons on the Formatting toolbar. Excel also has predefined worksheet formats to make formatting easier. Now that he has applied the appropriate fonts and font sizes to his worksheet labels, Evan wants to further enhance his worksheet's appearance by adding bold and underline formatting and centering some of the labels.

Steps

1. Press [Ctrl][Home] to select cell A1, then click the Bold button on the Formatting toolbar
   The title "Advertising Expenses" appears in bold.
2. Select the range A3:J3, then click the Underline button on the Formatting toolbar
   Excel underlines the column headings in the selected range.
3. Click cell A3, click the Italics button on the Formatting toolbar, then click
   The word "Type" appears in boldface, italic type. Notice that the Bold, Italics, and Underline buttons on the Formatting toolbar are indented. You decide you don't like the italic formatting. You remove it by clicking again.
4. Click
   Excel removes italics from cell A3.
5. Add bold formatting to the rest of the labels in the range B3:J3
   You want to center the title over the data.
6. Select the range A1:F1, then click the Merge and Center button on the Formatting toolbar
   The title Advertising Expenses is centered across six columns. Now you center the column headings in their cells.
7. Select the range A3:J3 then click the Center button on the Formatting toolbar
   You are satisfied with the formatting in the worksheet.
   Compare your screen to Figure C-8.

CourseHelp
The camera icon indicates there is a CourseHelp available with this lesson. Click the Start button, point to programs, point to CourseHelp, then click Word 97 Illustrated. Choose the CourseHelp that corresponds to this lesson.

QuickTip
Highlighting information on a worksheet can be useful, but overuse of any attribute can be distracting and make a document less readable. Be consistent by adding emphasis the same way throughout a workbook.

Time To
✔ Save

TABLE C-2: Attribute and Alignment buttons on the Formatting toolbar

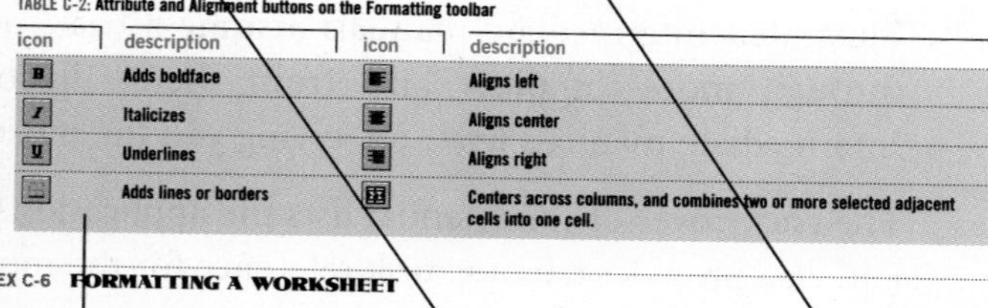

icon	description	icon	description
B	Adds boldface		Aligns left
I	Italicizes		Aligns center
U	Underlines		Aligns right
	Adds lines or borders		Centers across columns, and combines two or more selected adjacent cells into one cell.

▶ EX C-6 FORMATTING A WORKSHEET

Quickly accessible summaries of key terms, toolbar buttons, or keyboard alternatives are incorporated into the lesson material. Students can easily refer to this information when working on their own projects at a later time.

Hints as well as trouble-shooting advice are right where you need them – next to the step itself.

Clear step-by-step directions, with what students are to type in red, explain how to complete the specific task.

Every lesson features large, full-color representations of what the screen should look like as students complete the numbered steps.

The innovative design draws the students' eyes to important areas of the screens.

Brightly colored tabs above the program name indicate which section of the book you are in. Useful for finding your place within the book and for referencing information from the index.

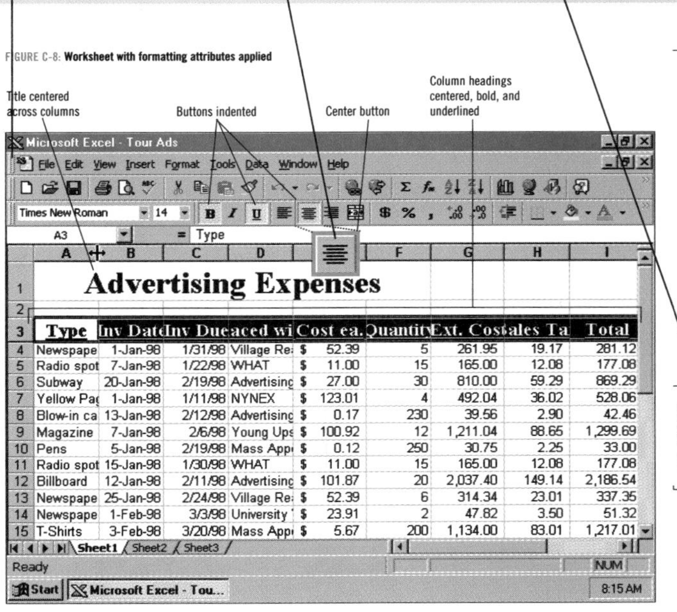

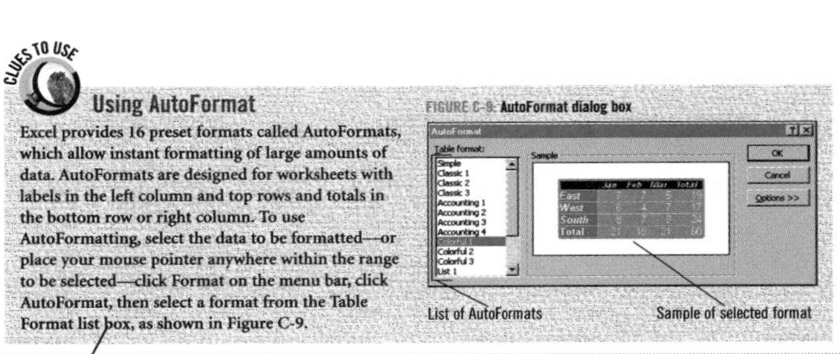
CLUES TO USE

Using AutoFormat

Excel provides 16 preset formats called AutoFormats, which allow instant formatting of large amounts of data. AutoFormats are designed for worksheets with labels in the left column and top rows and totals in the bottom row or right column. To use AutoFormatting, select the data to be formatted—or place your mouse pointer anywhere within the range to be selected—click Format on the menu bar, click AutoFormat, then select a format from the Table Format list box, as shown in Figure C-9.

FORMATTING A WORKSHEET EX C-7

Clues to Use Boxes provide concise information that either expands on the major lesson skill or describes an independent task that in some way relates to the major lesson skill.

The page numbers are designed like a road map. *EX* indicates the Excel section, *C* indicates the third unit, and *7* indicates the page within the unit. This map allows for the greatest flexibility in content – each unit stands completely on its own.

design makes information extremely accessible and easy to absorb, and provides a great reference for after the course is over. The modular structure of the book also allows for maximum flexibility; you can cover the units in any order you choose.

Each lesson, or "information display," contains the elements shown at left:

Other Features

The two-page lesson format featured in this book provides the new user with a powerful learning experience. Additionally, this book contains the following features:

▶ Real-World Case

The case study used throughout the textbook, a fictitious company called Nomad Ltd, is designed to be real-world in nature and introduces the kinds of activities people will encounter on the job. With a real-world case, the process of solving problems will be more meaningful to students.

▶ End of Unit Material

The single aspect most lacking in training materials today is the opportunity to practice. Illustrated manuals have just enough practice materials for trainers to assign or learners to progress through on their own. People learn by doing—it's a fact.

Each unit concludes with a Concepts Review that tests students' understanding of what they learned in the unit. A Skills Review follows the Concepts Review and provides students with additional hands-on practice of the skills they learned in the unit. The Skills Review is followed by Independent Challenges, which pose case problems for students to solve. At least one Independent Challenge in each unit asks students to use the World Wide Web to solve the problem, as indicated by a WebWork icon. The Visual Workshops that follow the Independent Challenges help students develop critical-thinking skills. Students are shown completed documents and must re-create them from scratch.

Instructor's Resource Kit

The Instructor's Resource Kit is Course Technology's way of putting into your hands the resources and information needed to teach and learn effectively. With an integrated array of teaching and learning tools that offer a broad range of instructional options, we believe that this kit represents the highest-quality and most cutting-edge resources available to corporate instructors today. The resources included with this book are:

Course Online Student Companion This book features its own Course Online Companion, where students can go to access Web sites that will help them complete the WebWork Independent Challenges.

Student files To use this book, you must have the student files. These files are contained on a diskette in the envelope affixed to the back cover of this book. Users of this text are granted the right to post the student files on any stand-alone computer or network.

Instructor's Guide in PDF format This is quality-assurance tested and includes:

- Solutions to all lessons and end-of-unit material
- Unit notes with teaching tips from the author
- Extra Independent Challenges
- Transparency Masters of key concepts
- Student Files
- Adobe Acrobat Reader

Contents

Excel 97

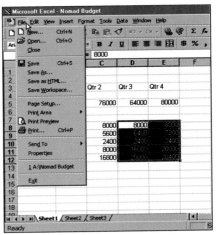

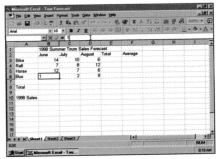

Contents

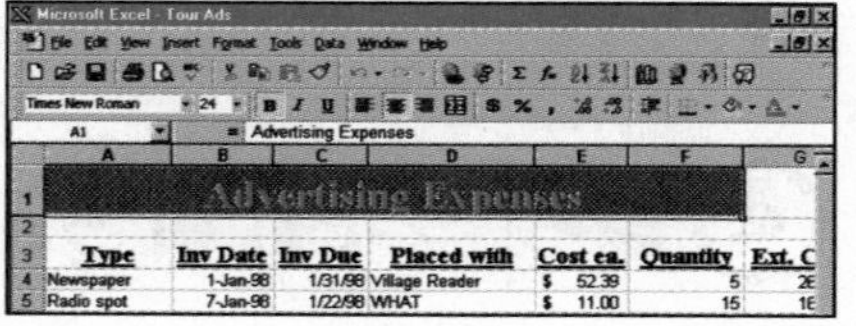

Advertising Expenses
Type
Inv Date
Inv Due
Placed with
Cost ea.
Quantity
Newspaper
Radio spot

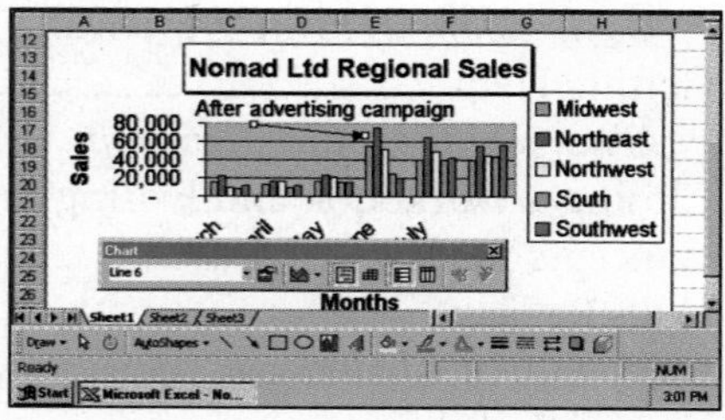

Nomad Ltd Regional Sales
After advertising campaign
Sales
80,000
60,000
40,000
20,000
Midwest
Northeast
Northwest
South
Southwest
Months

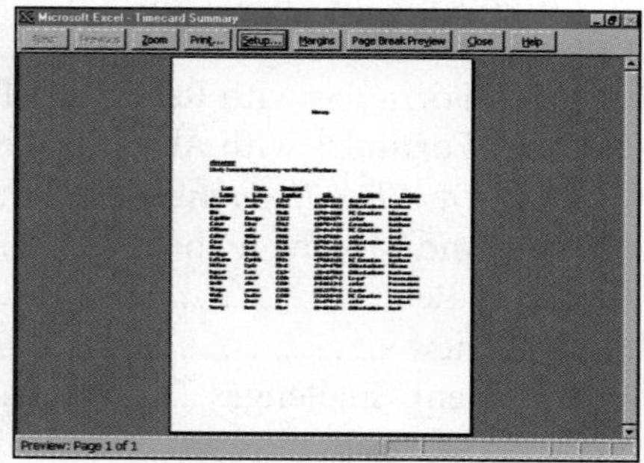

Excel 97

Getting
Started with Excel 97

Objectives

- ► Define spreadsheet software
- ► Start Excel 97
- ► View the Excel window
- ► Open and save an existing workbook
- ► Enter labels and values
- ► Preview and print a worksheet
- ► Get Help
- ► Close a workbook and exit Excel

In this unit, you will learn how to start Excel and recognize and use different elements of the Excel window and menus. You will also learn how to open existing files, enter data in a worksheet, and use the extensive online Help system. Evan Brillstein works in the Accounting Department at Nomad Ltd, an outdoor sporting gear and adventure travel company. Evan will use Excel to complete a worksheet that summarizes budget information and create a workbook to track tour sales.

Excel 97

Defining Spreadsheet Software

Excel is an electronic spreadsheet that runs on Windows computers. An **electronic spreadsheet** uses a computer to perform numeric calculations rapidly and accurately. See Table A-1 for common ways spreadsheets are used in business. An electronic spreadsheet is also referred to as a **worksheet**, which is the document that you produce when you use Excel. A worksheet created with Excel allows Evan to work quickly and efficiently, and to update the results accurately and easily. He will be able to produce more professional-looking documents with Excel. Figure A-1 shows a budget worksheet that Evan and his manager created using pencil and paper. Figure A-2 shows the same worksheet that they can create using Excel.

Details

Excel is better than the paper system for the following reasons:

Enter data quickly and accurately
With Excel, Evan can enter information faster and more accurately than he could using the pencil-and-paper method. For example, in the Nomad Ltd. Budget, Evan can use Excel to calculate Total Expenses and Net Income for each quarter by simply supplying the data and formulas, and Excel calculates the rest.

Recalculate easily
Fixing errors using Excel is easy, and any results based on a changed entry are recalculated automatically. If Evan receives updated Expense figures for Qtr 4, he can simply enter the new numbers and Excel will recalculate the spreadsheet.

Perform what-if analysis
One of the most powerful decision-making features of Excel is the ability to change data and then quickly recalculate changed results. Anytime you use a worksheet to answer the question "what if," you are performing a what-if analysis. For instance, if the advertising budget for May were increased to $3,000, Evan could enter the new figure into the spreadsheet and immediately find out the impact on the overall budget.

Change the appearance of information
Excel provides powerful features for enhancing a spreadsheet so that information is visually appealing and easy to understand. Evan can use boldface type and shading to add emphasis to key data in the worksheet.

Create charts
Excel makes it easy to create charts based on information in a worksheet. With Excel, charts are automatically updated as data changes. The worksheet in Figure A-2 includes a pie chart that graphically shows the distribution of Nomad Ltd. expenses for the first quarter.

Share information with other users
Because everyone at Nomad is now using Microsoft Office, it's easy for Evan to share information with his colleagues. If Evan wants to use the data from someone else's worksheet, he accesses their files through the network or by disk. For example, Evan can complete the budget for Nomad Ltd. that his manager started creating in Excel.

Create new worksheets from existing ones quickly
It's easy for Evan to take an existing Excel worksheet and quickly modify it to create a new one. When Evan is ready to create next year's budget, he can use this budget as a starting point.

FIGURE A-1: Traditional paper worksheet

Nomad Ltd					
	Qtr 1	Qtr 2	Qtr 3	Qtr 4	Total
Net Sales	48,000	76,000	64,000	80,000	268,000
Expenses:					
Salary	8,000	8,000	8,000	8,000	32,000
Interest	4,800	5,600	6,400	7,200	24,000
Rent	2,400	2,400	2,400	2,400	9,600
Ads	3,600	8,000	16,000	20,000	47,600
COG	16,000	16,800	20,000	20,400	73,200
Total Exp	34,800	40,800	52,800	58,000	186,400
Net Income	13,200	35,200	11,200	22,000	81,600

FIGURE A-2: Excel worksheet

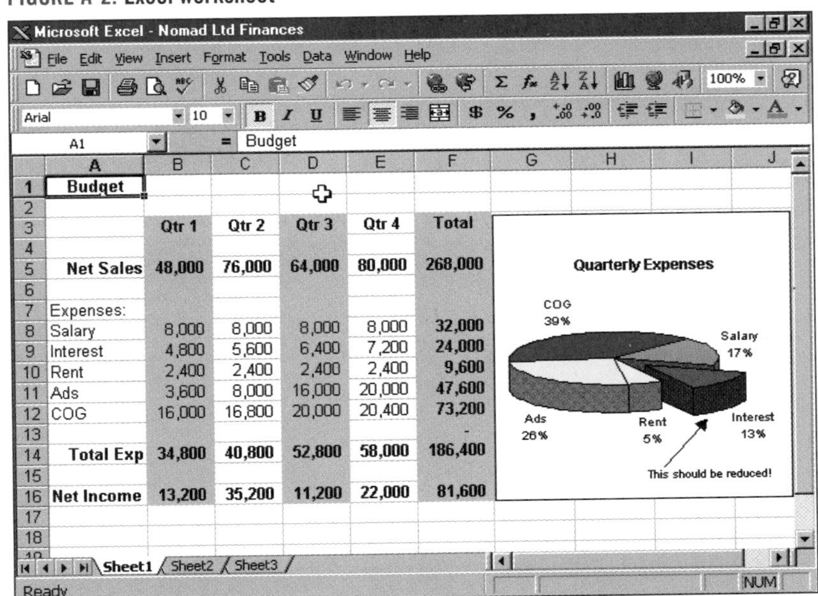

	A	B	C	D	E	F
1	Budget					
2						
3		Qtr 1	Qtr 2	Qtr 3	Qtr 4	Total
4						
5	Net Sales	48,000	76,000	64,000	80,000	268,000
6						
7	Expenses:					
8	Salary	8,000	8,000	8,000	8,000	32,000
9	Interest	4,800	5,600	6,400	7,200	24,000
10	Rent	2,400	2,400	2,400	2,400	9,600
11	Ads	3,600	8,000	16,000	20,000	47,600
12	COG	16,000	16,800	20,000	20,400	73,200
13						-
14	Total Exp	34,800	40,800	52,800	58,000	186,400
15						
16	Net Income	13,200	35,200	11,200	22,000	81,600

TABLE A-1: Common business spreadsheet uses

use	solution
Maintenance of values	Calculation of figures
Visual representation of values	Chart based on worksheet figures
Create consecutively numbered pages using multiple workbook sheets	Report containing workbook sheets
Organize data	Sort data in ascending or descending order
Analyze data	PivotTable or AutoFilter to create data summaries and short-lists
Create what-if data situations	Scenarios containing data outcomes using variable values

Excel 97

Starting Excel 97

To start Excel, you use the Start Button on the taskbar. Click Programs, then click the Microsoft Excel program icon. A slightly different procedure might be required for computers on a network and those that use utility programs to enhance Windows 95. If you need assistance, ask your instructor or technical support person for help. Evan's manager has started creating the Nomad Ltd budget and has asked Evan to finish it. He begins by starting Excel now.

1. **Point to the Start button on the taskbar**
   The Start button is on the left side of the taskbar and is used to start, or launch, programs on your computer.
2. **Click Start**
   Microsoft Excel is located in the Programs group—located at the top of the Start menu, as shown in Figure A-3.
3. **Point to Programs on the Start menu**
   All the programs, or applications, found on your computer can be found in this area of the Start menu.
   You can see the Microsoft Excel icon and other Microsoft programs, as shown in Figure A-4. Your desktop might look different depending on the programs installed on your computer.
4. **Click the Microsoft Excel program icon on the Program menu**
   Excel opens and a blank worksheet appears. In the next lesson, you will familiarize yourself with the elements of the Excel worksheet window.

Trouble?
If you don't see the Microsoft Excel icon, look for a program group called Microsoft Office.

Trouble?
If the Office Assistant appears on your screen, simply choose to start Excel.

FIGURE A-3: **Start menu**

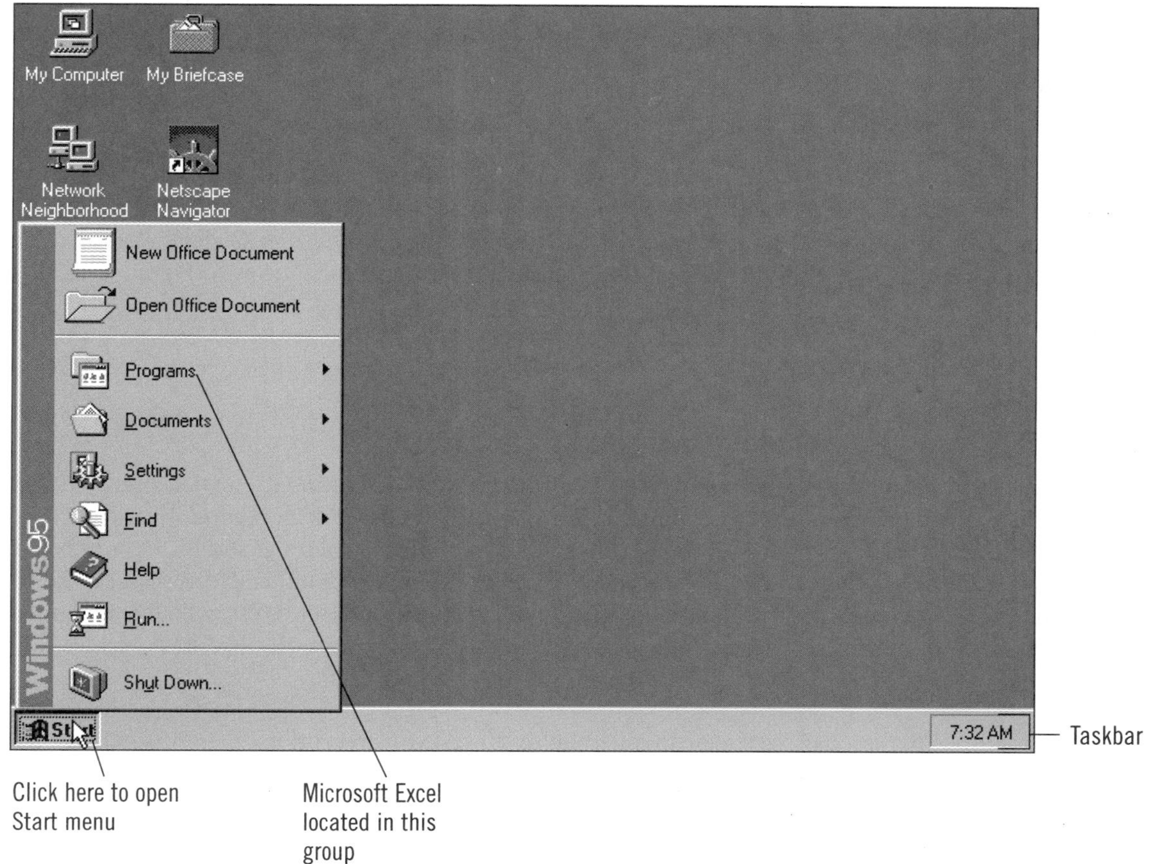

FIGURE A-4: **Programs available on your computer**

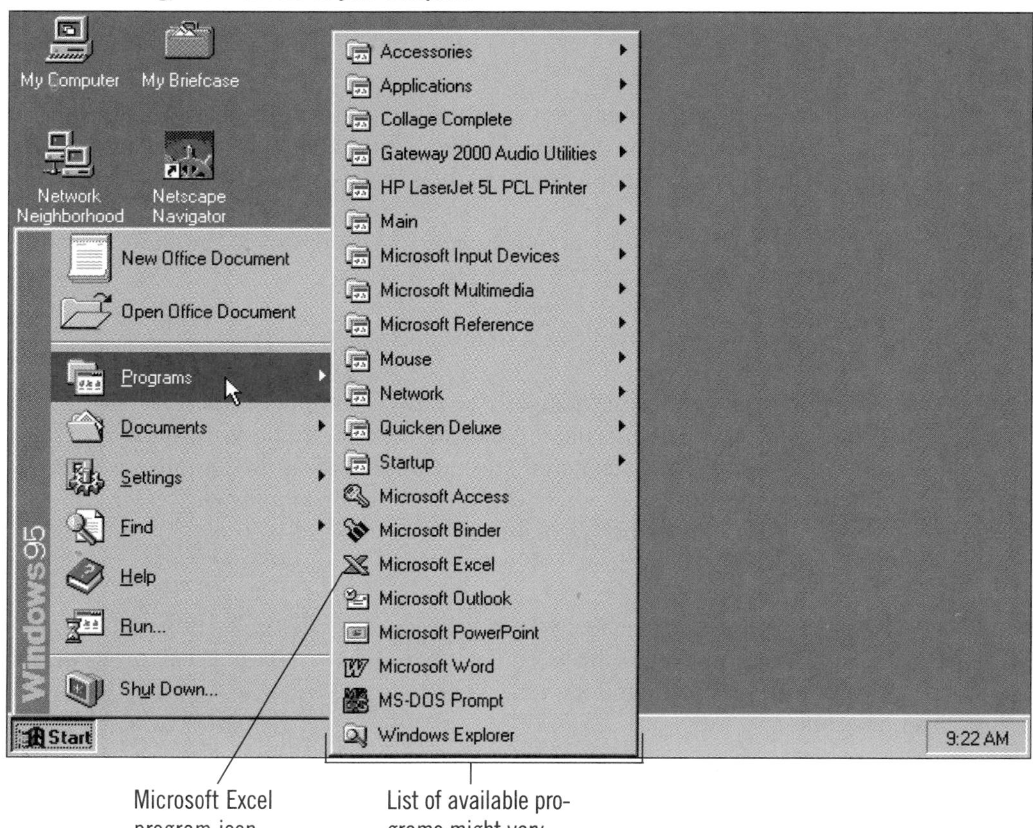

Excel 97

Viewing the Excel Window

When you start Excel, the computer displays the **worksheet window**, the area where you enter data, and the window elements that enable you to create and work with worksheets. Evan needs to familiarize himself with the Excel worksheet window and its elements before he starts working with the budget worksheet. Compare the descriptions below to Figure A-5.

Trouble?

If your worksheet does not fill the screen as shown in Figure A-5, click the Maximize button in the worksheet window.

The **worksheet window** contains a grid of columns and rows. Columns are labeled alphabetically (A, B, C, etc.) and rows are labeled numerically (1, 2, 3, etc.). The worksheet window displays only a tiny fraction of the whole worksheet, which has a total of 256 columns and 65,533 rows. The intersection of a column and a row is a **cell**. Cells can contain text, numbers, formulas, or a combination of all three. Every cell has its own unique location or **cell address**, which is identified by the coordinates of the intersecting column and row. For example, the cell address of the cell in the upper-left corner of a worksheet is A1.

The **cell pointer** is a dark rectangle that highlights the cell you are working in, or the **active cell**. In Figure A-5, the cell pointer is located at A1, so A1 is the active cell. To make another cell active, click any other cell or press the arrow keys on your keyboard to move the cell pointer to another cell in the worksheet.

The **title bar** displays the program name (Microsoft Excel) and the filename of the open worksheet (in this case, Book1). The title bar also contains a control menu box, a Close button, and resizing buttons.

The **menu bar** contains menus from which you choose Excel commands. As with all Windows programs, you can choose a menu command by clicking it with the mouse or by pressing [Alt] plus the underlined letter in the menu name, referred to as the command's **shortcut key**.

The **name box** displays the active cell address. In Figure A-5, "A1" appears in the name box, indicating that A1 is the active cell.

The **formula bar** allows you to enter or edit data in the worksheet.

The **toolbars** contain buttons for the most frequently used Excel commands. The **Standard** toolbar is located just below the menu bar and contains buttons corresponding to the most frequently used Excel features. The **Formatting** toolbar contains buttons for the most common commands used for improving the worksheet's appearance. To choose a button, simply click it with the left mouse button. The face of any button has a graphic representation of its function; for instance, the Printing button has a printer on its face.

Sheet tabs below the worksheet grid enable you to keep your work in collections called **workbooks**. Each workbook contains 3 worksheets by default and can contain a maximum of 255 sheets. Sheet tabs can be given meaningful names. **Sheet tab scrolling buttons** help you move from one sheet to another.

The **status bar** is located at the bottom of the Excel window. The left side of the status bar provides a brief description of the active command or task in progress. The right side of the status bar shows the status of important keys, such as the Caps Lock key and the Num Lock key.

FIGURE A-5: **Excel worksheet window elements**

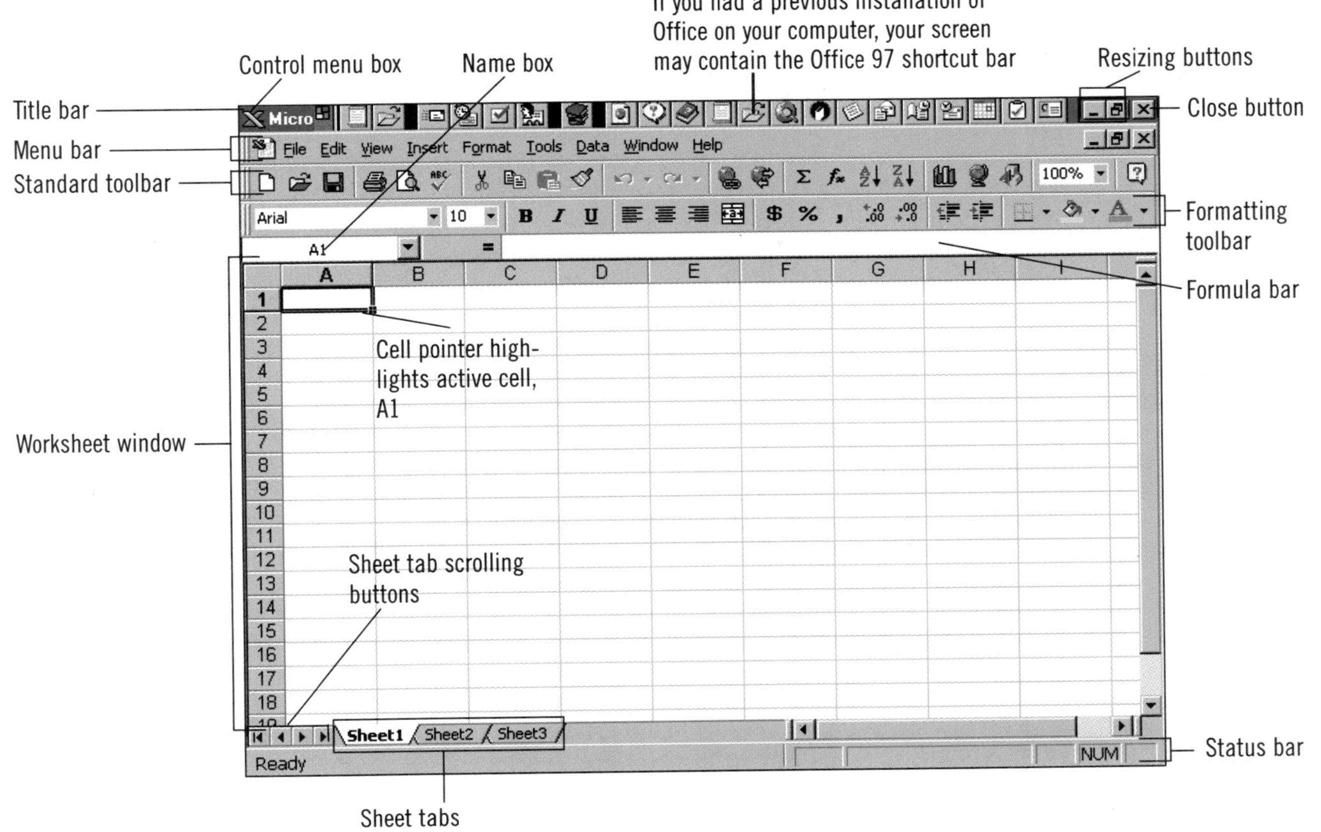

Excel 97

Excel 97

Opening and Saving an Existing Workbook

Sometimes it's more efficient to create a new worksheet by modifying one that already exists. This saves you from having to retype information. Throughout this book, you will be instructed to open a file from your Student Disk, use the Save As command to create a copy of the file with a new name, and then modify the new file by following the lesson steps. Saving the files with new names keeps your original Student Disk files intact in case you have to start the lesson over again or you wish to repeat an exercise. Evan's manager has asked Evan to enter information into the Nomad Ltd budget. Follow along as Evan opens the Budget workbook, then uses the Save As command to create a copy with a new name.

Trouble?

If necessary, you can download your student files from our Web Site at http:\\course.com.

1. ~~Insert your Student Disk in the appropriate disk drive~~ unzipped
2. Click the **Open button** on the Standard toolbar Ctl O – File open
   The Open dialog box opens. See Figure A-6.
3. Click the **Look in list arrow**
   A list of the available drives appears. Locate the drive that contains your Student Disk.
4. C: → Click the drive that contains your Student Disk
   A list of the files on your Student Disk appears in the Look in list box, with the default filename placeholder in the File name text box already selected.
5. In the File name list box click **XL A-1**, then click **Open**
   The file XL A-1 opens. You could also double-click the filename in the File name list box to open the file. To create and save a copy of this file with a new name, you use the Save As command.
6. Click **File** on the menu bar, then click **Save As**
   The Save As dialog box opens.
7. Make sure the Save in list box displays the drive containing your Student Disk
   You should save all your files to your Student Disk, unless instructed otherwise.
8. In the File name text box, double-click the current file name to select it (if necessary), then type **Nomad Budget** as shown in Figure A-7.
9. Click **Save** to save the file and close the Save As dialog box, then click **OK** to close the Summary Info dialog box if necessary
   The file XL A-1 closes, and a duplicate file named Nomad Budget opens, as shown in Figure A-8. To save the workbook in the future, you can click File on the menu bar, then click Save, or click the Save button on the Standard toolbar.

QuickTip

You can also click on the Standard Toolbar or use the shortcut key [Ctrl][S] to save.

QuickTip

Use the Save As command to create a new workbook from one that already exists; use the Save command to store any changes on your disk made to an existing file since the last time the file was saved.

FIGURE A-6: **Open dialog box**

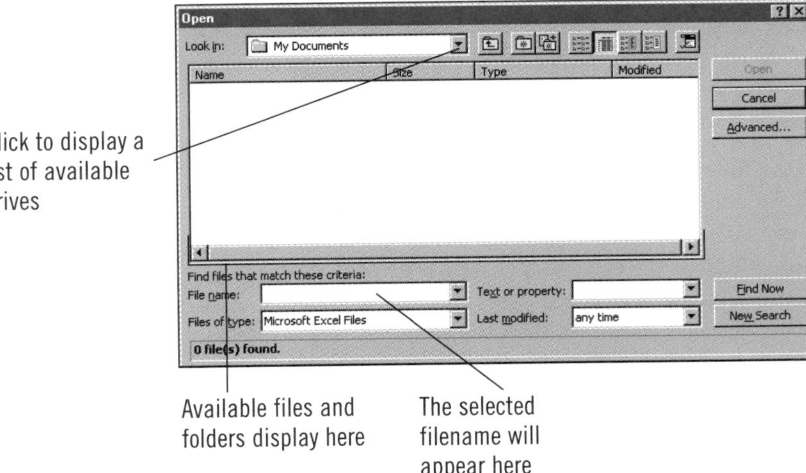

FIGURE A-7: **Save As dialog box**

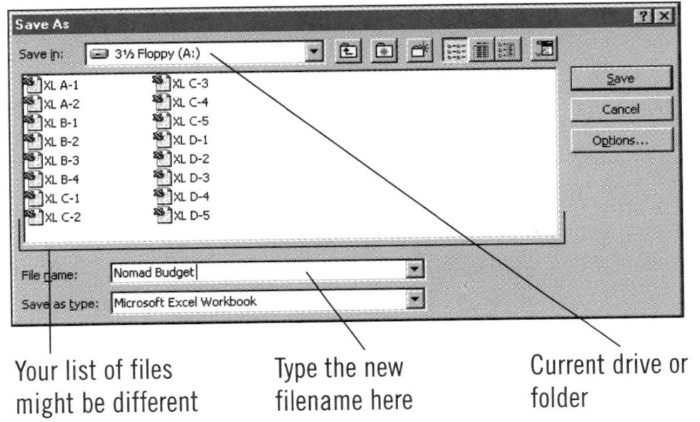

FIGURE A-8: **Nomad Budget workbook**

Microsoft Excel - Nomad Budget

A1 = Budget

	A	B	C	D	E	F	G	H	I
1	Budget								
2									
3		Qtr 1	Qtr 2	Qtr 3	Qtr 4				
4									
5	Net Sales	48000	76000	64000	80000				
6									
7	Expenses:								
8		8000	8000						
9		4800	5600						
10		2400	2400						
11	Ads	3600	8000						
12	COG	16000	16800						
13									
14									
15									
16									
17									

Sheet1 / Sheet2 / Sheet3

Ready NUM

Start | Microsoft Excel - No... 8:16 AM

Excel 97

Entering Labels and Values

Labels are used to identify the data in the rows and columns of a worksheet. They are also used to make your worksheet readable and understandable. For these reasons, you should enter all labels in your worksheet first. Labels can contain text and numerical information not used in calculations, such as dates, times, or addresses. Labels are left-aligned by default. **Values**, which include numbers, formulas, and functions, are used in calculations. Excel recognizes an entry as a value when it is a number or begins with one of these symbols: +, -, =, @, #, or $. All values are right-aligned by default. When a cell contains both text and numbers, Excel recognizes the entry as a label. Evan needs to enter labels identifying expense categories, and the values for Qtr 3 and Qtr 4 into the Nomad budget worksheet.

Steps

1. **Click cell A8 to make it the active cell**
   Notice that the cell address A8 appears in the name box. You will now enter text for the expenses.

2. **Type Salary, as shown in Figure A-9, then click the Enter button on the formula bar**
   You must click to confirm your entry. You can also confirm a cell entry by pressing [Enter], pressing [Tab], or by pressing one of the arrow keys on your keyboard. If a label does not fit in a cell, Excel displays the remaining characters in the next cell to the right as long as it is empty. Otherwise, the label is **truncated**, or cut off. The contents of A8, the active cell, display in the formula bar.

Trouble?

If you notice a mistake in a cell entry after it has been confirmed, double-click the cell and use [Backspace] or [Delete] to make your corrections, then press [Enter].

3. **Click cell A9, type Interest, then press [Enter] to complete the entry and move the cell pointer to cell A10; type Rent in cell A10, then press [Enter]**
   Now you enter the remaining expense values.

4. **Drag the mouse over cells D8 through E12**
   Two or more selected cells is called a **range**. Since these entries cover multiple columns and rows, you can pre-select the range to make the data entry easier.

5. **Type 8000, then press [Enter]; type 6400 in cell D9, then press [Enter]; type 2400 in cell D10, then press [Enter]; type 16000 in cell D11, then press [Enter]; type 20000 in cell D12, then press [Enter]**
   You have entered all the values in the Qtr 3 column. The cell pointer is now in cell E8. Finish entering the expenses in column E.

QuickTip

To enter a number, such as the year 1997, as a label so it will not be included in a calculation, type an apostrophe (') before the number.

6. **Type the remaining values for cells E8 through E12 using Figure A-10 as a guide**

7. **Click the Save button on the Standard toolbar**
   It is a good idea to save your work often. A good rule of thumb is to save every 15 minutes or so as you modify your worksheet, especially before making significant changes to the worksheet, or before printing.

FIGURE A-9: **Worksheet with initial label entered**

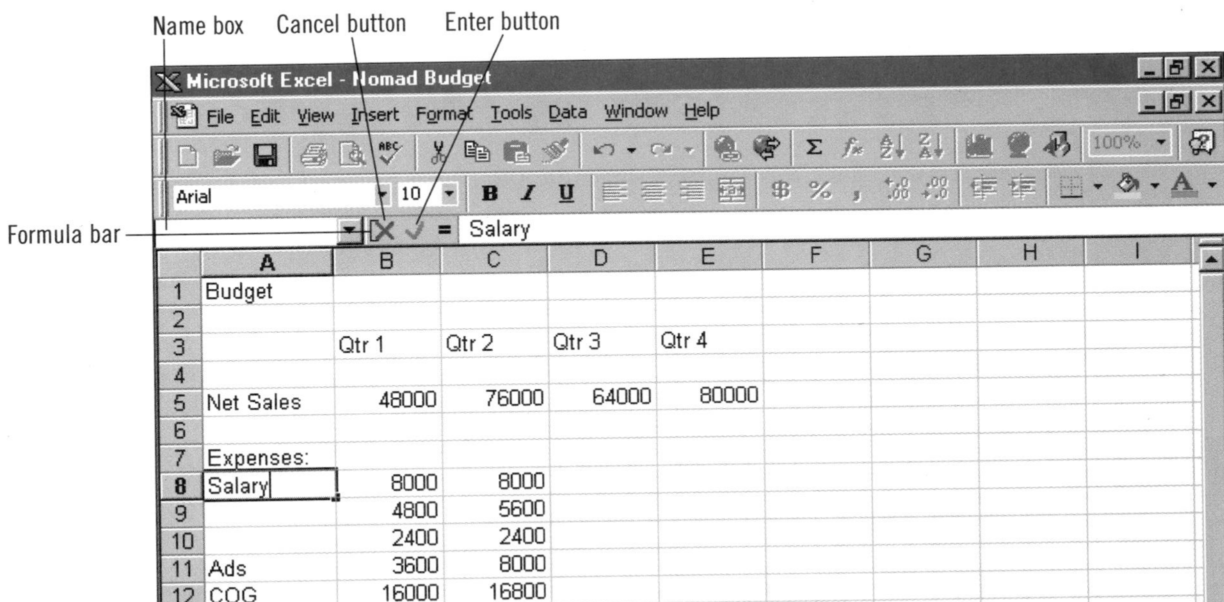

FIGURE A-10: **Worksheet with labels and values entered**

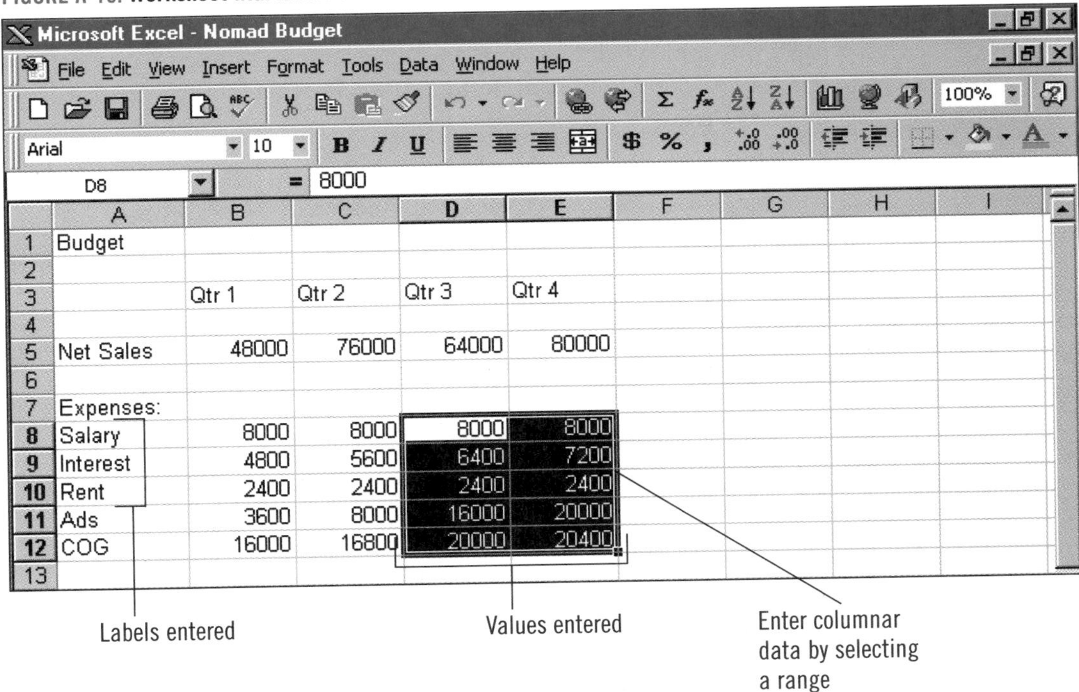

Navigating the worksheet

With over a billion cells available to you, it is important to know how to move around, or **navigate**, the worksheet. You can use the pointer-movement keys ([↑], [↓], [←], [→]) to move a cell or two at a time, or the [Page Up] or [Page Down] to move a screenful at a time. You can also simply use your mouse pointer to click the desired cell. If the desired cell is not visible in the worksheet window, you can use the scroll bars, or the Go To command to move the location into view. To return to the top of the worksheet, cell A1, press [Ctrl][Home].

Previewing and Printing a Worksheet

When a worksheet is completed, you print it to have a paper copy to reference, file, or send to others. You can also print a worksheet that is not complete to review it or work on when you are not at a computer. Before you print a worksheet, you should first save it, as you did at the end of the previous lesson. That way, if anything happens to the file as it is being sent to the printer, you will have a clean copy saved to your disk. Then you should preview it to make sure that it will fit on the page the way you want. When you preview a worksheet, you see a copy of the worksheet exactly as it will appear on paper. Table A-2 provides printing tips. Evan is finished entering the labels and values into the Nomad Ltd budget as his manager asked him to. Before he submits it to her for review, he previews it and then prints a copy.

Steps 1 2 3 4

1. Make sure the printer is on and contains paper
If a file is sent to print and the printer is off, an error message appears. You preview the worksheet to check its overall appearance.

2. Click the Print Preview button on the Standard toolbar
You could also click File on the menu bar, then click Print Preview. A miniature version of the worksheet appears on the screen, as shown in Figure A-11. If there was more than one page, you could click Next and Previous to move between pages. You can also enlarge the image by clicking the Zoom button. After verifying that the preview image is correct, print the worksheet.

3. Click Print
The Print dialog box opens, as shown in Figure A-12.

4. Make sure that the Active Sheet(s) radio button is selected and that 1 appears in the Number of Copies text box
Now you are ready to print the worksheet.

5. Click OK
The Printing dialog box appears while the file is sent to the printer. Note that the dialog box contains a Cancel button that you can use to cancel the print job.

Start - Programs-

TABLE A-2: Worksheet printing tips

before you print	recommendation
Check the printer	Make sure that the printer is turned on and online, that it has paper, and that there are no error messages or warning signals
Preview the worksheet	Check the formatted image for page breaks, page setup (vertical or horizontal), and overall appearance of the worksheet
Check the printer selection	Use the Printer setup command in the Print dialog box to verify that the correct printer is selected

FIGURE A-11: **Print Preview screen**

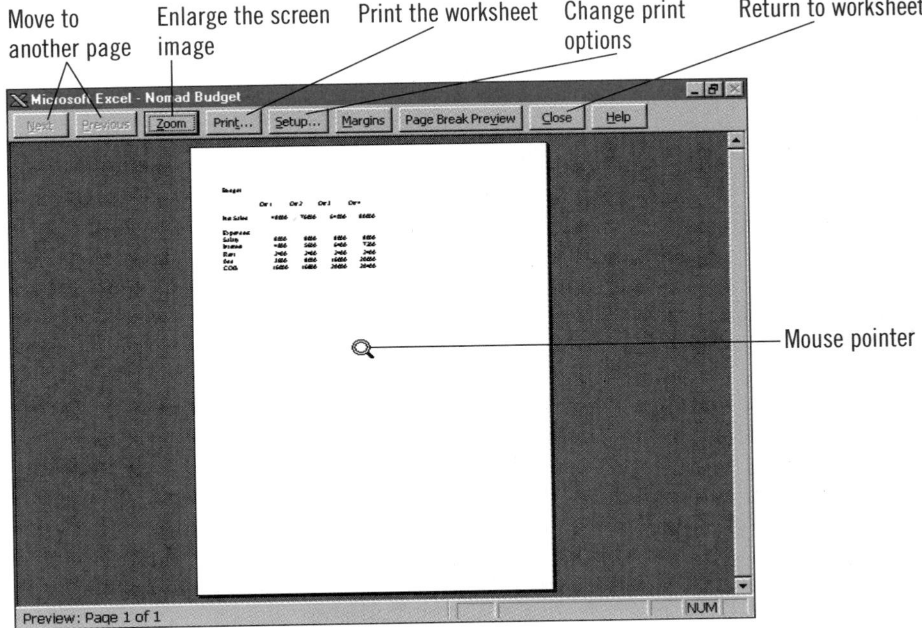

FIGURE A-12: **Print dialog box**

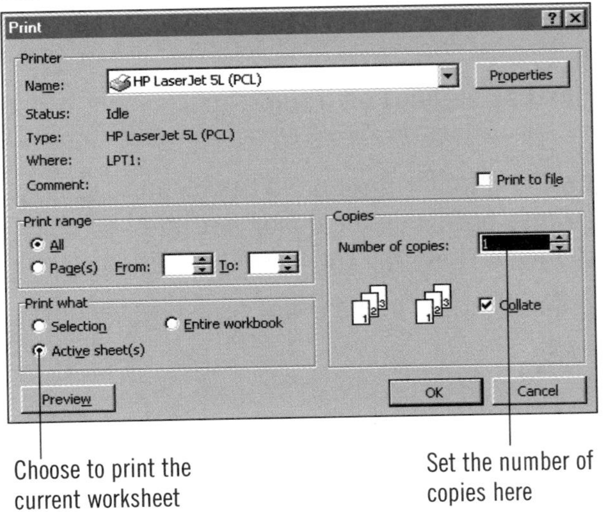

CLUES TO USE

Using Zoom in Print Preview

When you are in the Print Preview window, you can make the image of the page larger by clicking the Zoom button. You can also position the mouse pointer over a specific part of the worksheet page, then click to view that section of the page. While the image is zoomed in, use the scroll bars to view different sections of the page. See Figure A-13.

FIGURE A-13: **Enlarging the view using Zoom**

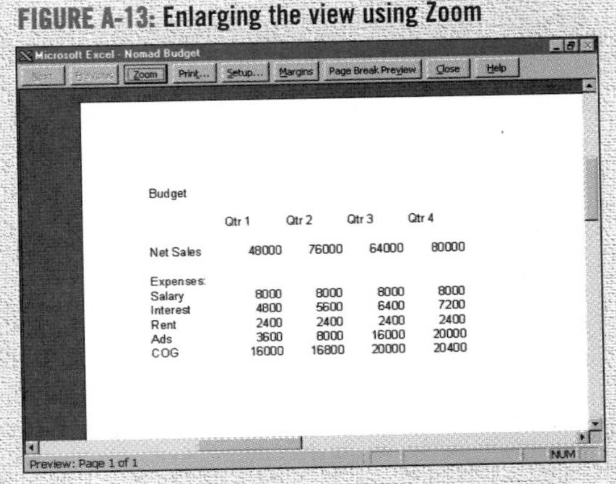

Excel 97

Getting Help

Excel features an extensive online Help system that gives you immediate access to definitions, explanations, and useful tips. The Office Assistant provides this information using a question and answer format. As you are working, the Office Assistant provides tips—indicated by a light bulb you can click—in response to your own working habits. Help appears in a separate balloon-shaped dialog box that you can resize and refer to as you work. You can press the F1 key at any time to get immediate help. Evan knows the manager will want to know the grand total of the expenses in the budget, and he thinks Excel can perform this type of calculation. He decides to use the animated Office Assistant to learn how to see the sum of a range using the AutoCalculate feature, located in the Status bar.

Steps

1. Click the **Office Assistant button** on the Standard toolbar
   The Office Assistant helps you find information using a question and answer format.
2. Once the Office Assistant is displayed, click its window to activate the query box
   You want information on calculating the sum of a range.
3. Type **How can I calculate a range?**
   See Figure A-15. Once you type a question, the Office Assistant can search for relevant topics from the help files in Excel, from which you can choose.
4. Click **Search**
   The Office Assistant displays several topics related to making quick calculations. See Figure A-16.
5. Click **Quick calculations on a worksheet**
   The Quick calculations on a worksheet help window opens.
6. Click **View the total for a selected range**, press **[Esc]** once you've read the text, then click the **Close button** on the dialog box title bar
   The Help window closes and you return to your worksheet.
7. Click the **Close button** in the Office Assistant window

QuickTip
Information in Help can be printed by clicking the Options button, then clicking Print Topic.

QuickTip
You can close the Office Assistant at any time by clicking its Close button.

CLUES TO USE

Changing the Office Assistant

The default Office Assistant is Clippit, but there are eight others from which you can choose. To change the appearance of the Office Assistant, right-click the Office Assistant window, then click Choose Assistant. Click the Gallery tab, click the Back and Next buttons until you find an Assistant you want to use, then click OK. (You may need your Microsoft Office 97 CD-ROM to change Office Assistants.) Each Office Assistant makes its own unique sounds and can be animated by right-clicking its window and clicking Animate! Figure A-16 displays the Office Assistant dialog box.

FIGURE A-14: Office Assistant dialog box

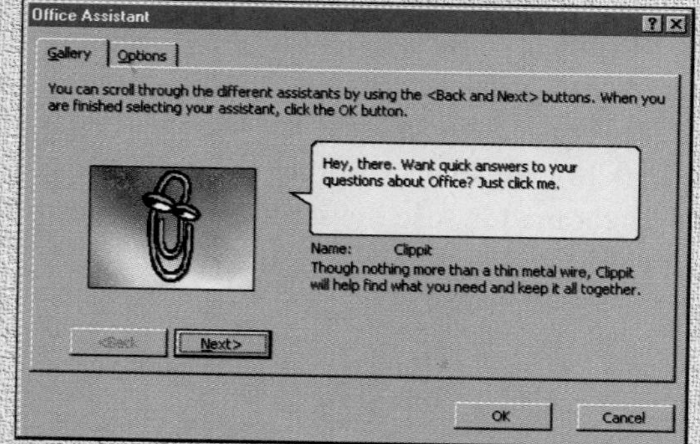

FIGURE A-15: Office Assistant

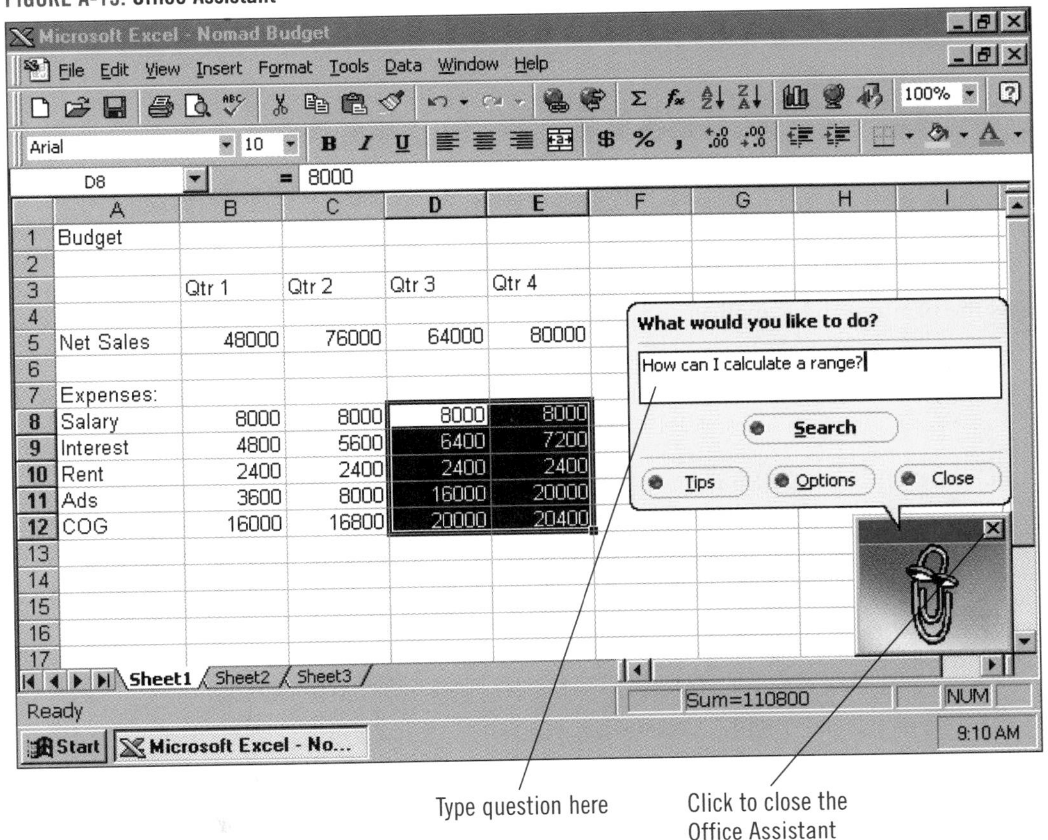

FIGURE A-16: Relevant Help Assistant topics

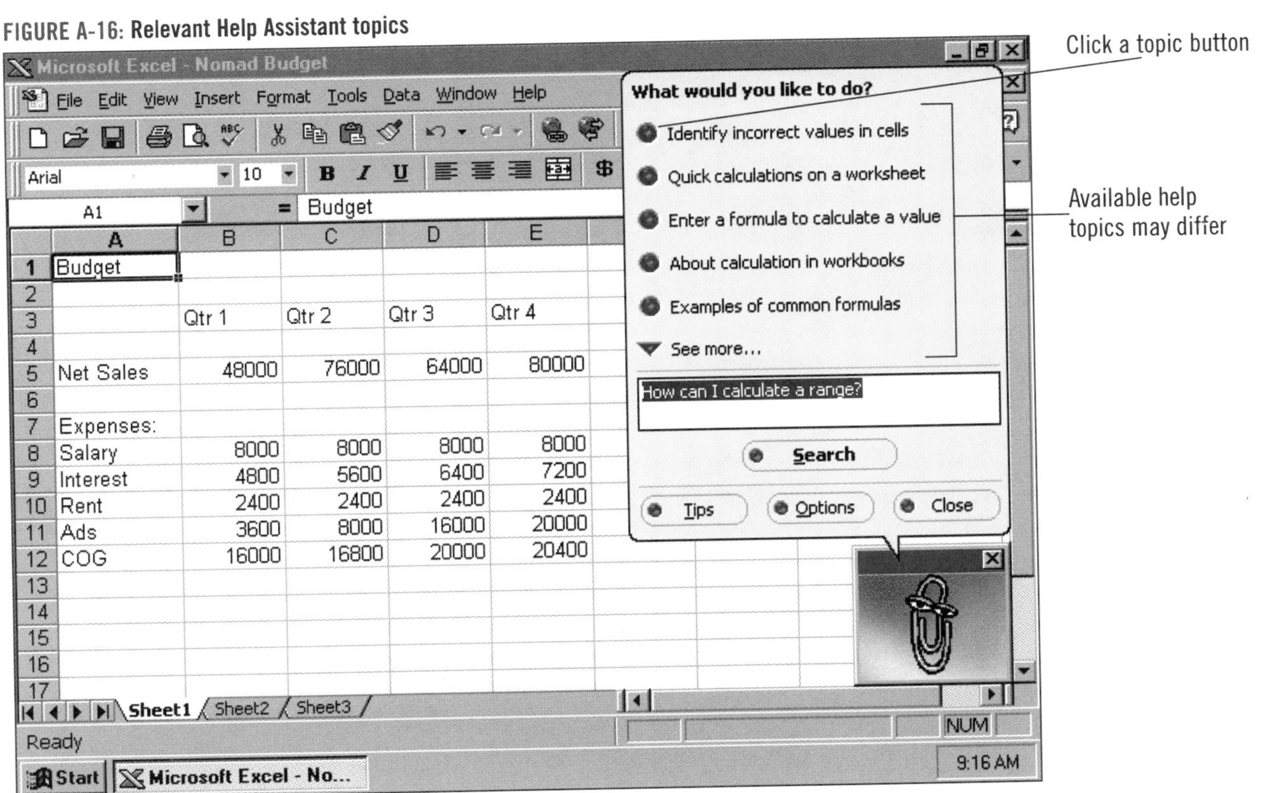

Excel 97

Excel 97

Closing a Workbook and Exiting Excel

When you have finished working on a workbook, you need to save the file and close it. Once you have saved a file and are ready to close it, click Close on the File menu. When you have completed all your work in Excel, you need to exit the program. To exit Excel, click Exit on the File menu. Evan is done adding the information to the Budget worksheet, and he is ready to pass the printout to his manger to review, so he closes the workbook and then exits Excel.

Steps

1. **Click File on the menu bar**
   The File menu opens as displayed in Figure A-17.
2. **Click Close**
   You could also click the workbook Close button instead of choosing File, then Close. Excel closes the workbook and asks you to save your changes; be sure that you do. A blank worksheet window appears.
3. **Click File, then click Exit**
   You could also click the program Close button to exit the program. Excel closes and computer memory is freed up for other computing tasks.

Trouble?

To exit Excel and close several files at once, choose Exit from the File menu. Excel will prompt you to save changes to each workbook before exiting.

FIGURE A-17: **Closing a workbook using the File menu**

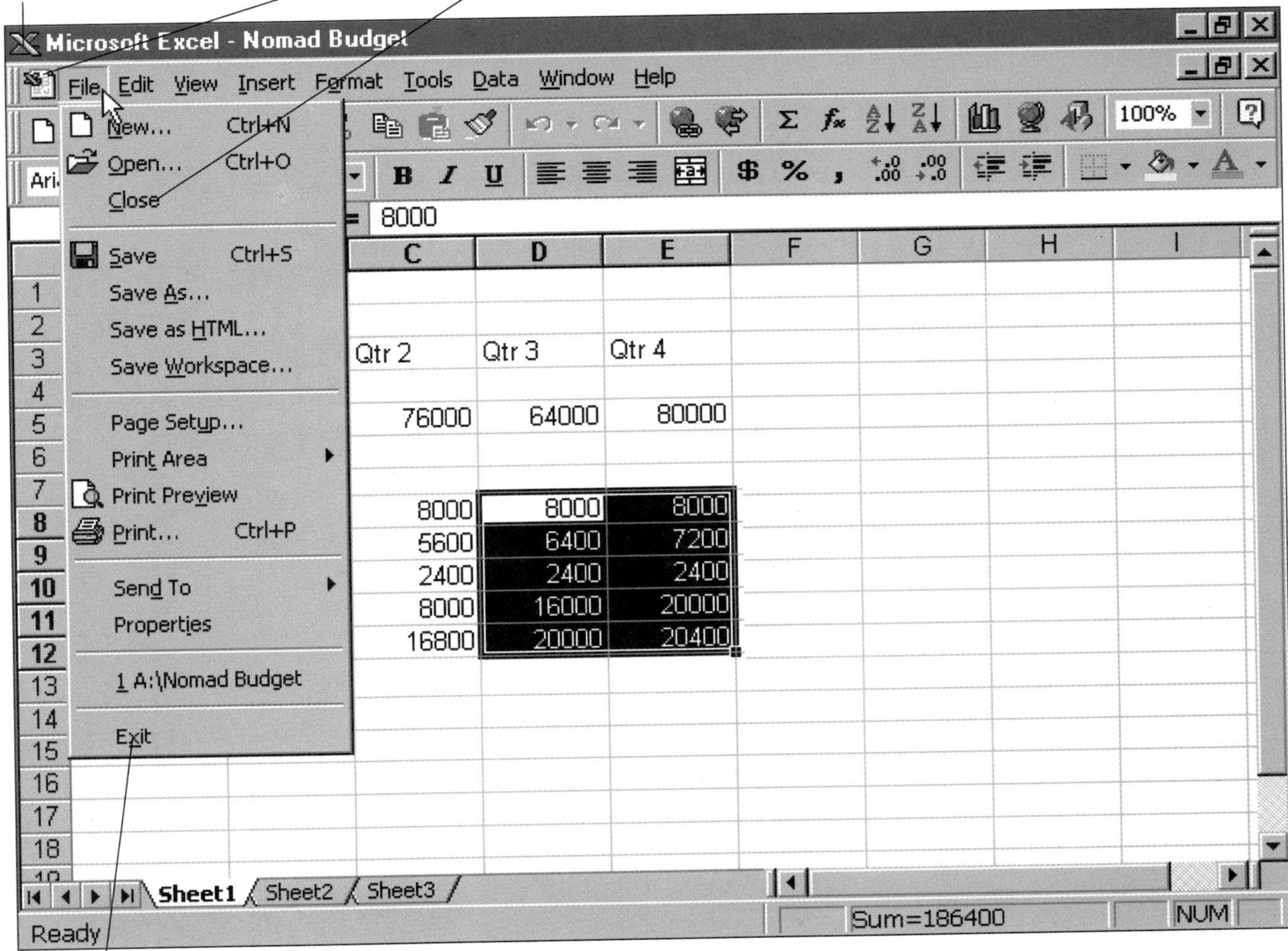

Excel 97

Practice

► Concepts Review

Label each of the elements of the Excel worksheet window shown in Figure A-18.

FIGURE A-18

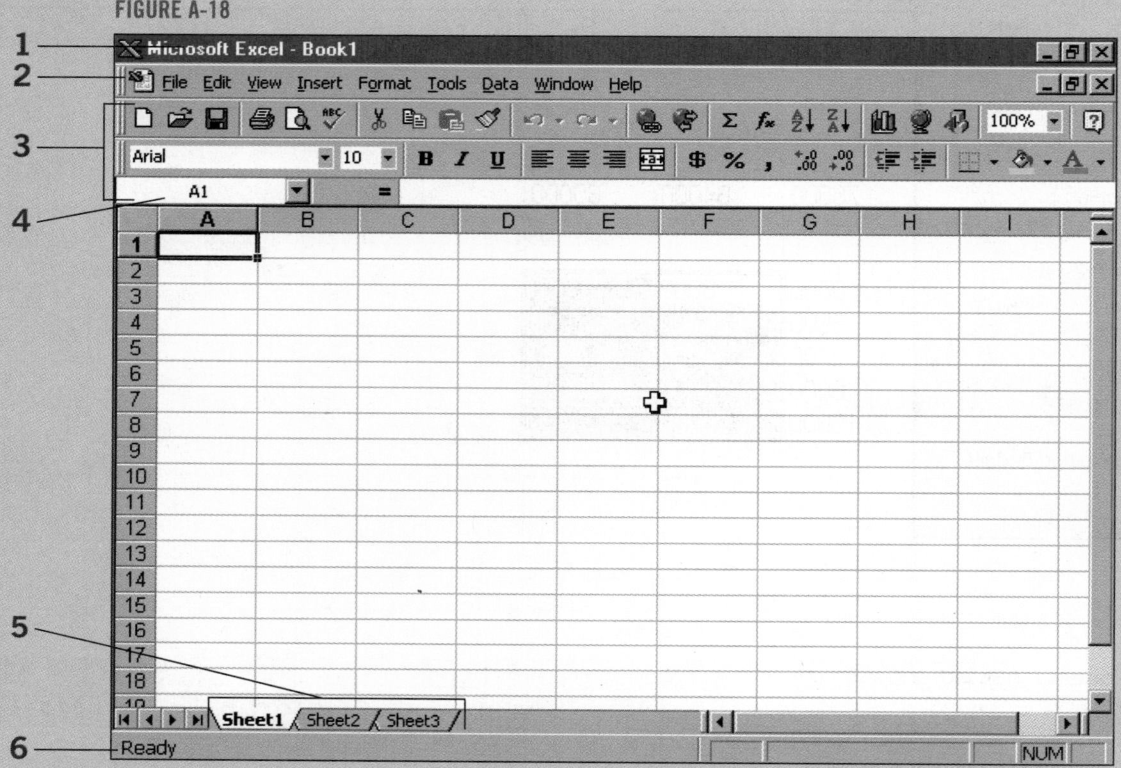

Match each of the terms with the statement that describes its function.

7. Cell pointer
8. Button
9. Worksheet window
10. Name box
11. Cell
12. Workbook

a. Area that contains a grid of columns and rows
b. The intersection of a column and row
c. Graphic symbol that depicts a task or function
d. Collection of worksheets
e. Rectangle that indicates the cell you are currently working in
f. Displays the active cell address

Select the best answer from the list of choices.

13. An electronic spreadsheet can perform all of the following tasks, *except*

a. Display information visually
b. Calculate data accurately
c. Plan worksheet objectives
d. Recalculate updated information

14. Each of the following is true about labels, *except*

a. They are left-aligned, by default
b. They are not used in calculations
c. They are right-aligned, by default
d. They can include numerical information

15. Each of the following is true about values, *except*

a. They can include labels
b. They are right-aligned, by default
c. They are used in calculations
d. They can include formulas

16. What symbol is typed before a number to make the number a label?

a. "
b. !
c. '
d. ;

17. You can get Excel Help by any of the following ways, *except*

a. Clicking Help on the menu bar
b. Pressing [F1]
c. Clicking the Help button on the Standard toolbar
d. Minimizing the application window

18. Each key(s) can be used to confirm cell entries, *except*

a. [Enter]
b. [Tab]
c. [Esc]
d. [Shift][Enter]

19. Which button is used to preview a worksheet?

a.
b.
c.
d.

20. Which feature is used to enlarge a print preview view?

a. Magnify
b. Enlarge
c. Amplify
d. Zoom

21. Each of the following is true about the Office Assistant, *except*

a. It provides tips based on your work habits
b. It provides help using a question and answer format
c. You can change the appearance of the Office Assistant
d. It can complete certain tasks for you

▶ Skills Review

1. **Start Excel and identify the elements in the worksheet window.**
   a. Point to Programs in the Start menu.
   b. Click the Microsoft Excel program icon.
   c. Try to identify as many elements in the Excel worksheet window as you can without referring to the unit material.

2. **Open an existing workbook.**
   a. Open the workbook XL A-2 by clicking the Open button on the Standard toolbar.
   b. Save the workbook as "Country Duds" by clicking File on the menu bar, then clicking Save As.

3. **Enter labels and values.**
   a. Enter labels shown in Figure A-19.
   b. Enter values shown in Figure A-19.
   c. Save the workbook by clicking the Save button on the Standard toolbar.

FIGURE A-19

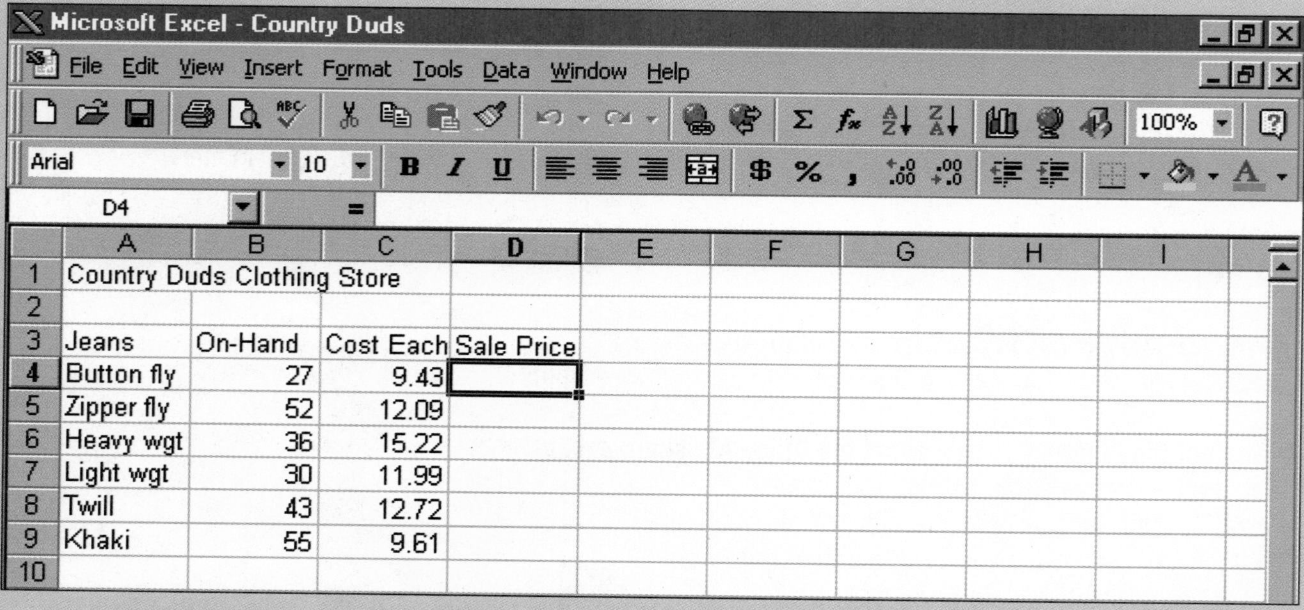
Microsoft Excel - Country Duds
File Edit View Insert Format Tools Data Window Help
100%
Arial
10
D4
=
A B C D E F G H I
1 Country Duds Clothing Store
2
3 Jeans On-Hand Cost Each Sale Price
4 Button fly 27 9.43
5 Zipper fly 52 12.09
6 Heavy wgt 36 15.22
7 Light wgt 30 11.99
8 Twill 43 12.72
9 Khaki 55 9.61
10

4. **Previewing and printing a worksheet.**
   a. Click the Print Preview button on the Standard toolbar.
   b. Use the Zoom button to see more of your worksheet.
   c. Print one copy of the worksheet.
   d. Hand in your printout.

5. **Get Help.**
   a. Click the Office Assistant button on the Standard toolbar if the Assistant is not displayed.
   b. Ask the Office Assistant for information about changing the Office Assistant character in Excel.
   c. Print information offered by the Office Assistant using the Print topic command on the Options menu.
   d. Close the Help window.
   e. Hand in your printout.

6. **Close the workbook and exit Excel.**
   a. Click File on the menu bar, then click Close.
   b. If asked if you want to save the worksheet, click No.
   c. If necessary, close any other worksheets you might have opened.
   d. Click File on the menu bar, then click Exit.

Independent Challenges

1. Excel's online Help provides definitions, explanations, procedures, and other helpful information. It also provides examples and demonstrations to show you how Excel features work. Topics include elements such as the active cell, status bar, buttons, and dialog boxes, as well as detailed information about Excel commands and options.

To complete this independent challenge:

1. Open a new workbook
2. Click the Office Assistant.
3. Type a question that will give you information about opening and saving a worksheet. (Hint: you may have to ask the Office Assistant more than one question.)
4. Print out the information and hand it in.
5. Return to your workbook when you are finished.

2. Spreadsheet software has many uses that can affect the way work is done. Some examples of how Excel can be used are discussed in the beginning of this unit. Use your own personal or business experiences to come up with five examples of how Excel could be used in a business setting.

To complete this independent challenge:

1. Open a new workbook.
2. Think of five business tasks that you could complete more efficiently by using an Excel worksheet.
3. Sketch a sample of each worksheet. See Figure A-20, a sample payroll worksheet.
4. Submit your sketches.

FIGURE A-20

Employee Names	Hours Worked	Hourly Wage	Gross Pay
Janet Bryce			
Anthony Krups			
Grant Miller			
Barbara Salazar			
Total			

Gross pay= Hours worked times Hourly wage

3. You are the office manager for Blossoms and Greens, a small greenhouse and garden center. Although the company is just three years old, it is expanding rapidly, and you are continually looking for ways to make your job easier. Last year you began using Excel to manage and maintain data on inventory and sales, which has greatly helped you to track this information accurately and efficiently. However, the job is still overwhelming for just one person. Fortunately, the owner of the company has just approved the hiring of an assistant for you. This person will need to learn how to use Excel. Create a short training document that your new assistant can use as a reference while becoming familiar with Excel.

To complete this independent challenge:

1. Draw a sketch of the Excel worksheet window, and label the key elements, such as toolbars, title bar, formula bar, scroll bars, etc.
2. For each labeled element, write a short description of its use.
3. List the main ways to get Help in Excel. (Hint: use the Office Assistant to learn of all the ways to get help in Excel..)
4. Identify five different ways to use spreadsheets in business.

4. Data on the World Wide Web is current and informative. It is a useful tool that can be used to gather the most up-to-date information which you can use to make smart buying decisions. Imagine that your supervisor has just told you that due to your great work, she has just found money in the budget to buy you a new computer. You can have whatever you want, but she wants you to justify the expense by creating a spreadsheet using data found on the World Wide Web to support your purchase decision.

To complete this independent challenge:

1. Open a new workbook and save it on your Student Disk as "New Computer Data."
2. Decide which features you want your ideal computer to have, and list these features.
3. Log on to the Internet and use your browser to go to the http://www.course.com. From there, click the link Student On Line Companions, then click the Microsoft Office 97 Professional Edition—Illustrated: A First Course page, then click on the Excel link for Unit A.
4. Use any of the following sites to compile your data: IBM [www.ibm.com], Gateway [www.gw2k.com], Dell [www.dell.com], or any other site you can find with related information.
5. Compile data for the components you want.
6. Make sure all components are listed and totaled. Include any tax and shipping costs the manufacturer charges.
7. Indicate on the worksheet your final purchase decision.
8. Save, print, and hand in your work.

► Visual Workshop

Create a worksheet similar to Figure A-21 using the skills you learned in this unit. Save the workbook as "Bea's Boutique" on your Student Disk. Preview, then print the worksheet.

FIGURE A-21

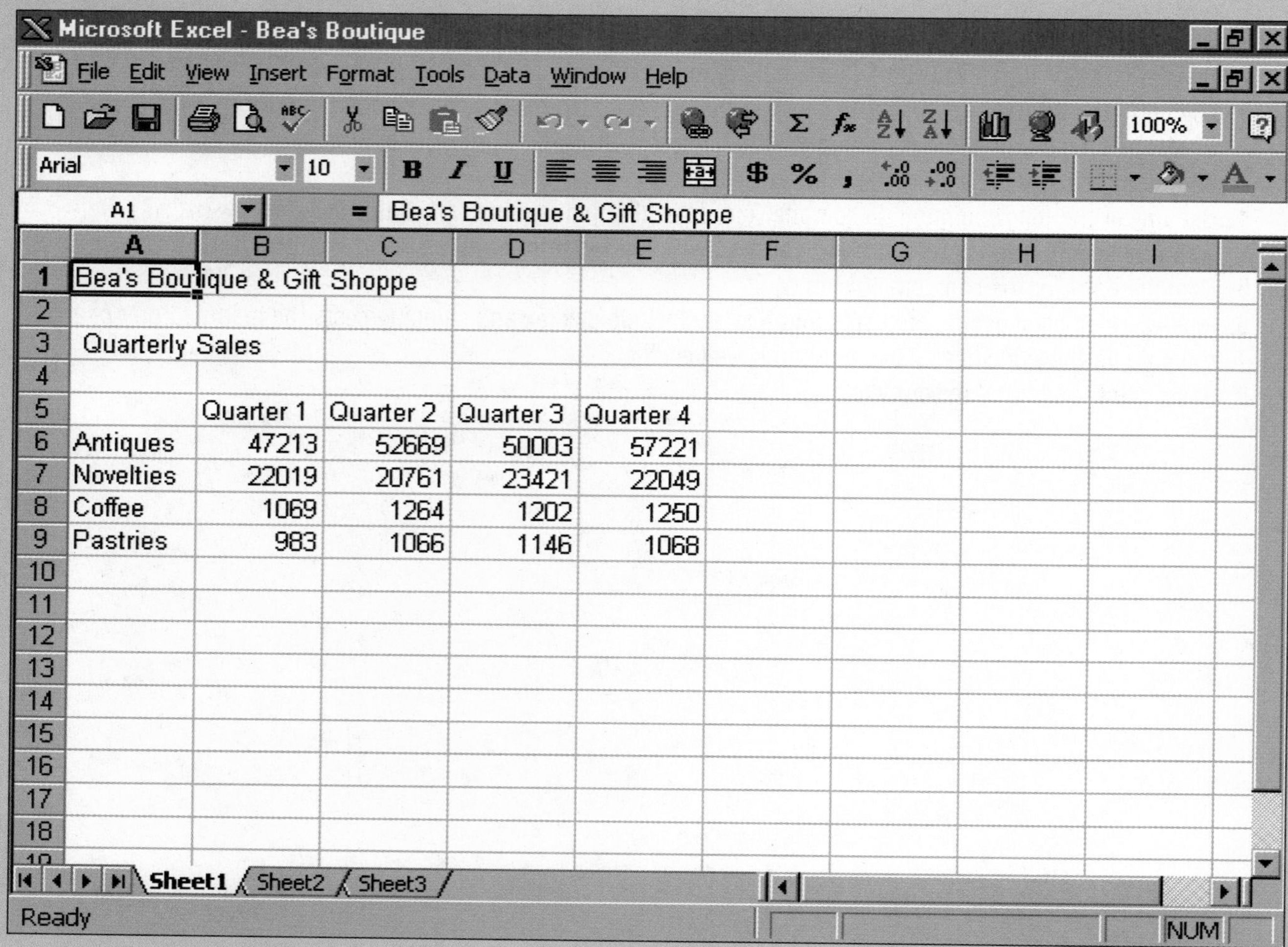

	A	B	C	D	E
1	Bea's Boutique & Gift Shoppe				
2					
3	Quarterly Sales				
4					
5		Quarter 1	Quarter 2	Quarter 3	Quarter 4
6	Antiques	47213	52669	50003	57221
7	Novelties	22019	20761	23421	22049
8	Coffee	1069	1264	1202	1250
9	Pastries	983	1066	1146	1068

Building and Editing Worksheets

Objectives

- Plan, design, and create a worksheet
- Edit cell entries and work with ranges
- Enter formulas
- Introduce functions
- Copy and move cell entries
- Copy formulas with relative cell references
- Copy formulas with absolute cell references
- Name and move a sheet

You will now plan and build your own worksheets. When you build a worksheet, you enter text, values, and formulas into worksheet cells. Once you create a worksheet, you can save it in a workbook file and then print it. Evan Brillstein has received a request from the Marketing Department for a forecast of this year's summer tour business, and an estimate of the average tour sales for each type of tour. Marketing hopes that the tour business will increase 20% over last year's figures. Evan needs to create a worksheet that summarizes tour sales for last year and a worksheet that forecasts the summer tour sales for this year.

Excel 97

Planning, Designing, and Creating a Worksheet

Before you start entering data into a worksheet, you need to know the purpose and approximate layout of the worksheet. Evan wants to forecast Nomad's 1998 summer tour sales. The sales goal, already identified by the Marketing Department, is to increase the 1997 summer sales by 20%. Using Figure B-1 and the planning guidelines below, work with Evan as he plans his worksheet.

Details

Determine the purpose of the worksheet and give it a meaningful title

Evan needs to forecast summer tour sales for 1998. Evan titles the worksheet "1998 Summer Tour Sales Forecast."

Determine your worksheet's desired results, sometimes called output

Evan needs to determine what the 1998 sales totals will be if sales increase by 20% over the 1997 sales totals, as well as the average number of tours per type.

Collect all the information, sometimes called input, that will produce the results you want to see

Evan gathers together the sales data for the 1997 summer tour season. The season ran from June through August. The types of tours sold in these months included Bike, Raft, Horse, and Bus.

Determine the calculations, or formulas, necessary to achieve the desired results

First, Evan needs to total the number of tours sold for each month of the 1997 summer season. Then he needs to add these totals together to determine the grand total of summer tour sales. Finally, the 1997 monthly totals and grand total must be multiplied by 1.2 to calculate a 20% increase for the 1998 summer tour season. He'll use the Paste Function to determine the average number of tours per type.

Sketch on paper how you want the worksheet to look; that is, identify where the labels and values will go

Evan decides to put tour types in rows and the months in columns. He enters the tour sales data in his sketch and indicates where the monthly sales totals and the grand total should go. Below the totals, he writes out the formula for determining a 20% increase in sales for 1997. He also includes a label for the location of the tour averages. Evan's sketch of his worksheet is shown in Figure B-1.

Create the worksheet

Evan enters his labels first to establish the structure of his worksheet. He then enters the values, the sales data into his worksheet. These values will be used to calculate the output Evan needs. The worksheet Evan creates is shown in Figure B-2.

FIGURE B-1: **Worksheet sketch showing labels, values, and calculations**

1998 Summer Tours Sales Forecast					
	June	July	August	Totals	Average
Bike	14	10	6	3 month total	
Raft	7	8	12		
Horse	12	7	6		
Bus	1	2	9		
Totals	June Total	July Total	August Total	Grand Total for 1997	
1998 Sales	Total X 1.2				

FIGURE B-2: **Evan's forecasting worksheet**

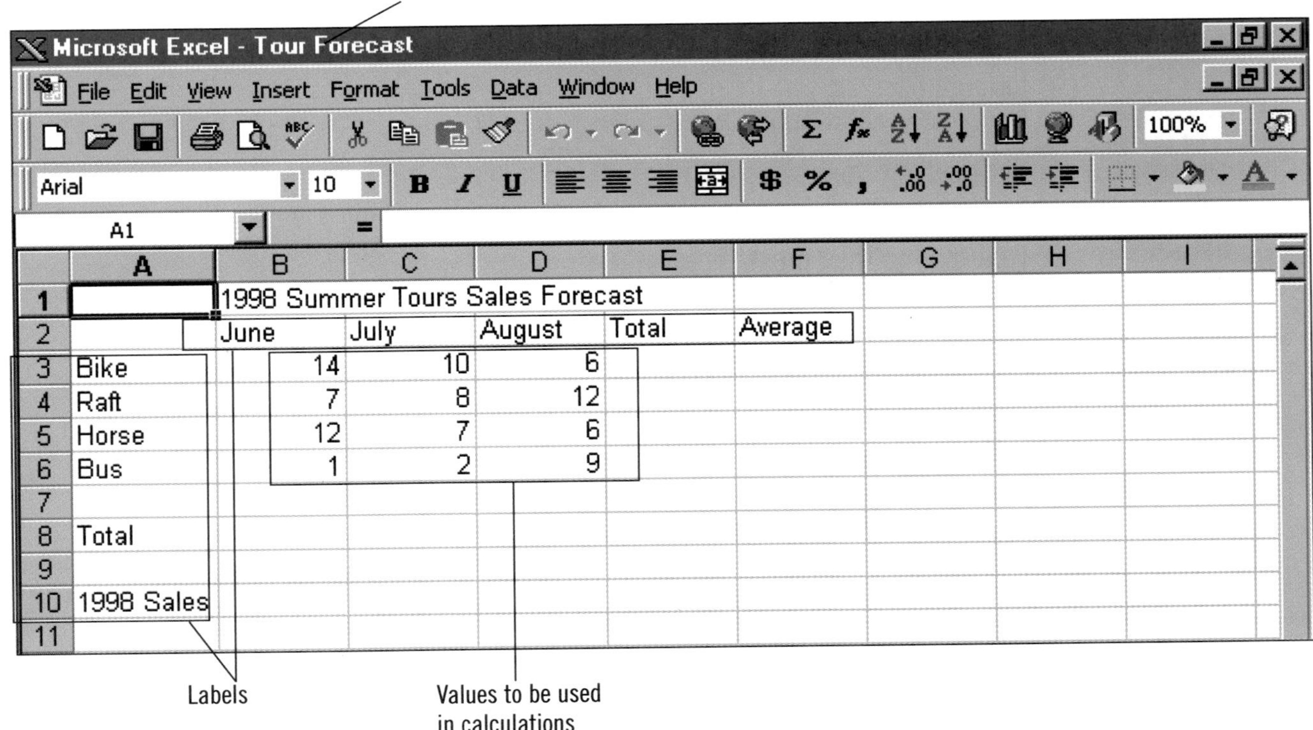

Excel 97

Editing Cell Entries and Working with Ranges

You can change the contents of any cells at any time. To edit the contents of a cell, you first select the cell you want to edit, then click the formula bar, double-click the selected cell, or press [F2]. This puts Excel into Edit mode. To make sure you are in Edit mode, check the **mode indicator** on the far left of the status bar. The mode indicator identifies the current Excel command or operation in progress. After planning and creating his worksheet, Evan notices that he entered the wrong value for the June bus tours and forgot to include the canoe tours. He fixes the bus tours figure, and he decides to add the canoe sales data to the raft sales figures.

Steps 1 2 3 4

1. **Start Excel, open the workbook XL B-1 from your Student Disk, then save it as Tour Forecast**
2. **Click cell B6**
   This cell contains June bus tours, which Evan needs to change to 2.
3. **Click anywhere in the formula bar**
   Excel goes into Edit mode, and the mode indicator displays "Edit." A blinking vertical line, called the **insertion point**, appears in the formula bar, and if you move the mouse pointer to the formula bar, the pointer changes to I as displayed in Figure B-3.
4. **Press [Backspace], type 2, then press [Enter] or click the Enter button on the formula bar**
   Evan now needs to add "/Canoe" to the Raft label.
5. **Click cell A4 then press [F2]**
   Excel is in Edit mode again, but this time, the insertion point is in the cell.
6. **Type /Canoe then press [Enter]**
   The label changes to Raft/Canoe.
7. **Double-click cell B4**
   Double-clicking a cell also puts Excel into Edit mode with the insertion point in the cell.
8. **Press [Delete], then type 9**
   See Figure B-4.
9. **Click to confirm the entry**

QuickTip

If you make a mistake, you can either click the Cancel button on the formula bar before accepting the cell entry, or click the Undo button on the Standard toolbar if you notice the mistake after you have accepted the cell entry. The Undo button allows you to reverse up to 16 previous actions, one at a time.

FIGURE B-3: Worksheet in Edit mode

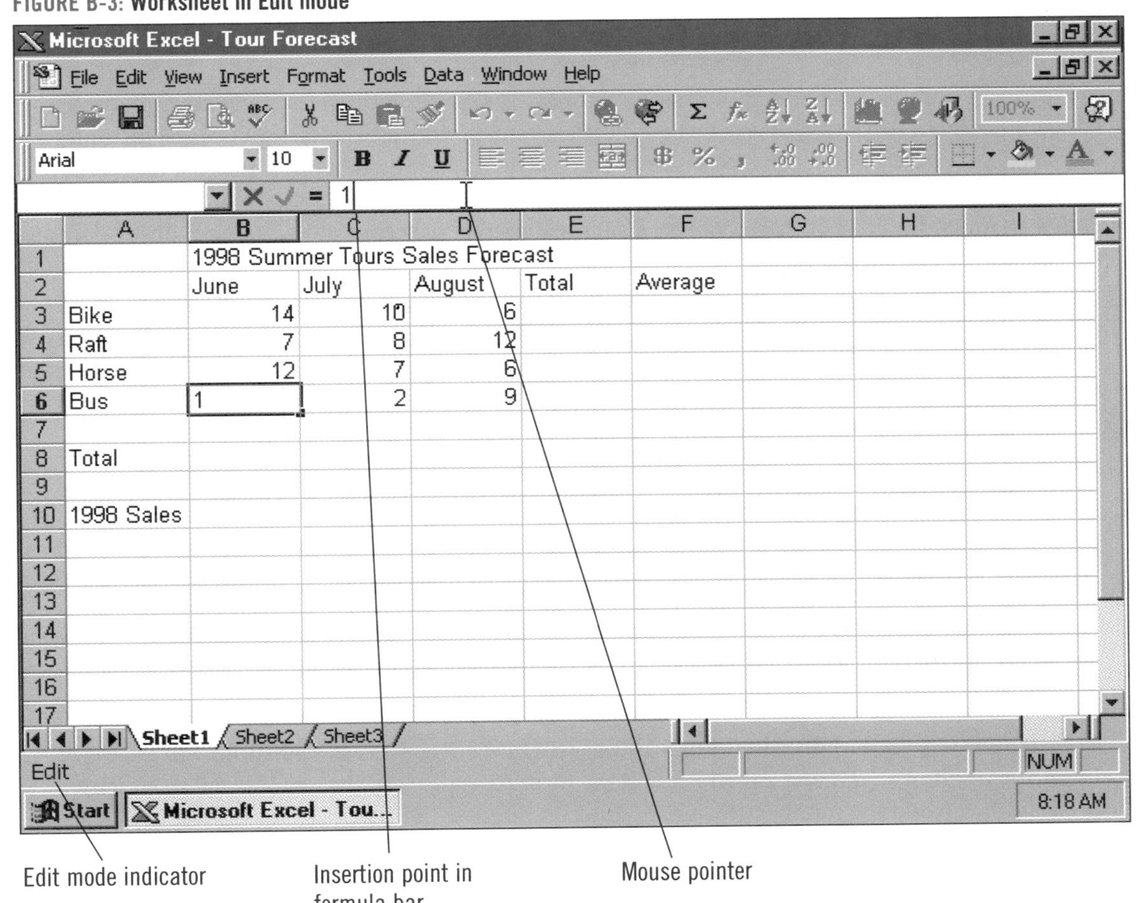

FIGURE B-4: Edited worksheet

Microsoft Excel - Tour Forecast

	A	B	C	D	E	F
1		1998 Summer Tours Sales Forecast				
2		June	July	August	Total	Average
3	Bike	14	10	6		
4	Raft/Canoe	9	8	12		
5	Horse	12	7	6		

Insertion point in cell

Using range names in a workbook

Any group of cells (two or more) is called a range. To select a range, click the first cell and drag to the last cell you want included in the range. The range address is defined by noting the first and last cells in the range. Give a meaningful name to a range by selecting cells, clicking the name box, and then typing a name. Range names—meaningful English names that Evan uses in this worksheet—are usually easier to remember than cell addresses, they can be used in formulas, and they also help you move around the workbook quickly. Click the name box list arrow, then click the name of the range you want to go to. The cell pointer moves immediately to that range.

Excel 97

Entering Formulas

Formulas are used to perform numeric calculations such as adding, multiplying, and averaging. Formulas in an Excel worksheet start with the formula prefix—the equal sign (=). All formulas use one or more **arithmetic operators** to perform calculations. See Table B-1 for a list of Excel operators. Formulas often contain cell addresses and range names. Using a cell address or range name in a formula is called **cell referencing.** Using cell references keeps your worksheet up-to-date and accurate. If you change a value in a cell, any formula containing that cell reference will be automatically recalculated using the new value. In formulas using more than one arithmetic operator, Excel decides which operation to perform first. Evan needs to add the monthly tour totals for June, July, and August, and calculate a 20% increase in sales. He can perform these calculations using formulas.

Steps

1. **Click cell B8**
   This is the cell where you want to put the calculation that will total the June sales.
2. **Type = (the equal sign)**
   Placing an equal sign at the beginning of an entry tells Excel that a formula is about to be entered rather than a label or a value. The total June sales is equal to the sum of the values in cells B3, B4, B5, and B6.
3. **Type b3+b4+b5+b6, then click the Enter button on the formula bar**
   The result of 37 appears in cell B8, and the formula appears in the formula bar. See Figure B-5. Next, you add the number of tours in July and August.
4. **Click cell C8, type =c3+c4+c5+c6, then press [Tab]; in cell D8, type =d3+d4+d5+d6, then press [Enter]**
   The total tour sales for July, 27, and for August, 33, appear in cells C8 and D8 respectively.
5. **Click cell B10, type =B8*1.2, then click on the formula bar**
   To calculate the 20% increase, you multiply the total by 1.2. This formula calculates the result of multiplying the total monthly tour sales for June, cell B8, by 1.2. The result of 44.4 appears in cell B10.
   Now you need to calculate the 20% increase for July and August. You can use the **pointing method**, by which you specify cell references in a formula by selecting the desired cell with your mouse instead of typing its cell reference into the formula.
6. **Click cell C10, type =, click cell C8, type *1.2, then press [Tab]**
7. **Click cell D10, type =, click cell D8, type *1.2, then click**
   Compare your results with Figure B-6.

Trouble?

If the formula instead of the result appears in the cell after you click , make sure you began the formula with = (the equal sign).

QuickTip

It does not matter if you type the column letter in lower case or upper case when entering formulas. Excel is not case-sensitive—B3 and b3 both refer to the same cell.

TABLE B-1: Excel arithmetic operators

operator	purpose	example
+	Performs addition	=A5+A7
–	Performs subtraction	=A5-10
*	Performs multiplication	=A5*A7
/	Performs division	=A5/A7

FIGURE B-5: Worksheet showing formula and result

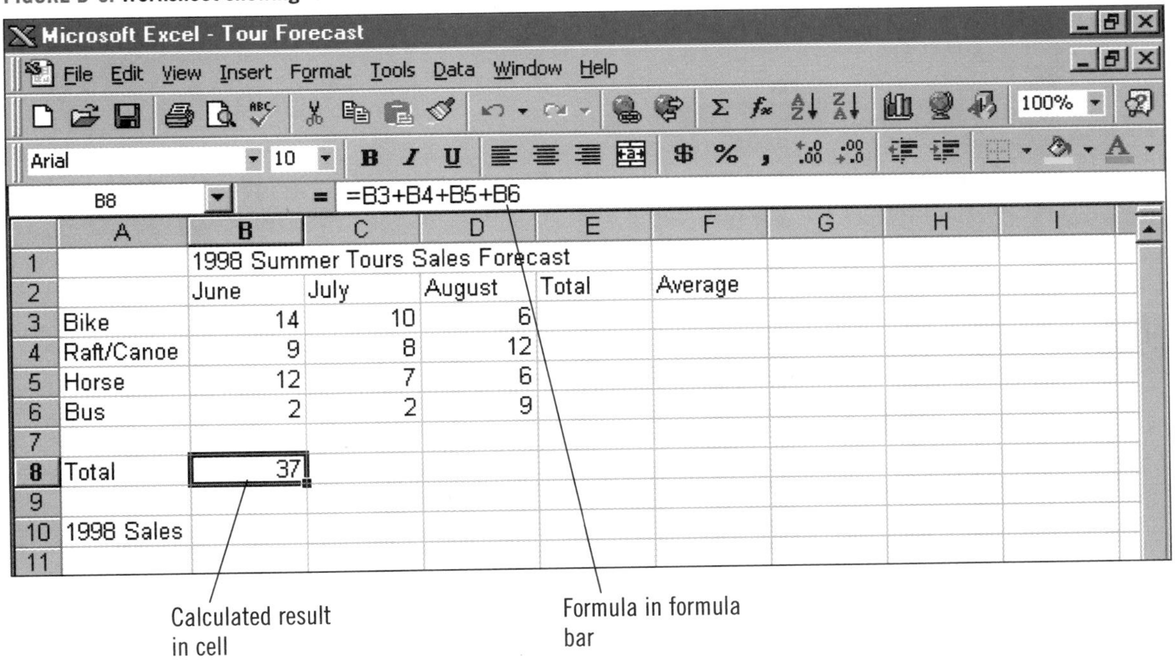

Microsoft Excel - Tour Forecast

B8 = =B3+B4+B5+B6

	A	B	C	D	E	F	G	H	I
1		1998 Summer Tours Sales Forecast							
2		June	July	August	Total	Average			
3	Bike	14	10	6					
4	Raft/Canoe	9	8	12					
5	Horse	12	7	6					
6	Bus	2	2	9					
7									
8	Total	37							
9									
10	1998 Sales								
11									

Calculated result in cell

Formula in formula bar

FIGURE B-6: Calculated results for 20% increase

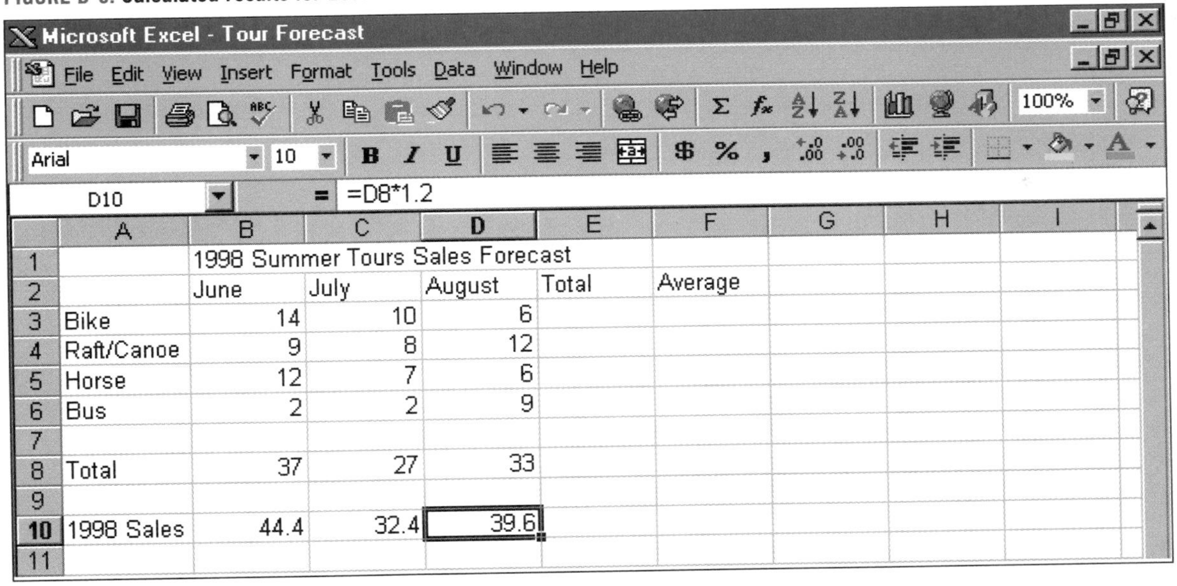

Microsoft Excel - Tour Forecast

D10 = =D8*1.2

	A	B	C	D	E	F	G	H	I
1		1998 Summer Tours Sales Forecast							
2		June	July	August	Total	Average			
3	Bike	14	10	6					
4	Raft/Canoe	9	8	12					
5	Horse	12	7	6					
6	Bus	2	2	9					
7									
8	Total	37	27	33					
9									
10	1998 Sales	44.4	32.4	39.6					
11									

CLUES TO USE

Order of precedence in Excel formulas

A formula can include several operations. When you work with formulas that have more than one operator, the order of precedence is very important. If a formula contains two or more operators, such as 4 + .55/4000 * 25, the computer performs the calculations in a particular sequence based on these rules:

Calculated 1st	Calculation of exponents
Calculated 2nd	Multiplication and division, left to right
Calculated 3rd	Addition and subtraction, left to right

In the example 4 + .55/4000 * 25, Excel performs the arithmetic operations by first dividing 4000 into .55, then multiplying the result by 25, then adding 4. You can change the order of calculations by using parentheses. For example, in the formula (4+.55)/4000 * 25, Excel would first add 4 and .55, then divide that amount by 4000, then finally multiply it by 25. Operations inside parentheses are calculated before any other operations.

Introducing Excel Functions

Functions are predefined worksheet formulas that enable you to do complex calculations easily. Like formulas, functions always begin with the formula prefix = (the equal sign). You can enter functions manually, or you can use the Paste Function. Evan uses the SUM function to calculate the grand totals in his worksheet, and the AVERAGE function to calculate the average number of tours per type.

Steps

1. **Click cell E3**
   This is the cell where you want to display the total of all bike tours for June, July, and August. You use the AutoSum button to create the totals. AutoSum sets up the SUM function to add the values in the cells above the cell pointer. If there are no values in the cells above the cell pointer, AutoSum adds the values in the cells to the left of the cell pointer—in this case, the values in cells B3, C3, and D3.

2. **Click the AutoSum button on the Standard toolbar, then click the Enter button on the formula bar**
   The formula =SUM(B3:D3) appears in the formula bar. The information inside the parentheses is the **argument**, or the information to be used in calculating a result of the function. An argument can be a value, a range of cells, text, or another function.
   The result appears in cell E3. Next, you calculate the total of raft and canoe tours.

3. **Click cell E4, click Σ, then click ✓**
   Now you calculate the three-month total of the horse tours.

4. **Click cell E5 then click Σ**
   AutoSum sets up a function to sum the two values in the cells above the active cell, which is not what you intended. You need to change the argument.

5. **Click cell B5, then drag to select the range B5:D5, then click ✓ to confirm the entry**
   As you drag, the argument in the SUM function changes to reflect the range being chosen, and a tip box appears telling you the size of the range you are selecting.

6. **Enter the SUM function in cells E6, E8, and E10**
   Make sure you add the values to the left of the active cell, not the values above it. See Figure B-7. Next, you calculate the average number of Bike tours using the Paste Function.

7. **Click cell F3, then click the Paste Function button on the Standard toolbar**
   The Paste Function dialog box opens. See Table B-2 for frequently used functions.
   The function needed to calculate averages—named AVERAGE—is included in the Most Recently Used category.

8. **Click the function name AVERAGE in the Function name list box, click OK, then in the AVERAGE dialog box type B3:D3 in the Number 1 text box, as shown in Figure B-8**

9. **Click OK, then repeat steps 7, 8 and 9 to calculate the Raft/Canoe (cell F4), Horse (cell F5), and Bus tours (cell F6) averages**
   The Time To checklist in the left margin contains Steps for routine actions. Everytime you see a Time To checklist, perform the actions listed.

FIGURE B-7: **Worksheet with SUM functions entered**

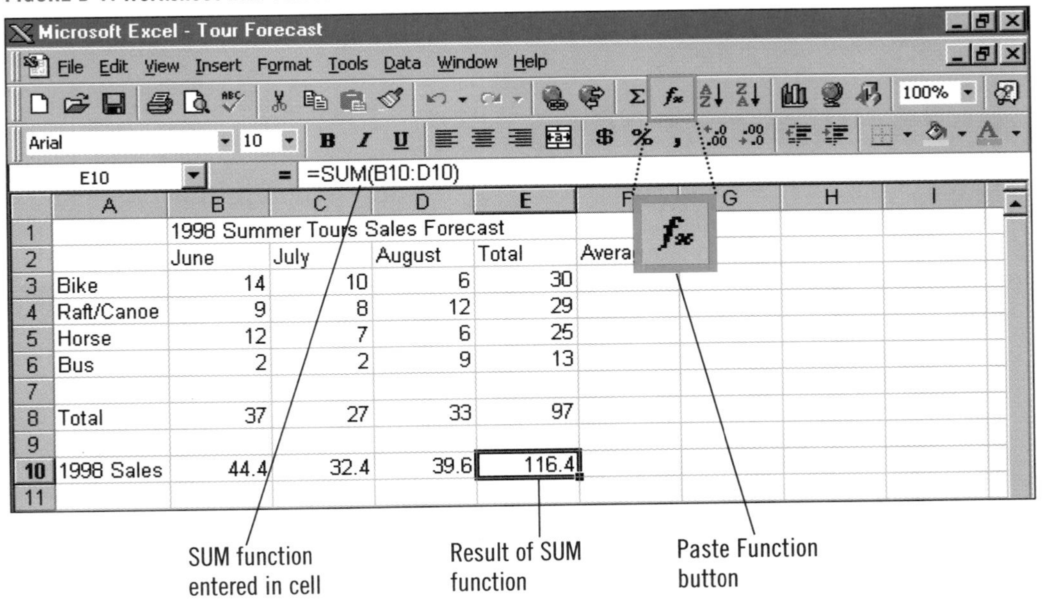

FIGURE B-8: **Using the Paste Function to create a formula**

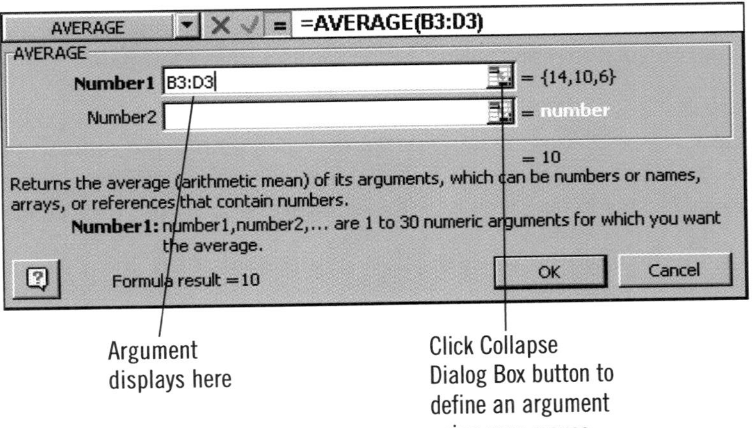

TABLE B-2: **Frequently Used Functions**

function	description
SUM(*argument*)	**Calculates the sum of the arguments**
AVERAGE(*argument*)	**Calculates the average of the arguments**
MAX(*argument*)	**Displays the largest value among the arguments**
MIN(*argument*)	**Displays the smallest value among the arguments**
COUNT(*argument*)	**Calculates the number of values in the arguments**

Introducing the Paste Function

The Paste Function button is located to the right of the AutoSum button on the Standard toolbar. To use the Paste Function, click. In the Paste Function dialog box, click the category containing the function you want, then click the desired function. The function appears in the formula bar. Click OK to fill in values or cell addresses for the arguments, then click OK.

Excel 97

Copying and Moving Cell Entries

Using the Cut, Copy, and Paste buttons or Excel's drag-and-drop feature, you can copy or move information from one cell or range in your worksheet to another. You can also cut, copy, and paste data from one worksheet to another. Evan included the 1998 forecast for spring and fall tours sales in his Tour Info workbook. He already entered the spring report in Sheet2 and will finish entering the labels and data for the fall report. Using the Copy and Paste buttons and drag-and-drop, Evan copies information from the spring report to the fall report.

Steps

CourseHelp

The camera icon indicates there is a CourseHelp available with this lesson. Click the Start button, point to programs, point to CourseHelp, then click Excel 97 Illustrated. Choose the CourseHelp that corresponds to this lesson.

Trouble?

When you drag-and-drop into occupied cells, Excel asks if you want to replace the existing cells. Click OK to replace the contents with the cells you are moving.

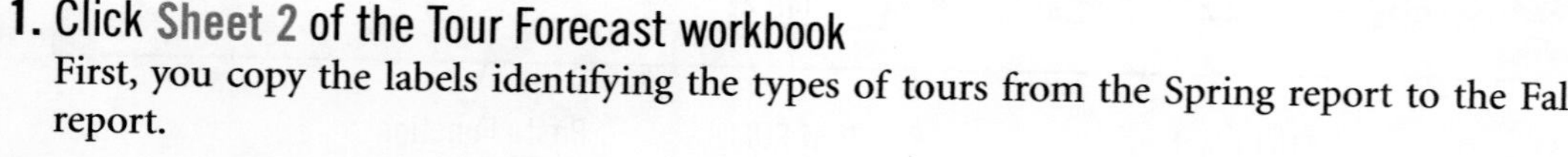

1. **Click Sheet 2 of the Tour Forecast workbook**
   First, you copy the labels identifying the types of tours from the Spring report to the Fall report.
2. **Select the range A4:A9, then click the Copy button on the Standard toolbar**
   The selected range (A4:A9) is copied to the **Clipboard**, a temporary storage file that holds all the selected information you copy or cut. The Cut button removes the selected information from the worksheet and places it on the Clipboard. To copy the contents of the Clipboard to a new location, you click the new cell and then use the Paste command.
3. **Click cell A13, then click the Paste button on the Standard toolbar**
   The contents of the Clipboard are copied into the range A13:A18. When pasting the contents of the Clipboard into the worksheet, you need to specify only the first cell of the range where you want the copied selection to go. Next, you decide to use drag-and-drop to copy the Total label.
4. **Click cell E3, then position the pointer on any edge of the cell until the pointer changes to**
5. **While the pointer is , press and hold down [Ctrl]**
   The pointer changes to .
6. **While still pressing [Ctrl], press and hold the left mouse button, then drag the cell contents to cell E12**
   As you drag, an outline of the cell moves with the pointer, as shown in Figure B-9, and a tip box appears tracking the current position of the item as you move it. When you release the mouse button, the Total label appears in cell E12. You now decide to move the worksheet title over to the left. To use drag-and-drop to move data to a new cell without copying it, do not press [Ctrl] while dragging.
7. **Click cell C1, then position the mouse on the edge of the cell until it changes to , then drag the cell contents to A1**
   You now enter fall sales data into the range B13:D16.
8. **Using the information shown in Figure B-10, enter the sales data for the fall tours into the range B13:D16**
   Compare your worksheet to Figure B-10.

FIGURE B-9: Using drag-and-drop to copy information

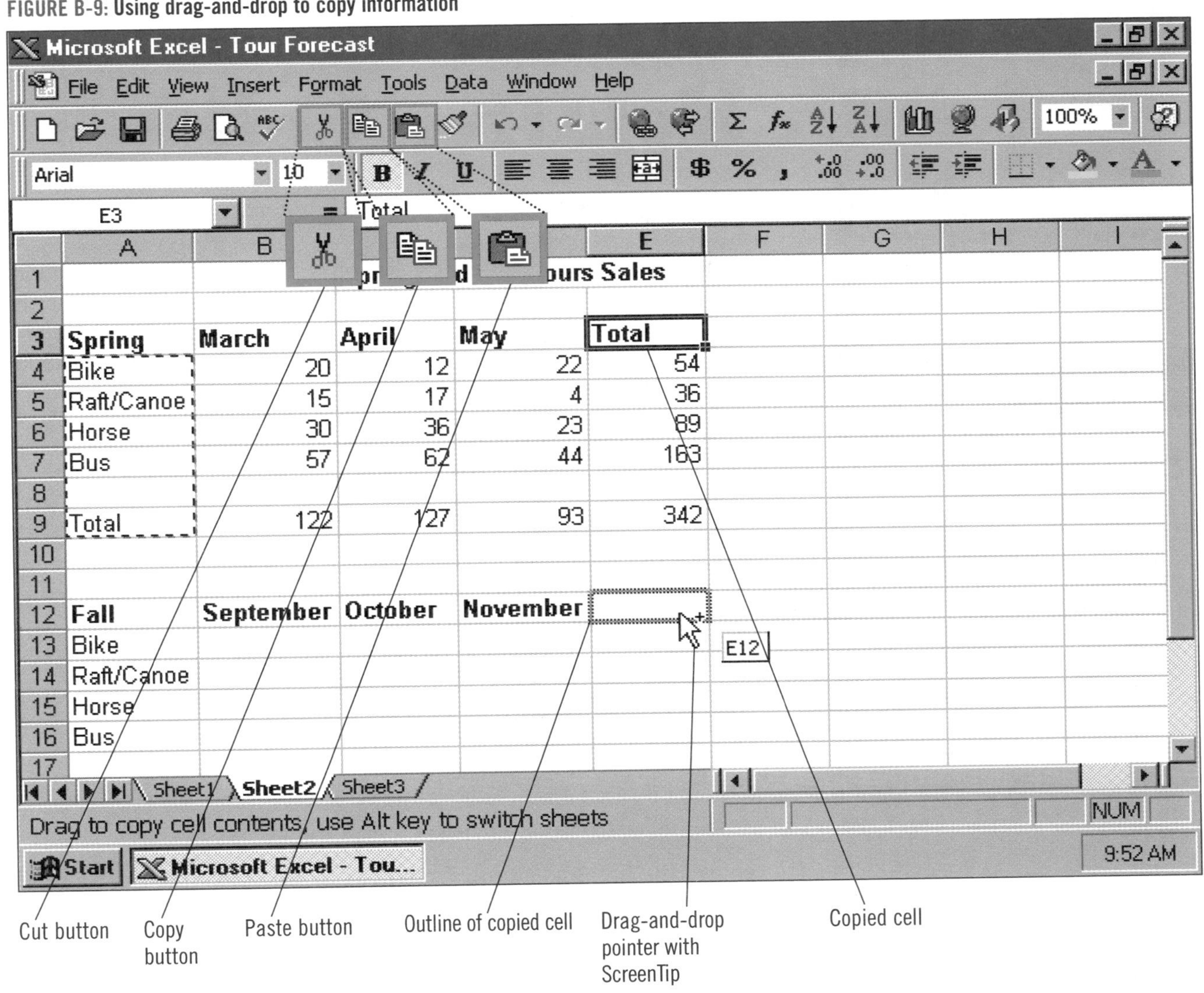

FIGURE B-10: Worksheet with Fall tours data entered

	A	B	C	D	E
11					
12	Fall	September	October	November	Total
13	Bike	17	15	18	
14	Raft/Canoe	21	8	5	
15	Horse	12	21	14	
16	Bus	25	12	18	
17					

Sheet1 Sheet2 Sheet3

Ready Sum=186 NUM

Start Microsoft Excel - Tou... 9:55 AM

Excel 97

Excel 97

Copying Formulas with Relative Cell References

Copying and moving formulas allows you to reuse formulas you've already created. Copying formulas, rather than retyping them, helps to prevent typing errors. Evan wants to copy from the Spring tours report to the Fall tours report the formulas that total the tours by type and by month. He can use Copy and Paste commands and the Fill right method to copy this information.

Steps

CourseHelp

If you have trouble with the concepts in this lesson, be sure to view the CourseHelp entitled Relative versus Absolute Cell Referencing

1. **Click cell E4, then click the Copy button on the Standard toolbar**
   The formula for calculating the total number of spring Bike tours is copied to the Clipboard. Notice that the formula in the formula bar appears as =SUM(B4:D4).

2. **Click cell E13, then click the Paste button on the Standard toolbar**
   The formula from cell E4 is copied into cell E13, where the new result of 50 appears. Notice in the formula bar that the cell references have changed, so that the range B13:D13 appears in the formula. Formulas in Excel contain **relative cell references.** A relative cell reference tells Excel to copy the formula to a new cell, but to substitute new cell references so that the relationship of the cells to the formula in its new location remains unchanged. In this case, Excel inserted cells D13, C13, and B13, the three cell references immediately to the left of E13.
   Notice that the bottom right corner of the active cell contains a small square, called the **fill handle.** Evan uses the fill handle to copy the formula in cell E13 to cells E14, E15, and E16. You can also use the fill handle to copy labels.

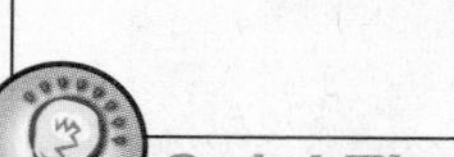

QuickTip

You can fill cells with sequential months, days of the week, years, and text plus a number (Quarter 1, Quarter 2, . . .) by dragging the fill handle. As you drag the fill handle, the contents of the last filled cell appears in the name box.

3. **Position the pointer over the fill handle until it changes to +, then drag the fill handle to select the range E13:E16**
   See Figure B-11.

4. **Release the mouse button**
   Once you release the mouse button, the fill handle copies the formula from the active cell (E13) and pastes it into each cell of the selected range. Again, because the formula uses relative cell references, cells E14 through E16 correctly display the totals for Raft and Canoe, Horse, and Bus tours

5. **Click cell B9, click Edit on the menu bar, then click Copy**
   The Copy command on the Edit menu has the same effect as clicking the Copy button on the Standard toolbar.

6. **Click cell B18, click Edit on the menu bar, then click Paste**
   See Figure B-12. The formula for calculating the September tours sales appears in the formula bar. Now you use the Fill Right command to copy the formula from cell B18 to cells C18, D18, and E18.

7. **Select the range B18:E18**

QuickTip

Use the Fill Series command on the Edit menu to examine all of Excel's available fill series options.

8. **Click Edit on the menu bar, point to Fill, then click Right**
   The rest of the totals are filled in correctly. Compare your worksheet to Figure B-13.

9. **Click the Save button on the Standard toolbar**
   Your worksheet is now saved.

FIGURE B-11: Selected range using the fill handle

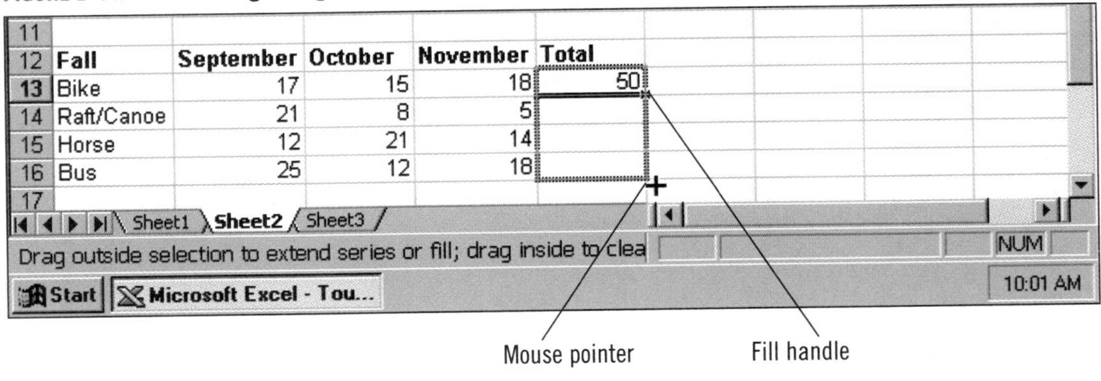

FIGURE B-12: Worksheet with copied formula

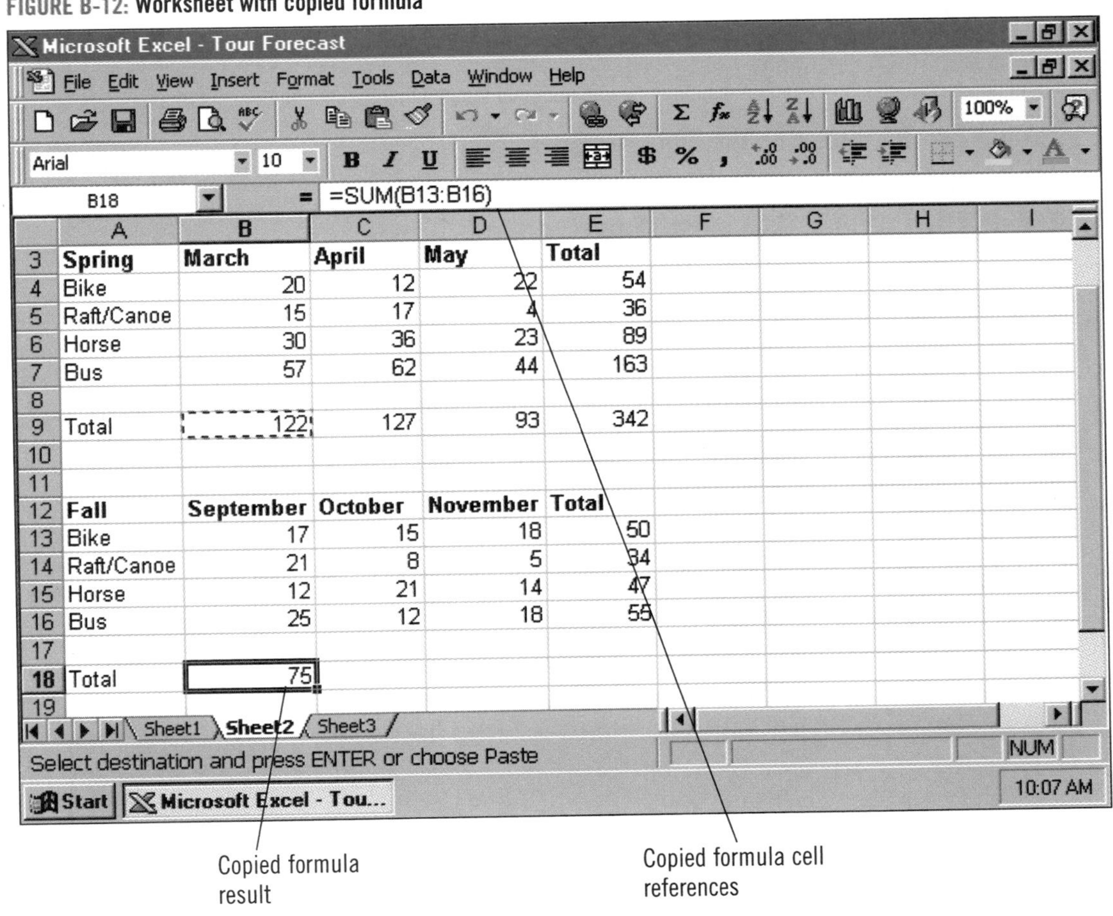

FIGURE B-13: Completed worksheet with all formulas copied

11					
12	**Fall**	**September**	**October**	**November**	**Total**
13	Bike	17	15	18	50
14	Raft/Canoe	21	8	5	34
15	Horse	12	21	14	47
16	Bus	25	12	18	55
17					
18	Total	75	56	55	186
19					

Sheet1 Sheet2 Sheet3

Ready Sum=372 NUM

Start Microsoft Excel - Tou... 10:09 AM

Excel 97

Copying Formulas with Absolute Cell References

Sometimes you might want a cell reference to always refer to a particular cell address. In such an instance, you would use an **absolute cell reference**. An absolute cell reference is a cell reference that always refers to a specific cell address, even if you move the formula to a new location. You identify an absolute reference by placing a dollar sign ($) before the column letter and row number of the address (for example A1). Marketing hopes the tour business will increase by 20% over last year's figures. Evan decides to add a column that calculates a possible increase in the number of spring tours in 1998. He wants to do a what-if analysis and recalculate the spreadsheet several times, changing the percentage that the tours might increase each time.

Steps 1 2 3 4

1. **Click cell G1, type Change, and then press [→]**
   You can store the increase factor that will be used in the what-if analysis in cell H1.
2. **Type 1.1 in cell H1, then press [Enter]**
   This represents a 10% increase in sales.
3. **Click cell F3, type 1998?, then press [Enter]**
   Now, you create a formula that references a specific address: cell H1.
4. **In cell F4, type =E4*H1, then click the Enter button on the formula bar**
   The result of 59.4 appears in cell F4. Now use the fill handle to copy the formula in cell F4 to F5:F7.
5. **Drag the fill handle to select the range F4:F7**
   The resulting values in the range F5:F7 are all zeros. When you look at the formula in cell F5, which is =E5*H2, you realize you need to use an absolute reference to cell H1. You can correct this error by editing cell F4 using [F4], a shortcut key, to change the relative cell reference to an absolute cell reference.
6. **Click cell F4, press [F2] to change to Edit mode, then press [F4]**
   When you pressed [F2], the **range finder** outlined the equations arguments in blue and green. When you pressed [F4], dollar signs appeared, changing the H1 cell reference to an absolute reference. See Figure B-14.
7. **Click the on the formula bar**
   Now that the formula correctly contains an absolute cell reference, use the fill handle to copy the formula in cell F4 to F5:F7.
8. **Drag the fill handle to select the range F4:F7**
   Now you can complete your what-if analysis by changing the value in cell H1 from 1.1 to 1.25 to indicate a 25% increase in sales.
9. **Click cell H1, type 1.25, then click the on the formula bar**
   The values in the range F4:F7 change. Compare your worksheet to Figure B-15.

QuickTip

Before you copy or move a formula, check to see if you need to use an absolute cell reference.

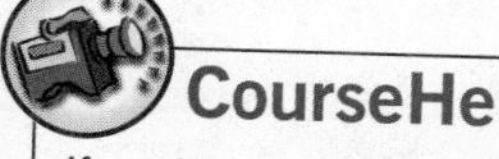

CourseHelp

If you have trouble with the concepts in this lesson, be sure to view the CourseHelp entitled Copying Formulas.

FIGURE B-14: **Absolute cell reference in cell F4**

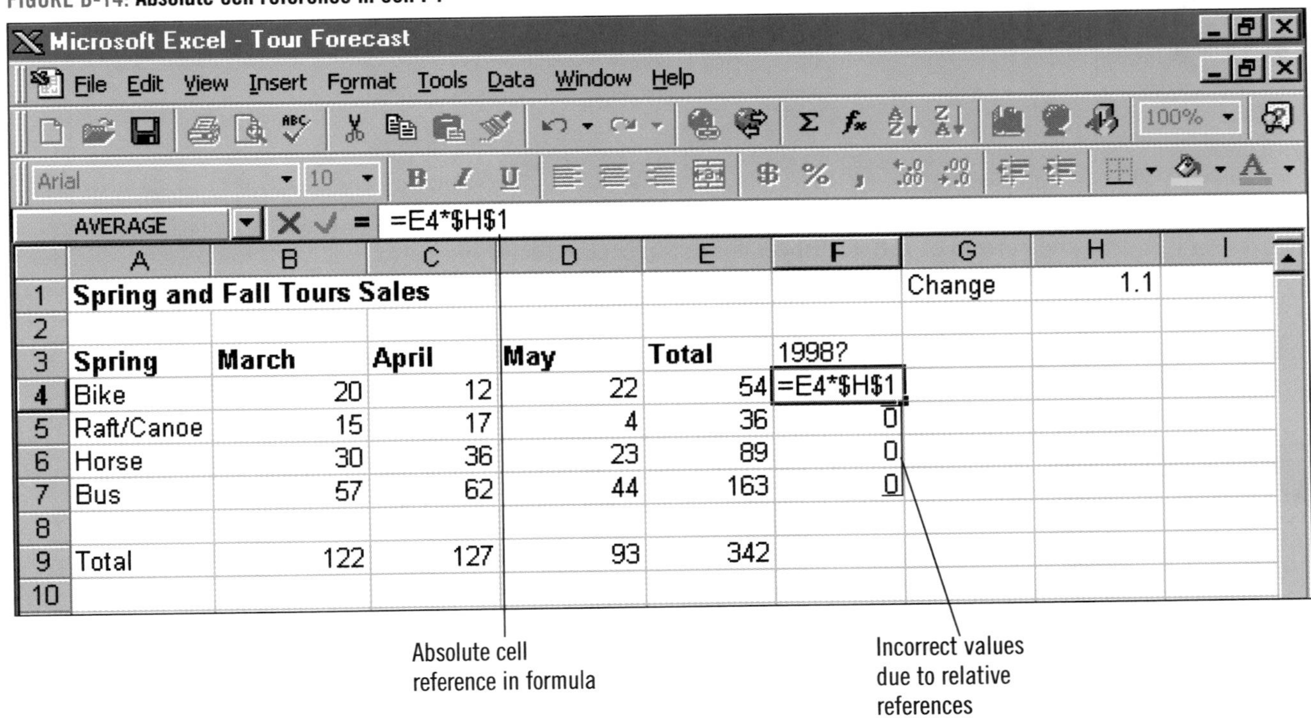

FIGURE B-15: **Worksheet with what-if value**

Microsoft Excel - Tour Forecast

H1 = 1.25

	A	B	C	D	E	F	G	H	I
1	**Spring and Fall Tours Sales**						Change	1.25	
2									
3	**Spring**	**March**	**April**	**May**	**Total**	1998?			
4	Bike	20	12	22	54	67.5			
5	Raft/Canoe	15	17	4	36	45			
6	Horse	30	36	23	89	111.25			
7	Bus	57	62	44	163	203.75			
8									
9	Total	122	127	93	342				
10									

Absolute cell reference in formulas

Excel 97

CLUES TO USE

Project a What-If Analysis

The ability to "plug in" values in a worksheet means you can create countless what-if analyses. A what-if analysis occurs when you insert different values into a worksheet model. This type of analysis can help you determine budgetary constraints, and can influence corporate economic decisions.

Naming and Moving a Sheet

Each workbook initially contains three worksheets. When the workbook is opened, the first worksheet is the active sheet. To move from sheet to sheet, click the desired sheet tab located at the bottom of the worksheet window. Sheet tab scrolling buttons, located to the left of the sheet tabs, allow rapid movement among the sheets. To make it easier to identify the sheets in a workbook, you can name each sheet. The name appears on the sheet tab. For instance, sheets within a single workbook could be named for individual sales people to better track performance goals. To better organize a workbook, you can easily rearrange sheets within it. Evan wants to be able to easily identify the Tour Information and the Tour Forecast sheets. He decides to name the two sheets in his workbook, then changes their order.

Steps

1. **Click the Sheet1 tab**
   Sheet1 becomes active; this is the worksheet that contains the Fall Tour Forecast information you compiled for the Marketing department. Its tab moves to the front, and the tab for Sheet2 moves to the background.
2. **Click the Sheet2 tab**
   Sheet2, containing last year's Tour Information, becomes active. Now that you have confirmed which sheet is which, rename Sheet1 so it has a name that identifies its contents.
3. **Double-click the Sheet1 tab**
   The Sheet1 text ("Sheet1") is selected. You could also click Format in the menu bar, point to Sheet, then click Rename to select the sheet name.
4. **Type Forecast, then press [Enter]**
   See Figure B-16. The new name automatically replaced the default name on the tab. Worksheet names can have up to 31 characters, including spaces and punctuation.
5. **Double-click the Sheet2 tab, then rename this sheet Information**
   You decide to rearrange the order of the sheets, so that Forecast comes after Information.
6. **Drag the Forecast sheet after the Information sheet**
   As you drag, the pointer changes to a sheet relocation indicator.
   See Figure B-17.
7. **Save and close the workbook, then exit Excel**

FIGURE B-16: **Renamed sheet in workbook**

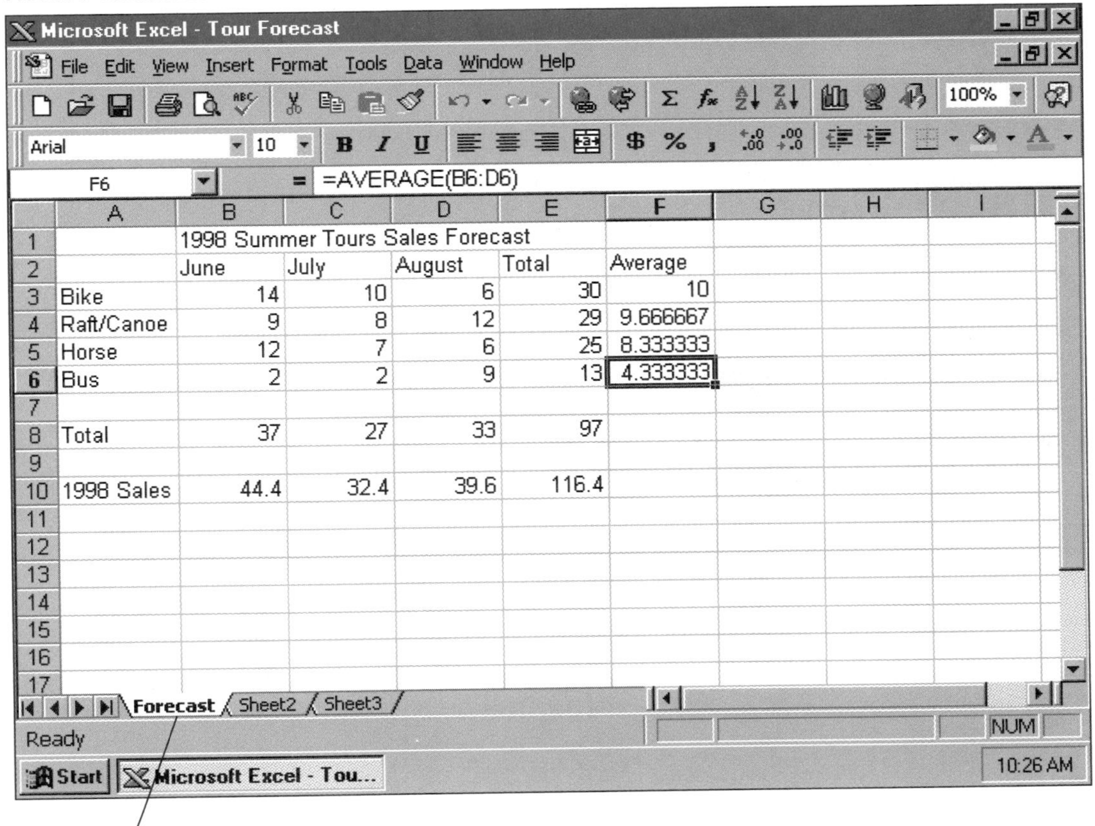

FIGURE B-17: **Moving Forecast after Information sheet**

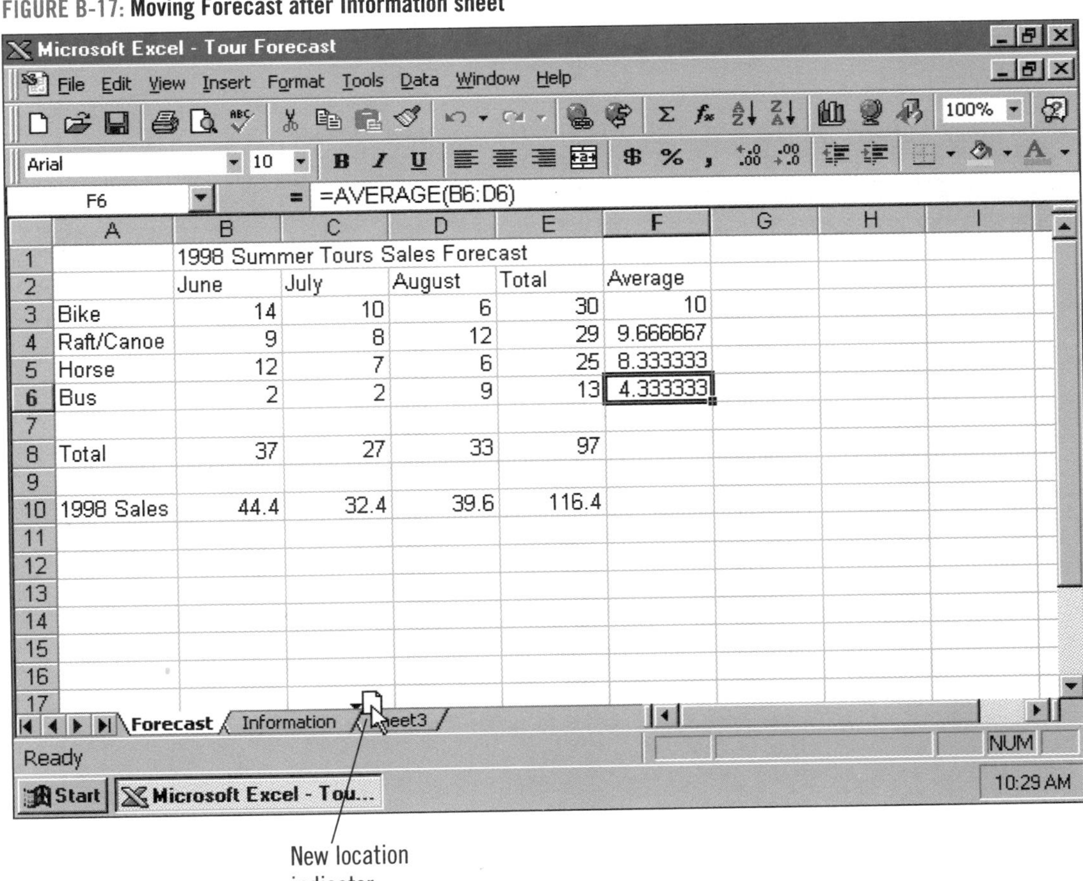

Practice

▶ Concepts Review

Label each of the elements of the Excel worksheet window shown in Figure B-18.

FIGURE B-18

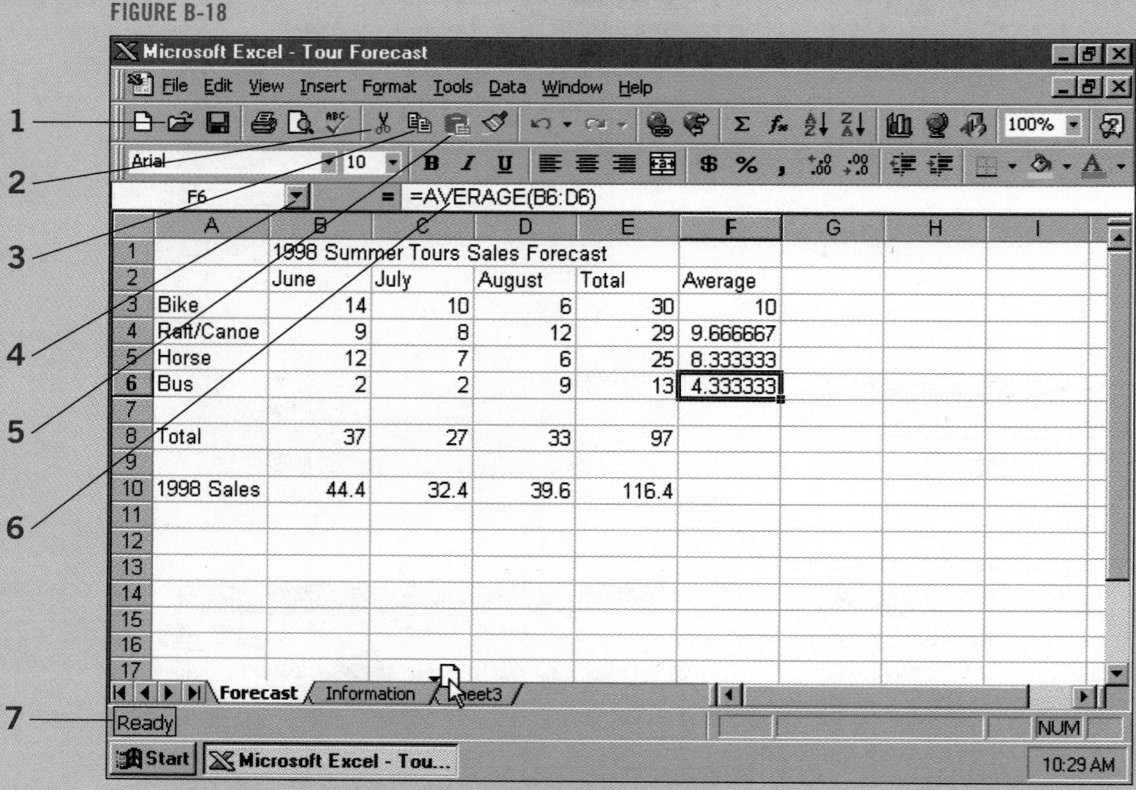

Match each of the terms with the statement that describes its function.

8. **Range**
9. **Function**
10. [Paste button]
11. [Copy button]
12. **Formula**

a. A predefined formula that provides a shortcut for commonly used calculations
b. A cell entry that performs a calculation in an Excel worksheet
c. A specified group of cells, which can include the entire worksheet
d. Used to copy cells
e. Used to paste cells

Select the best answer from the list of choices.

13. What type of cell reference changes when it is copied?
  a. Absolute
  b. Circular
  c. Looping
  d. Relative

14. Which character is used to make a reference absolute?
  a. &
  b. ^
  c. $
  d. @

Skills Review

1 Edit cell entries and work with ranges.
  a. Open workbook XL B-2 and save it as "Mutual Funds" on your Student Disk.
  b. Change the number of Arch shares to 210.
  c. Change the price per share of RST stock to 18.45.
  d. Change the number of United shares to 100.
  e. Name the range B2:B5 "Shares".
  f. Name the range C2:C5 "Price".
  g. Save, preview, and print your worksheet.

2 Enter formulas.
  a. Click cell B6.
  b. Enter the formula B2+B3+B4+B5.
  c. Click cell C6.
  d. Enter the formula C2+C3+C4+C5.
  e. Save your work, then preview and print the data in the Mutual Funds worksheet.

3 Introduce functions.
  a. Click cell C7.
  b. Enter the MIN function for the range C2:C5.
  c. Type the label Min Price in cell A7.
  d. Save your work.
  e. Preview and print this worksheet.

4 Copy and move cell entries.
  a. Select the range A1:E6.
  b. Use drag-and-drop to copy the range to cell A10.
  c. Delete the range B11:C14.
  d. Save your work.
  e. Preview and print this worksheet.

5 Copy formulas with relative cell references.

- **a.** Click cell D2.
- **b.** Create a formula that multiplies B2 and C2.
- **c.** Copy the formula in D2 into cells D3:D5.
- **d.** Copy the formula in D2 into cells D11:D14.
- **e.** Save, preview, and print this worksheet.

6 Copy formulas with absolute cell references.

- **a.** Click cell G2.
- **b.** Type the value 1.375.
- **c.** Click cell E2.
- **d.** Create a formula containing an absolute reference that multiplies D2 and G2.
- **e.** Copy the formula in E2 into cells E3:E5.
- **f.** Copy the formula in E2 into cells E11:E14.
- **g.** Change the amount in cell G2 to 2.873.
- **h.** Save, preview, and print this worksheet.

7 Name a sheet.

- **a.** Name the Sheet1 tab "Funds".
- **b.** Move the Funds sheet so it comes after Sheet3.
- **c.** Save and close this worksheet.

Independent Challenges

1. You are the box-office manager for Lightwell Players, a regional theater company. Your responsibilities include tracking seasonal ticket sales for the company's main stage productions and anticipating ticket sales for the next season. Lightwell Players sells four types of tickets: reserved seating, general admission, senior citizen tickets, and student tickets. The 1993–94 season included productions of *Hamlet, The Cherry Orchard, Fires in the Mirror, The Shadow Box,* and *Heartbreak House.*

Open a new workbook and save it as "Theater" on your Student Disk. Plan and build a worksheet that tracks the sales of each of the four ticket types for all five of the plays. Calculate the total ticket sales for each play, the total sales for each of the four ticket types, and the total sales for all tickets.

Enter your own sales data, but assume the following: the Lightwell Players sold 800 tickets during the season; reserved seating was the most popular ticket type for all of the shows except for *The Shadow Box*; no play sold more than 10 student tickets. Plan and build a second worksheet in the workbook that reflects a 5% increase in sales of all ticket types.

To complete this independent challenge:

1. Think about the results you want to see, the information you need to build into these worksheets, and what types of calculations must be performed.
2. Sketch sample worksheets on a piece of paper to indicate how the information should be laid out. What information should go in the columns? In the rows?
3. Build the worksheets by entering a title, row labels, column headings, and formulas. Use named ranges to make the worksheet easier to use, and rename the sheet tabs to easily identify the contents of each sheet. (Hint: If your columns are too narrow, position the cell pointer in the column you want to widen. To widen the column, click Format on the menu bar, click Column, click Width, choose a new column width, and then click OK.)
4. Use separate worksheets for existing ticket sales and projected sales showing the 5% increase.
5. Save your work, then preview and print the worksheets.
6. Submit your sketches and printed worksheets.

2. You have been promoted to computer lab manager at your school, and it is your responsibility to make sure there are enough computers for students during scheduled classes. Currently, you have four classrooms: three with IBM PCs and one with Macintoshes. Classes are scheduled Monday, Wednesday, and Friday in two-hour increments from 9 a.m. to 5 p.m. (the lab closes at 7 p.m.), and each room can currently accommodate 20 computers.

Open a new workbook and save it as "Lab Manager" on your Student Disk. Plan and build a worksheet that tracks the number of students who can currently use available computers per two-hour class. Create your enrollment data, but assume that current enrollment averages 85% of each room's daily capacity. Using an additional worksheet, show the impact of an enrollment increase of 25%.

To complete this independent challenge:

1. Think about how to construct these worksheets to create the desired output.
2. Sketch sample paper worksheets, to indicate how the information should be laid out.
3. Build the worksheets by entering a title, row labels, column headings, and formulas. Use named ranges to make the worksheet easier to use, and rename the sheets to identify their contents easily.
4. Use separate sheets for actual enrollment and projected changes.
5. Save your work, then preview and print the worksheets.
6. Submit your sketches and printed worksheets.

3. Nuts and Bolts is a small but growing hardware store that has hired you to organize its accounting records using Excel. The store hopes to track its inventory using Excel once its accounting records are under control. Before you were hired, one of the accounting staff started to enter expenses in a workbook, but the work was never completed. Open the workbook XL B-3 and save it as "Nuts and Bolts Finances" on your Student Disk. Include functions such as the Average, Maximum, and Minimum amounts of each of the expenses in the worksheet.

To complete this independent challenge:

1. Think about what information would be important for the accounting staff to know.
2. Use the existing worksheet to create a paper sketch of the types of functions and formulas you will use and of where they will be located. Indicate where you will have named ranges.
3. Create your sketch using the existing worksheet as a foundation. Your worksheet should use range names in its formulas and functions.
4. Rename Sheet1 "Expenses".
5. Save your work, and then preview and print the worksheet.
6. Submit your sketches and printed worksheets.

4. The immediacy of the World Wide Web allows you to find comparative data on any service or industry of interest to you. Your company is interested in investing in one of any of the most actively traded stocks in the three primary trading houses, and you have been asked to retrieve this information. To complete this independent challenge:

1. Open a new workbook and save it on your Student Disk as Stock Data.
2. Log on to the Internet and use your browser to go to the http://www.course.com. From there, click the link Student On Line Companions, then click the Microsoft Office 97 Professional Edition — Illustrated: A First Course page, then click on the Excel link for Unit B.
3. Use each of the following sites to compile your data: NASDAQ [www.nasdaq.com], the New York Stock Exchange [www.nyse.com], and the American Stock Exchange [www.amex.com].
4. Using one worksheet per exchange, locate data for the 10 most actively traded stocks.
5. Make sure all stocks are identified using their commonly known names.
6. Your company will invest a total of $100,000 and wants to make that investment in only one exchange. Still, they are asking you to research the types of stocks that could be purchased in each exchange.
7. Assume an even distribution of the original investment in the stocks, and total pertinent columns. Determine the total number of shares that will be purchased.
8. Save, print, and hand in a print of your work.

Visual Workshop

Create a worksheet similar to Figure B-19 using the skills you learned in this unit. Save the workbook as "Annual Budget" on your Student Disk. Preview, and then print the worksheet.

FIGURE B-19

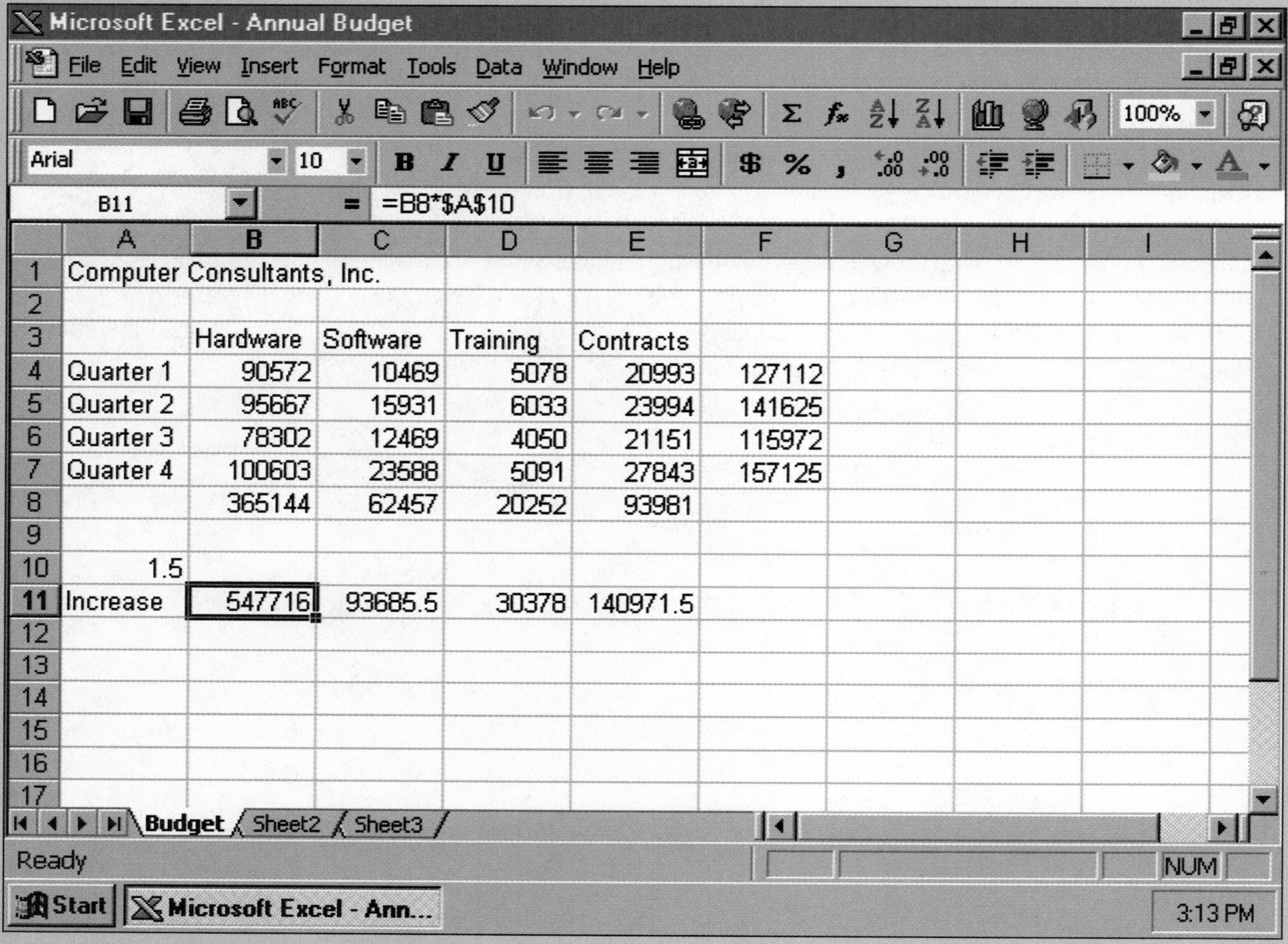

Microsoft Excel - Annual Budget

B11 = =B8*A10

	A	B	C	D	E	F
1	Computer Consultants, Inc.					
2						
3		Hardware	Software	Training	Contracts	
4	Quarter 1	90572	10469	5078	20993	127112
5	Quarter 2	95667	15931	6033	23994	141625
6	Quarter 3	78302	12469	4050	21151	115972
7	Quarter 4	100603	23588	5091	27843	157125
8		365144	62457	20252	93981	
9						
10	1.5					
11	Increase	547716	93685.5	30378	140971.5	

Formatting a Worksheet

Objectives

- Format values
- Select fonts and point sizes
- Change attributes and alignment of labels
- Adjust column widths
- Insert and delete rows and columns
- Apply colors, patterns, and borders
- Use conditional formatting
- Check spelling

Now you will learn how to format a worksheet to make it easier to read and to emphasize key data. You do this by formatting cell contents, adjusting column widths, and inserting and deleting columns and rows. The marketing managers at Nomad Ltd have asked Evan Brillstein to create a worksheet that tracks tour advertising expenses. Evan has prepared a worksheet containing this information, and now he needs to use formatting techniques to make the worksheet easier to read and to call attention to important data.

Excel 97

Formatting Values

Formatting is how information appears in cells; it does not alter the data in any way. To format a cell, you select it, then apply the formatting you want. You can also format a range of cells. Cells and ranges can be formatted before or after data is entered. If you enter a value in a cell, and the cell appears to display the data incorrectly, you need to format the cell to display the value correctly. You might also want more than one cell to have the same format. The Marketing Department has requested that Evan track tour advertising expenses. Evan developed a worksheet that tracks invoices for tour advertising. He has entered all the information and now wants to format some of the labels and values in the worksheet. Because some of the format changes he will make to labels and values might also affect column widths, Evan decided to make all his formatting changes before changing the column widths. He formats his values first.

Steps

1. **Open the worksheet XL C-1 from your Student Disk, then save it as Tour Ads**
   The tour advertising worksheet appears in Figure C-1.
   You want to format the data in the Cost ea. column so it displays with a dollar sign.
2. **Select the range E4:E32, then click the Currency Style button on the Formatting toolbar**
   Excel adds dollar signs and two decimal places to the Cost ea. column data. When the new format is applied, Excel automatically resizes the columns to display all the information. Columns G, H, and I contain dollar values also, but you decide to apply the comma format instead of currency.
3. **Select the range G4:I32, then click the Comma Style button on the Formatting toolbar**
   Column J contains percentages.
4. **Select the range J4:J32, click the Percent Style button on the Formatting toolbar, then click the Increase Decimal button on the Formatting toolbar to show one decimal place**
   Data in the % of Total column is now formatted in Percent style. Next, you reformat the invoice dates.
5. **Select the range B4:B31, click Format on the menu bar, then click Cells**
   The Format Cells dialog box appears with the Number tab in front and the Date format already selected. See Figure C-2. You can also use this dialog box to format ranges with currency, commas, and percentages.
6. **Select the format 4-Mar-97 in the Type list box, then click OK**
   You decide you don't need the year to appear in the Inv Due column.
7. **Select the range C4:C31, click Format on the menu bar, click Cells, click 4-Mar in the Type list box, then click OK**
   Compare your worksheet to Figure C-3.
8. **Save your work**

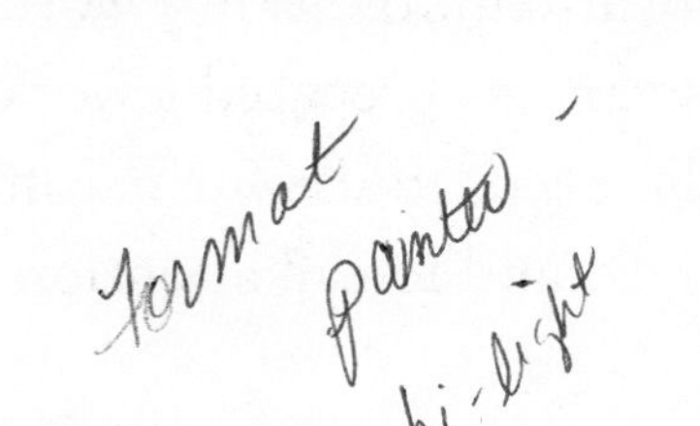

FIGURE C-1: **Tour advertising worksheet**

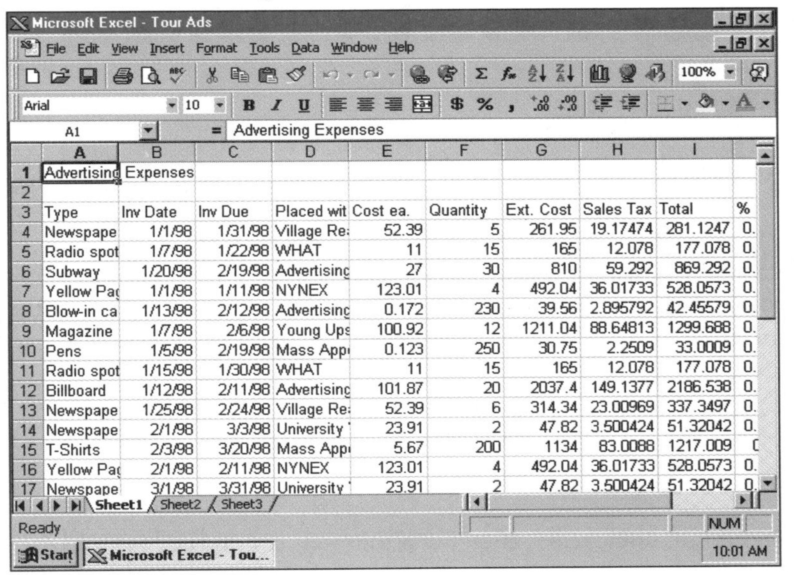

FIGURE C-2: **Format Cells dialog box**

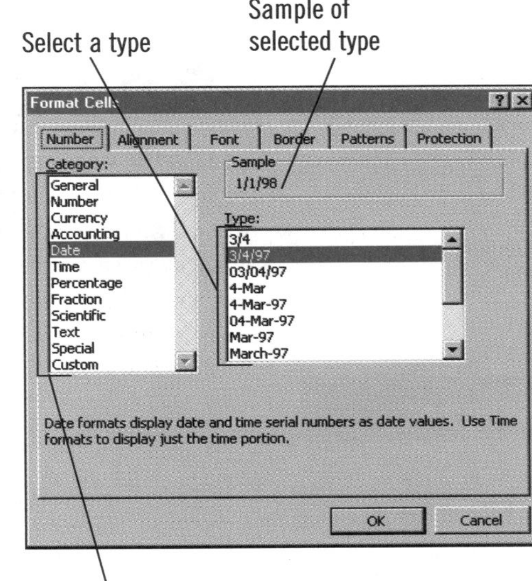

FIGURE C-3: **Worksheet with formatted values**

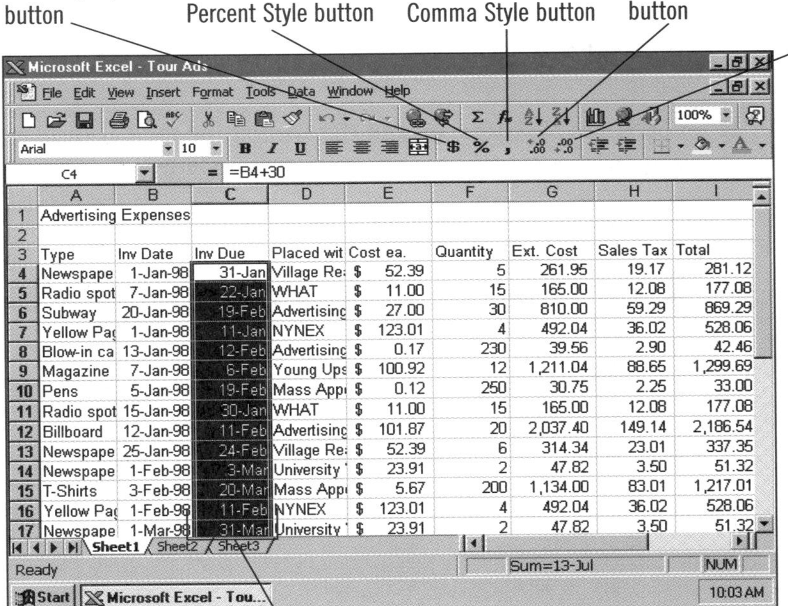

CLUES TO USE

Using the Format Painter

A cell's format can be "painted" into other cells using the Format Painter button on the Formatting toolbar. This is similar to using drag-and-drop to copy information, but instead of copying cell contents, you copy only the cell format. Select the cell containing the desired format, then click. The pointer changes to, as shown in Figure C-4. Use this pointer to select the cell or range you want to contain the painted format.

FIGURE C-4: **Using the Format Painter**

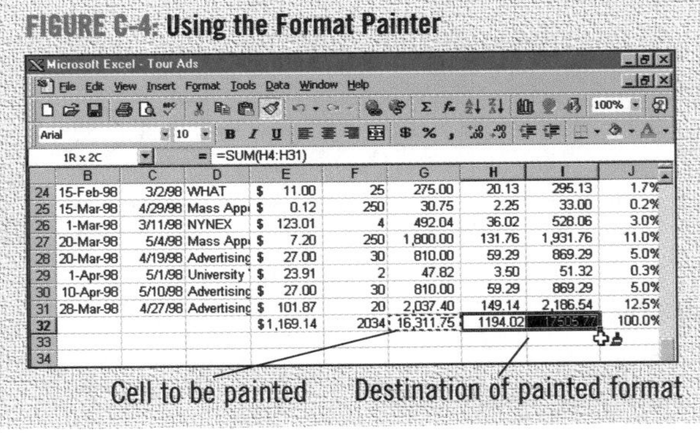

Excel 97

Selecting Fonts and Point Sizes

A **font** is the name given to a collection of characters (letters, numerals, symbols, and punctuation marks) with a specific design. The **point size** is the physical size of the text, measured in points. The default font in Excel is 10 point Arial. You can change the font, the size, or both of any entry or section in a worksheet by using the Format command on the menu bar or by using the Formatting toolbar. Table C-1 shows several fonts in different sizes. Now that the data is formatted, Evan wants to change the font and size of the labels and the worksheet title so that they stand out.

QuickTip

You can also open the Format Cells dialog box by right-clicking the mouse after selecting cells, then selecting Format Cells.

Trouble?

If you don't have Times New Roman in your list of fonts, choose another font.

QuickTip

The Format Cells dialog box displays a sample of the selected font. Use the Format Cells command to access the Format Cells dialog box if you're unsure of a font's appearance.

1. **Press [Ctrl][Home] to select cell A1**
2. **Click Format on the menu bar, click Cells, then click the Font tab in the Format Cells dialog box**
   See Figure C-5.
   You decide to change the font of the title from Arial to Times New Roman, and increase the font size to 24.
3. **Click Times New Roman in the Font list box, click 24 in the Size list box, then click OK**
   The title font appears in 24 point Times New Roman, and the Formatting toolbar displays the new font and size information. Next, you make the column headings larger.
4. **Select the range A3:J3, click Format on the menu bar, then click Cells**
   The Font tab should still be the front-most tab in the Format Cells dialog box.
5. **Click Times New Roman in the Font list box, click 14 in the Size list box, then click OK**
   Compare your worksheet to Figure C-6.
6. **Save your work**

TABLE C-1: Types of fonts

font	12 point	24 point
Arial	Excel	Excel
Helvetica	Excel	Excel
Palatino	Excel	Excel
Times	Excel	Excel

FIGURE C-5: **Font tab in the Format Cells dialog box**

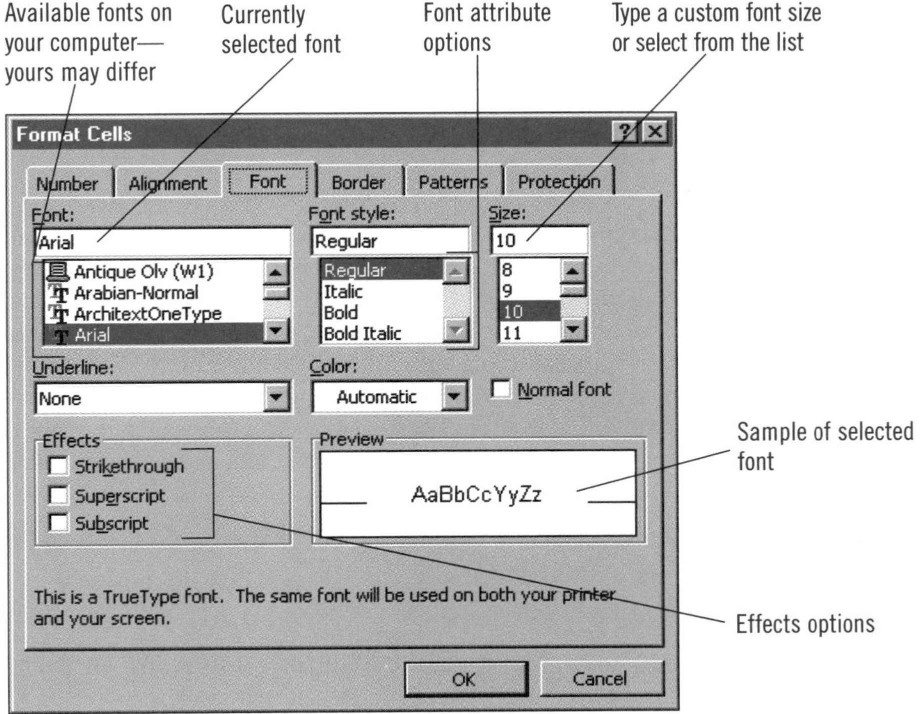

FIGURE C-6: **Worksheet with enlarged title and labels**

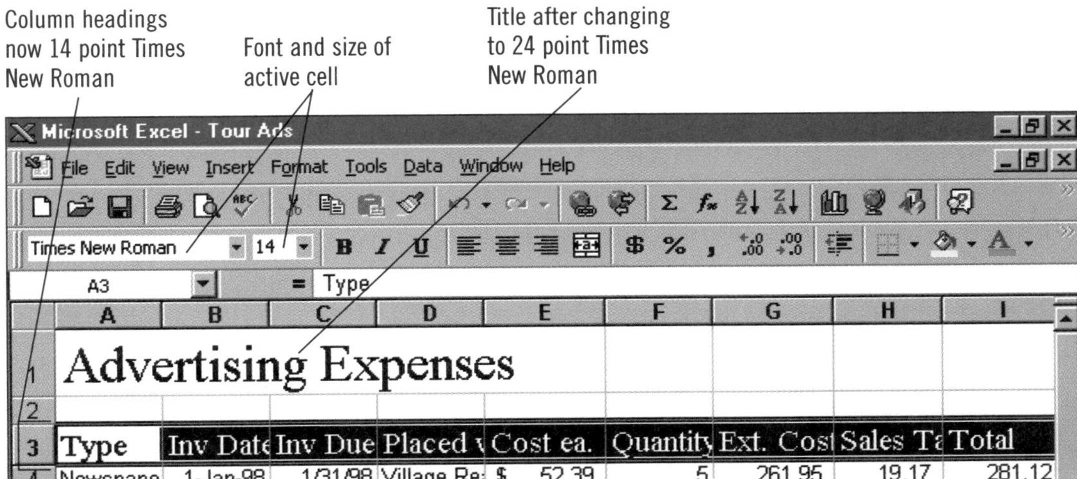

Clues to Use: Using the Formatting toolbar to change fonts and sizes

The font and size of the active cell appear on the Formatting toolbar. Click the Font list arrow, as shown in Figure C-7, to see a list of available fonts. If you want to change the font, first select the cell, click the Font list arrow, then choose the font you want. You can change the size of selected text in the same way, by clicking the Size list arrow on the Formatting toolbar to display a list of available point sizes.

FIGURE C-7: **Available fonts on the Formatting toolbar**

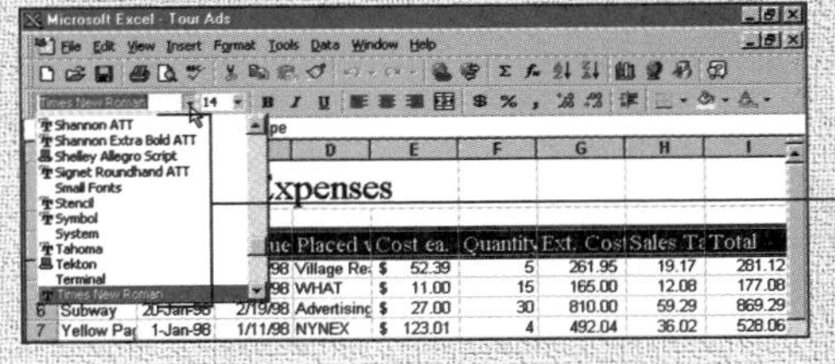

Excel 97

Changing Attributes and Alignment of Labels

Attributes are font styling features such as bold, italics, and underlining. You can apply bold, italics, and underlining from the Formatting toolbar or from the Font tab in the Format Cells dialog box. You can also change the alignment of text in cells. Left, right, or center alignment can be applied from the Formatting toolbar, or from the Alignment tab in the Format Cells dialog box. See Table C-2 for a description of the available attribute and alignment buttons on the Formatting toolbar. Excel also has predefined worksheet formats to make formatting easier. Now that he has applied the appropriate fonts and font sizes to his worksheet labels, Evan wants to further enhance his worksheet's appearance by adding bold and underline formatting and centering some of the labels.

Steps

1. **Press [Ctrl][Home] to select cell A1, then click the Bold button on the Formatting toolbar**
   The title "Advertising Expenses" appears in bold.
2. **Select the range A3:J3, then click the Underline button on the Formatting toolbar**
   Excel underlines the column headings in the selected range.
3. **Click cell A3, click the Italics button on the Formatting toolbar, then click**
   The word "Type" appears in boldface, italic type. Notice that the Bold, Italics, and Underline buttons on the Formatting toolbar are indented. You decide you don't like the italic formatting. You remove it by clicking again.
4. **Click**
   Excel removes italics from cell A3.
5. **Add bold formatting to the rest of the labels in the range B3:J3**
   You want to center the title over the data.
6. **Select the range A1:F1, then click the Merge and Center button on the Formatting toolbar**
   The title Advertising Expenses is centered across six columns. Now you center the column headings in their cells.
7. **Select the range A3:J3 then click the Center button on the Formatting toolbar**
   You are satisfied with the formatting in the worksheet.
   Compare your screen to Figure C-8.

QuickTip

Highlighting information on a worksheet can be useful, but overuse of any attribute can be distracting and make a document less readable. Be consistent by adding emphasis the same way throughout a workbook.

Time To

✓ Save

FIGURE C-8: Worksheet with formatting attributes applied

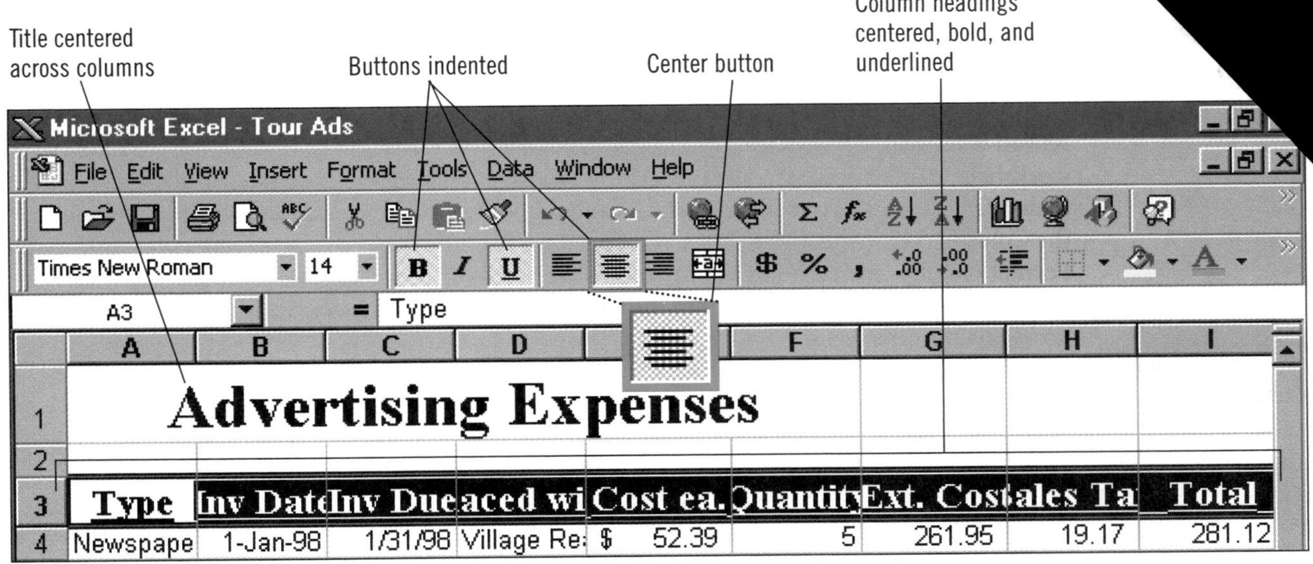

TABLE C-2: Attribute and Alignment buttons on the Formatting toolbar

icon	description	icon	description
B	Adds boldface		Aligns left
I	Italicizes		Aligns center
U	Underlines		Aligns right
	Adds lines or borders		Centers across columns, and combines two or more selected adjacent cells into one cell.

Using AutoFormat

Excel provides 16 preset formats called AutoFormats, which allow instant formatting of large amounts of data. AutoFormats are designed for worksheets with labels in the left column and top rows and totals in the bottom row or right column. To use AutoFormatting, select the data to be formatted—or place your mouse pointer anywhere within the range to be selected—click Format on the menu bar, click AutoFormat, then select a format from the Table Format list box, as shown in Figure C-9.

FIGURE C-9: AutoFormat dialog box

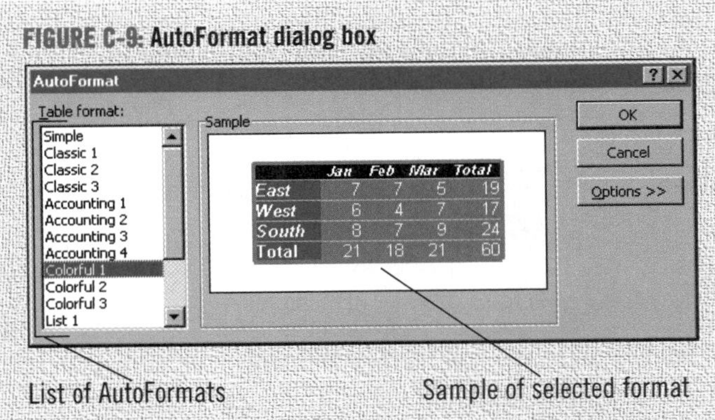

Excel 97

djusting Column Vidths

work with a worksheet, you might need to adjust the width of the columns to make your
eet more usable. The default column width is 8.43 characters wide, a little less than one
th Excel, you can adjust the column width for one or more columns using the mouse or
mn command on the Format menu. Table C-3 describes the commands available on the
Column menu. You can also adjust the height of rows. Evan notices that some
of the labels in column A don't fit in the cells. He decides to adjust the widths of columns so that the labels fit in the cells.

Steps

1. **Position the pointer on the column line between columns A and B in the column header area**
   The pointer changes to ✛, as shown in Figure C-10. You make the column wider.
2. **Drag the line to the right until column A is wide enough to accommodate all of the labels for types of advertising**
   You decide to resize the columns so they automatically accommodate the widest entry in a cell.
3. **Position the pointer on the column line between columns B and C in the column header area until it changes to ✛, then double-click the left mouse button**
   The width of column B is automatically resized to fit the widest entry, in this case, the column head. This feature is called **AutoFit**.
4. **Repeat step 3 to use AutoFit to automatically resize columns C, D, and J**
   You can also use the Column Width command on the Format menu to adjust several columns to the same width.
5. **Select the range F5:I5**
   Any cells in the columns you want to resize can be selected.
6. **Click Format on the menu bar, point to Column, then click Width**
   The Column Width dialog box appears. Move the dialog box, if necessary, by dragging it by its title bar so you can see the contents of the worksheet.
7. **Type 12 in the Column Width text box, then click OK**
   The column widths change to reflect the new settings. See Figure C-11. You are satisfied and decide to save the worksheet.
8. **Save your work**

QuickTip

To reset columns to the default width, select the range of cells, then use the Column Standard Width command on the Format menu. Click OK in the Standard Width dialog box to accept the default width.

TABLE C-3: Format Column commands

command	description
Width	Sets the width to a specific number of characters
AutoFit Selection	Fits the widest entry
Hide	Hide(s) column(s)
Unhide	Unhide(s) column(s)
Standard Width	Resets to default widths

FIGURE C-10: **Preparing to change the column width**

	A	B	C	D	E	F	G	H	I
1	**Advertising Expenses**								
2									
3	**Type**	**Inv Datd**	**Inv Due**	**aced wi**	**Cost ea.**	**Quantity**	**Ext. Cost**	**ales Ta**	**Total**
4	Newspape	1-Jan-98	1/31/98	Village Re:	$ 52.39	5	261.95	19.17	281.12
5	Radio spot	7-Jan-98	1/22/98	WHAT	$ 11.00	15	165.00	12.08	177.08
6	Subway	20-Jan-98	2/19/98	Advertising	$ 27.00	30	810.00	59.29	869.29

Resize pointer between columns A and B

FIGURE C-11: **Worksheet with column widths adjusted**

	D	E	F	G	H	I	
1	**ng Expenses**						
2							
3	**Placed with**	**Cost ea.**	**Quantity**	**Ext. Cost**	**Sales Tax**	**Total**	**% o**
4	Village Reader	$ 52.39	5	261.95	19.17	281.12	
5	WHAT	$ 11.00	15	165.00	12.08	177.08	
6	Advertising Concepts	$ 27.00	30	810.00	59.29	869.29	
7	NYNEX	$ 123.01	4	492.04	36.02	528.06	
8	Advertising Concepts	$ 0.17	230	39.56	2.90	42.46	

Specifying row height

The Row Height command on the Format menu allows you to customize row height to improve readability. Row height is calculated in points, units of measure also used for fonts—one inch equals 72 points. The row height must exceed the size of the font you are using. For example, if you are using a 12 point font, the row height must be more than 12 points. Normally, you don't need to adjust row heights manually. If you format something in a row to be a larger point size, Excel will adjust the row height to fit the largest point size in the row.

Excel 97

Inserting and Deleting Rows and Columns

As you modify a worksheet, you might find it necessary to insert or delete rows and columns. For example, you might need to insert rows to accommodate new inventory products or remove a column of yearly totals that are no longer current. Inserting or deleting rows or columns can help to make your worksheet more readable. Evan has already improved the appearance of his worksheet by formatting the labels and values in the worksheet. Now he decides to improve the overall appearance of the worksheet by inserting a row between the last row of data and the totals. This will help make the totals stand out more. Evan has also located a row of inaccurate data that should be deleted.

Steps

1. **Click cell A32, click Insert on the menu bar, then click Cells**
   The Insert dialog box opens. See Figure C-12. You can choose to insert a column or a row, or you can shift the data in the cells in the active column right or in the active row down. You want to insert a row to add some space between the last row of data and the totals.

2. **Click the Entire Row radio button, then click OK**
   A blank row is inserted between the title and the month labels. When you insert a new row, the contents of the worksheet shift down from the newly inserted row. When you insert a new column, the contents of the worksheet shift to the right from the point of the new column. Now delete the row containing information about hats, as this information is inaccurate.

3. **Click the row 27 selector button (the gray box containing the row number to the left of the worksheet)**
   All of row 27 is selected as shown in Figure C-13.

4. **Click Edit on the menu bar, then click Delete**
   Excel deletes row 27, and all rows below this shift up one row. You are satisfied with the appearance of the worksheet.

5. **Save your work**

QuickTip

Inserting or deleting rows or columns can also cause problems with formulas that reference cells in that area, so be sure to consider this when inserting or deleting rows or columns.

FIGURE C-12: Insert dialog box

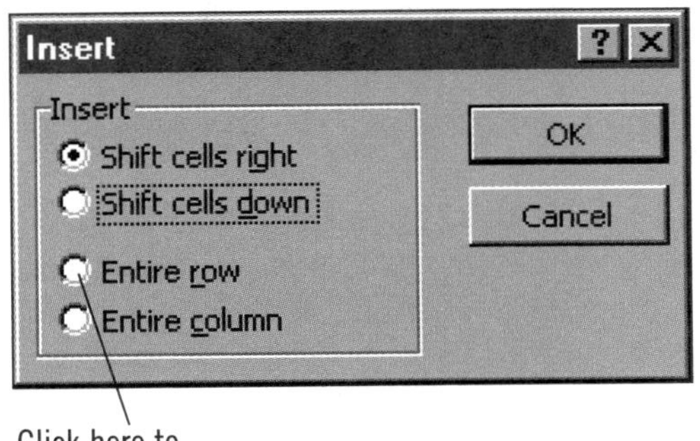

FIGURE C-13: Worksheet with row 27 selected

25	Pens	15-Mar-98	4/29/98	Mass Appeal, Inc.	$ 0.12	250	3
26	Yellow Pages	1-Mar-98	3/11/98	NYNEX	$ 123.01	4	49
27	Hats	20-Mar-98	5/4/98	Mass Appeal, Inc.	$ 7.20	250	1,80
28	Subway	20-Mar-98	4/19/98	Advertising Concepts	$ 27.00	30	81
29	Newspaper	1-Apr-98	5/1/98	University Voice	$ 23.91	2	4
30	Subway	10-Apr-98	5/10/98	Advertising Concepts	$ 27.00	30	81
31	Billboard	28-Mar-98	4/27/98	Advertising Concepts	$ 101.87	20	2,03
32							
33					$1,169.14	2034	16,31
34							
35							

Sheet1 / Sheet2 / Sheet3

Ready — Sum=75913.83035 — NUM

Start — Microsoft Excel - Tou... — 8:26 AM

Row 27 selector button

Inserted row

Clues to Use

Using dummy columns and rows

You use cell references and ranges in formulas. When you add or delete a column or row within a range used in a formula, Excel automatically adjusts the formula to reflect the change. However, when you add a column or row at the end of a range used in a formula, you must modify the formula to reflect the additional column or row. To avoid having to edit the formula, you can include a dummy column and dummy row within the range you use for that formula. A dummy column is a blank column included to the right of but within a range. A dummy row is a blank row included at the bottom of but within a range, as shown in Figure C-14. Then if you add another column or row to the end of the range, the formula will automatically be modified to include the new data.

FIGURE C-14: Formula with dummy row

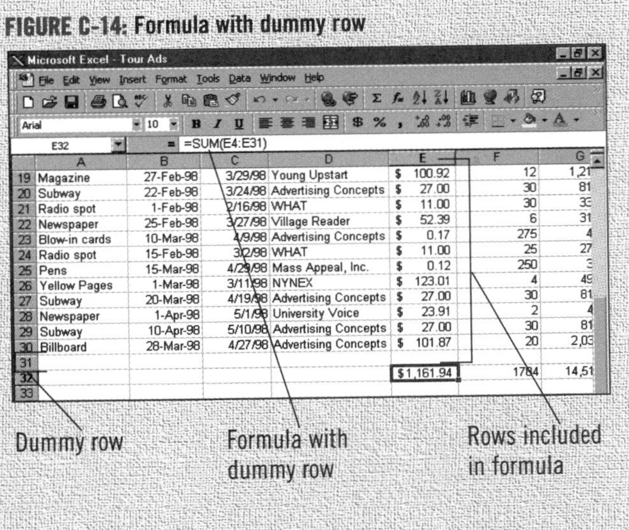

Excel 97

Applying Colors, Patterns, and Borders

You can use colors, patterns, and borders to enhance the overall appearance of a worksheet and to improve its readability. You can add these enhancements using the Patterns tab in the Format Cells dialog box or by using the Borders and Color buttons on the Formatting toolbar. When you use the Format Cells dialog box, you can see what your enhanced text will look like in the Sample box. You can apply color to the background of a cell or range or to cell contents. If you do not have a color monitor, the colors appear in shades of gray. You can apply patterns to the background of a cell or range. And, you can apply borders to all the cells in a worksheet or only to selected cells. See Table C-4 for a list of border buttons and their functions. Evan decides to add a pattern, a border, and color to the title of the worksheet. This will give the worksheet a more professional appearance.

1. Click cell **A1**, then click the **Fill Color button list arrow** on the Formatting toolbar
   The color palette appears, as shown in Figure C-15.
2. Click **Turquoise** (fourth row, fourth color from the right)
3. Click **Format** on the menu bar, then click **Cells**
   The Format Cells dialog box opens.
4. Click the **Patterns tab**, as shown in Figure C-16, if it is not already displayed
   When choosing a background pattern, consider that the more cell contents contrast with the background, the more readable the contents will be. You choose the diamond pattern.
5. Click the **Pattern list arrow**, click the **thin diagonal crosshatch pattern** (third row, last pattern on the right), then click **OK**
   Now you add a border.
6. Click the **Borders button list arrow** on the Formatting toolbar, then click the **heavy bottom border** (second row, second border from the left)
   Next, you change the font color.
7. Click the **Font Color button list arrow** on the Formatting toolbar, then click **blue** (second row, third color from the right)
   The text changes color, as shown in Figure C-17.
8. Preview and print the first page of the worksheet

QuickTip

Use color sparingly. Excessive use can divert the reader's attention away from the data in the worksheet.

Time To

Save

TABLE C-4: Border buttons

button	description	button	description
	No border		Thin border around range
	Single underline		Left border
	Double underline		Right border
	Thick bottom, thin top border		Double bottom, single top
	Outline all in range		Thick bottom border
	Thick border around range		

FIGURE C-15: Fill Color palette

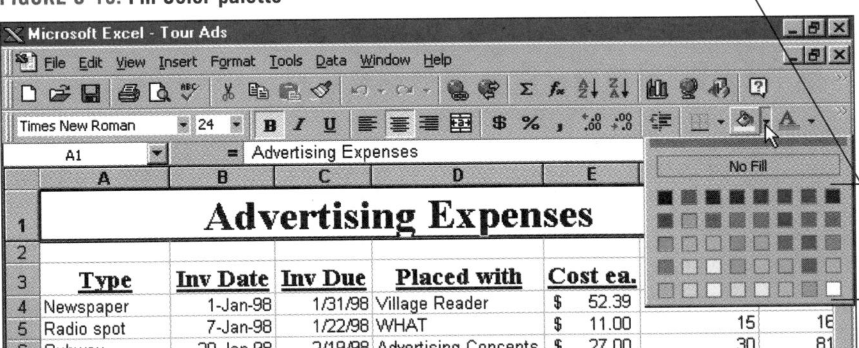

FIGURE C-16: Patterns tab in the Format Cells dialog box

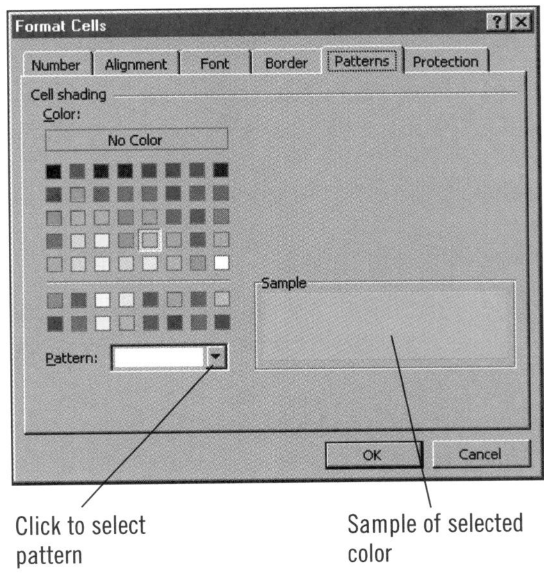

FIGURE C-17: Worksheet with color, patterns, and border

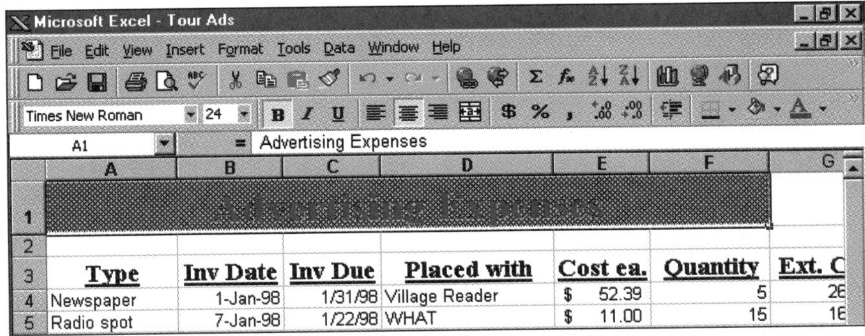

Using color to organize a worksheet

You can use color to give a distinctive look to each part of a worksheet. For example, you might want to apply a light blue to all the rows containing the subway data and a light green to all the rows containing the newspaper data. Be consistent throughout a group of worksheets, and try to avoid colors that are too bright and distracting.

Excel 97

Using Conditional Formatting

Formatting attributes make worksheets look professional, and these same attributes can be applied depending on specific outcomes in cells. Automatically applying formatting attributes based on cell values is called **conditional formatting**. You might, for example, want advertising costs above a certain number to display in red boldface, and lower values to display in blue. Evan wants his worksheet to include conditional formatting so that extended advertising costs greater than $175 display in red boldface. He creates the conditional format in the first cell in the extended cost column.

1. **Click cell G4**
   Use the scroll bars if necessary, to make column G visible.
2. **Click Format on the menu bar, then click Conditional Formatting**
   The Conditional Formatting dialog box opens, as shown in Figure C-18. The number of input fields varies depending on which operator is selected. You can define up to 3 different conditions that let you determine outcome parameters and then assign formatting attributes to each one.
   You begin by defining the first part of the condition.
3. **Click the Operator list arrow, then click greater than or equal to**
   Next, you define the value in this condition that must be met for the formatting to be applied.
4. **Click the Value text box, then type 175**
   Once the value has been assigned, you define this condition's formatting attributes.
5. **Click Format, click the Color list arrow, click Red (third row, first color from the left), click Bold in the Font Style list box, click OK, then click OK again to close the Conditional Formatting dialog box**
   Next, you copy the formatting to the other cells in the column.
6. **Click the Format Painter button on the Formatting toolbar, then select the range G5:G30**
   Once the formatting is copied, you reposition the cell pointer to review the results.
7. **Click cell G4**
   Compare your results to Figure C-19.
8. **Press [Ctrl][Home] to move to cell Al**
9. **Save your work**

Trouble?

If the Office Assistant appears, click the No, don't provide help now button to close the Office Assistant.

FIGURE C-18: **Conditional Formatting dialog box**

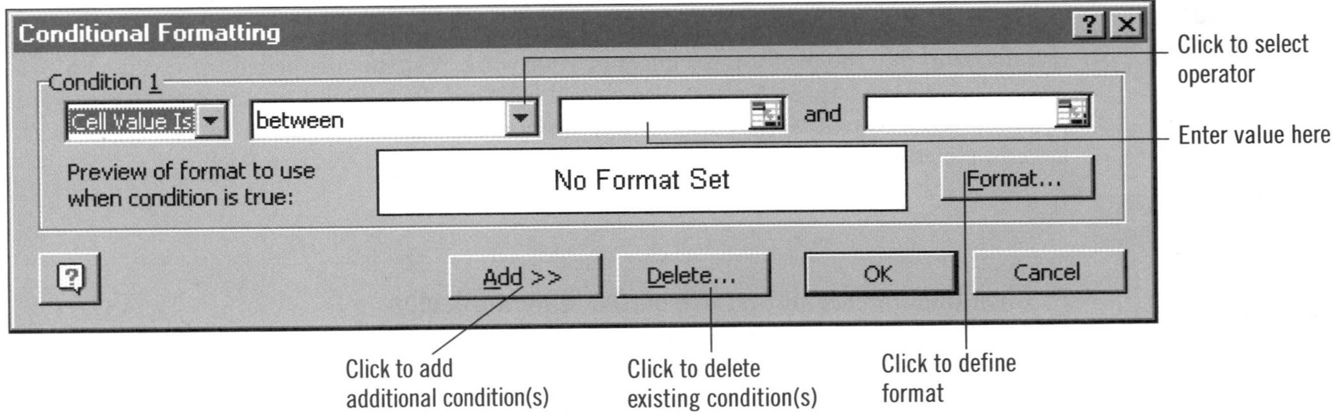

FIGURE C-19: **Worksheet with conditional formatting**

Microsoft Excel - Tour Ads

G4 = =E4*F4

	B	C	D	E	F	G	H
1	Advertising Expenses						
2							
3	Inv Date	Inv Due	Placed with	Cost ea.	Quantity	Ext. Cost	Sales T
4	1-Jan-98	1/31/98	Village Reader	$ 52.39	5	261.95	19
5	7-Jan-98	1/22/98	WHAT	$ 11.00	15	165.00	12
6	20-Jan-98	2/19/98	Advertising Concepts	$ 27.00	30	810.00	59
7	1-Jan-98	1/11/98	NYNEX	$ 123.01	4	492.04	36
8	13-Jan-98	2/12/98	Advertising Concepts	$ 0.17	230	39.56	2
9	7-Jan-98	2/6/98	Young Upstart	$ 100.92	12	1,211.04	88
10	5-Jan-98	2/19/98	Mass Appeal, Inc.	$ 0.12	250	30.75	2
11	15-Jan-98	1/30/98	WHAT	$ 11.00	15	165.00	12
12	12-Jan-98	2/11/98	Advertising Concepts	$ 101.87	20	2,037.40	149
13	25-Jan-98	2/24/98	Village Reader	$ 52.39	6	314.34	23
14	1-Feb-98	3/3/98	University Voice	$ 23.91	2	47.82	3
15	3-Feb-98	3/20/98	Mass Appeal, Inc.	$ 5.67	200	1,134.00	83

Sheet1 / Sheet2 / Sheet3

Ready NUM

Start | Microsoft Excel - Tou... 10:32 AM

Results of conditional formatting

CLUES TO USE

Deleting conditional formatting

Because its likely that the conditions you define will change, any of the conditional formats defined can be deleted. Select the cell(s) containing conditional formatting, click Format, click Conditional Formatting, then click the Delete button. The Delete Conditional Format dialog box opens, as shown in Figure C-20. Click the checkboxes for any of the conditions you want to delete, then click OK. The previously assigned formatting is deleted—leaving the cell's contents intact.

FIGURE C-20: **Delete Conditional Format dialog box**

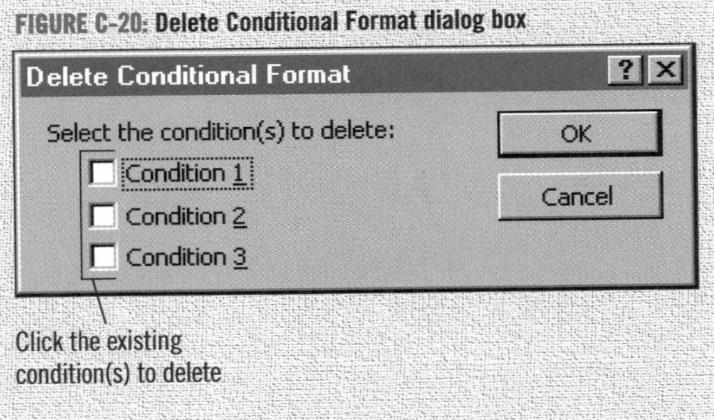

Excel 97

Excel 97

Checking Spelling

You may think your worksheet is complete, but if you haven't checked for spelling errors, you risk undermining the professional effect of your work. A single misspelled word can ruin your work. The spell checker in Excel is also shared by Word, PowerPoint, and Access, so any words you've added to the dictionary using those programs are also available in Excel. Evan has completed the formatting for his worksheet and is ready to check its spelling.

Steps 1 2 3 4

1. **Click the Spelling button on the Standard toolbar**
   The Spelling dialog opens, as shown in Figure C-21, with the abbreviation Inv selected as the first misspelled word in the worksheet. The spell checker starts from the active cell and compares words in the worksheet to those in its dictionary. Any word not found in the dictionary causes the spell checker to stop. At that point, you can decide to Ignore, Change, or Add the word.
   You decide to Ignore All cases of Inv, the abbreviation of invoice.
2. **Click Ignore All, then click Ignore All again when the spell checker stops on T-Shirts**
   The spell checker found the word 'cards' misspelled. You find the correct spelling and fix the error.
3. **Scroll through the Suggestions list, click Cards, then click Change**
   The word 'Concepts' is also misspelled. Make this correction.
4. **Click Concepts in the Suggestions list, then click Change**
   When no more incorrect words are found, Excel displays the message box shown in Figure C-22.
5. **Click OK**
6. **Press [Ctrl][Home] to move to cell A1**
7. **Save your work**
8. **Preview and print the worksheet, then close the workbook and exit Excel**

FIGURE C-21: **Spelling dialog box**

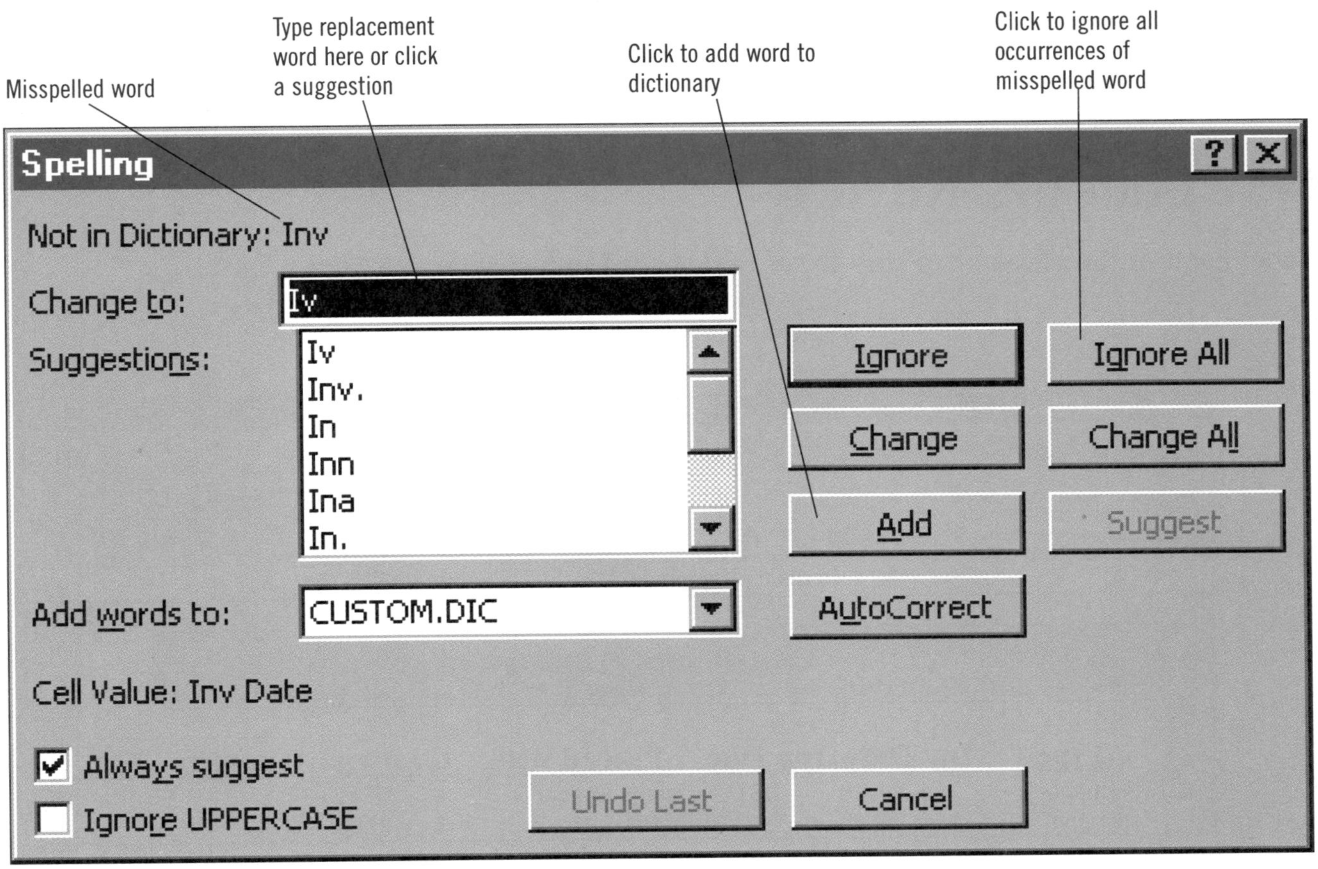

Misspelled word

Type replacement word here or click a suggestion

Click to add word to dictionary

Click to ignore all occurrences of misspelled word

FIGURE C-22: **Spelling completed warning box**

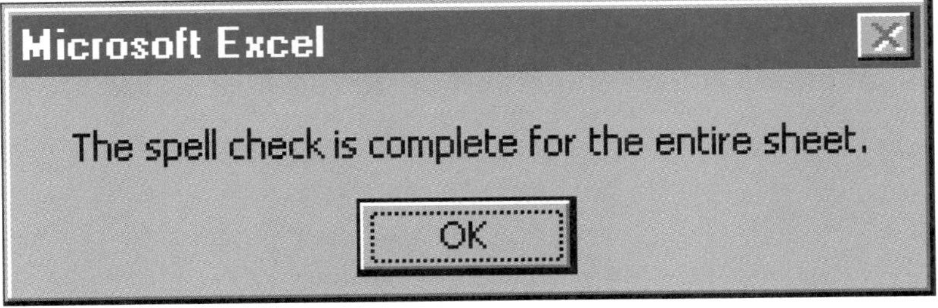

CLUES TO USE

Modifying the spell checker

Each of us use words specific to our profession or task. Because the dictionary supplied with Microsoft Office cannot possibly include all the words that each of us needs, it is possible to add words to the dictionary shared by all the components in the suite.

To customize the Microsoft Office dictionary used by the spell checker, click Add when a word not in the dictionary is found. From then on, that word will no longer be considered misspelled by the spell checker.

Practice

Concepts Review

Label each of the elements of the Excel worksheet window shown in Figure C-23.

FIGURE C-23

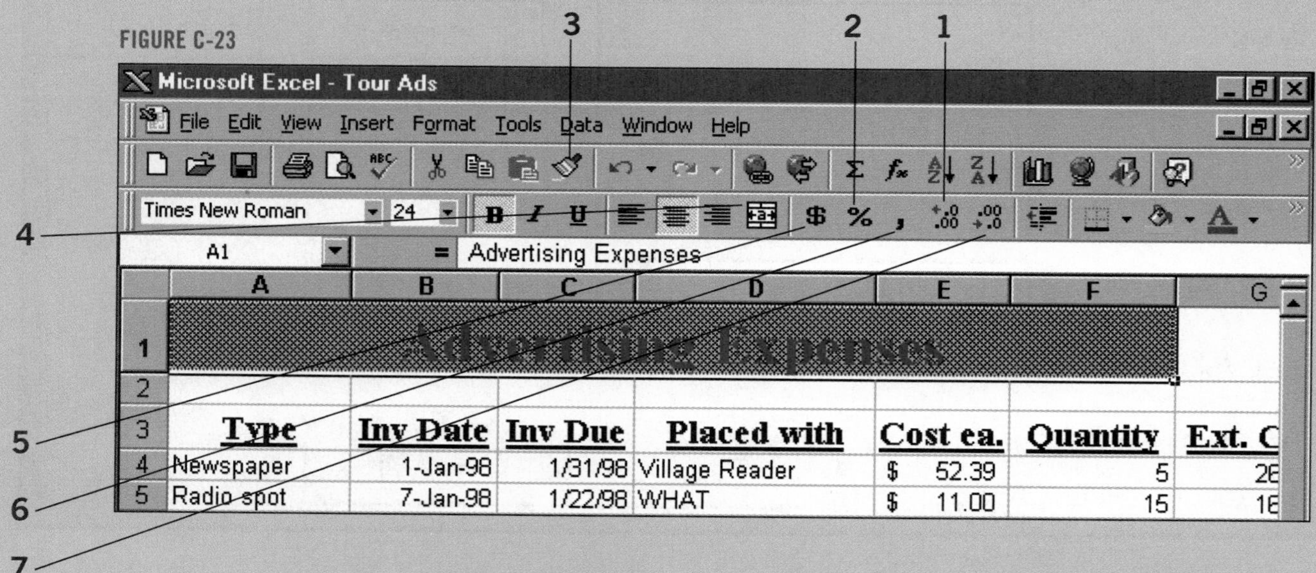

Match each of the statements to the command or button it describes.

8. **Format Cells**
9. **Edit Clear**
10. **Insert Row/Column**
11.
12.
13.

a. Adds a new row or column
b. Erases the contents of a cell
c. Checks the spelling in a worksheet
d. Changes the point size of selected cells
e. Pastes the contents of the Clipboard in the current cell
f. Changes the format to Currency

Select the best answer from the list of choices.

14. Which button increases the number of decimal places in selected cells?

a. [button] b. [button] c. [button] d. [button]

15. Each of the following operators can be used in conditional formatting, *except*

a. equal to b. greater than c. similar to d. not between

16. How many conditional formats can be created in any cell?

a. 1 b. 2 c. 3 d. 4

► Skills Review

1. Format values.

a. Open a new workbook.
b. Enter the information from Table C-5 in your worksheet. Make sure you put "Quarterly Sales Sheet" on the next line.
c. Select the range of values in the Price and Totals columns.
d. Click the Currency Style button.
e. Calculate the Totals column by multiplying the price by the number sold.
f. Save this workbook as Chairs on your Student Disk.

TABLE C-5

Country Oak Chairs, Inc.
Quarterly Sales Sheet

Description	Price	Sold	Totals
Rocker	1299	1104	
Recliner	800	1805	
Bar stool	159	1098	
Dinette	369	1254	

2. Select fonts and point sizes.

a. Select the range of cells containing the column titles.
b. Change the font of the column titles to Times New Roman.
c. Increase the point size of the column titles to 14 point.
d. Resize columns as necessary.
e. Save your workbook changes.

3. Change attributes and alignment of labels.

a. Select the worksheet title Country Oak Chairs, Inc.
b. Click the Bold button to apply boldface to the title.
c. Select the label Quarterly Sales Sheet.
d. Click the Underline button to apply underlining to the label.
e. Add the bold attribute to the furniture descriptions, as well as the Totals label.
f. Make the Price and Sold labels italics.
g. Select the range of cells containing the column titles.
h. Click the Center button to center the column titles.
i. Save your changes, then preview and print the worksheet.

4. Adjust column widths.

a. Change the width of the Price column to 11.
b. Use the Format menu to make the Description and Sold columns the same size as the Price column.
c. Save your workbook changes.

5. **Insert and delete rows and columns.**
   a. Insert a new row between rows 4 and 5.
   b. Add Country Oak Chairs' newest product—a Shaker bench—in the newly inserted row. Enter "239" for the price and "360" for the number sold.
   c. Use the fill handle to copy the formula in cell D4 to D5.
   d. Save your changes, then preview and print the workbook.

6. **Apply colors, patterns, and borders.**
   a. Add a border around the data entered from Table C-5.
   b. Apply a light green background color to the Descriptions column.
   c. Apply a light pattern to the Descriptions column.
   d. Apply a dark green background to the column labels.
   e. Change the color of the font in the first row of the data to light green.
   f. Save your work.
   g. Preview and print the worksheet, then close the workbook.

7. **Use conditional formatting.**
   a. Open the file XL C-2 from your Student Disk.
   b. Save it as "Recap" on your Student Disk.
   c. Create conditional formatting that changes values to blue if they are greater than 35000, and changes values to green if they are less than 21000.
   d. Use the Bold button and Center button to format the column headings and row titles.
   e. Autofit the other columns as necessary.
   f. Save your changes.

8. **Check spelling.**
   a. Open the spell checker.
   b. Check the spelling in the worksheet.
   c. Correct any spelling errors.
   d. Save your changes, then preview and print the workbook.
   e. Close the workbook, then exit Excel.

Independent Challenges

1. Nuts and Bolts is a small but growing hardware store that has hired you to organize its accounting records using Excel. Now that the Nuts and Bolts hardware store's accounting records are on Excel, they would like you to work on the inventory. Although more items will be added later, enough have been entered in a worksheet for you to begin your modifications.

Open the workbook XL C-3 on your Student Disk, and save it as "NB Inventory."

To complete this independent challenge:

1. Create a formula that calculates the Value of the inventory on-hand for each item.
2. Use an absolute reference to calculate the Sale Price of each item.
3. Use enhancements to make the title, column headings, and row headings more attractive.
4. Make sure all columns are wide enough to see the data.
5. Before printing, preview the file so you know what the worksheet will look like. Adjust any items as needed, check spelling, and print a copy. Save your work before closing the file.
6. Submit your final printout.

2. You recently moved to a small town and joined the Chamber of Commerce. Since the other members are not computer-literate, you volunteered to organize the member organizations in a worksheet. As part of your efforts with the Chamber of Commerce, you need to examine more closely the membership in comparison to the community. To make the existing data more professional-looking and easier to read, you've decided to use attributes and your formatting abilities.

Open the workbook XL C-4 on your Student Disk, and save it as "Community."

To complete this independent challenge:

1. Remove any blank columns.
2. Format the Annual Revenue column using the Currency format.
3. Make all columns wide enough to fit their data.
4. Use formatting enhancements, such as fonts, font sizes, and text attributes, to make the worksheet more attractive.
5. Before printing, preview the file so you know what the worksheet will look like. Adjust any items as needed, check spelling, and print a copy. Save your work before closing the file.
6. Submit your final printout.

3. Write Brothers is a Houston-based company that manufactures high-quality pens and markers. As the finance manager, one of your responsibilities is to analyze the monthly reports from your five district sales offices. Your boss, Joanne Parker, has just told you to prepare a quarterly sales report for an upcoming meeting. Because several top executives will be attending this meeting, Joanne reminds you that the report must look professional. In particular, she asks you to emphasize the company's surge in profits during the last month and to highlight the fact that the Northeastern district continues to outpace the other districts.

Plan and build a worksheet that shows the company's sales during the last three months. Make sure you include:

- The number of pens sold (units sold) and the associated revenues (total sales) for each of the five district sales offices. The five Write Brothers sales districts include: Northeastern, Midwestern, Southeastern, Southern, and Western.
- Calculations that show month-by-month totals and a three-month cumulative total.
- Calculations that show each district's share of sales (percent of units sold).
- Formatting enhancements to emphasize the recent month's sales surge and the Northeastern district's sales leadership.

To complete this independent challenge:

1. Prepare a worksheet plan that states your goal, lists the worksheet data you'll need, and identifies the formulas for the different calculations.
2. Sketch a sample worksheet on a piece of paper, indicating how the information should be organized and formatted. How will you calculate the totals? What formulas can you copy to save time and keystrokes? Do any of these formulas need to use an absolute reference? How will you show dollar amounts? What information should be shown in bold? Do you need to use more than one font? More than one point size?
3. Build the worksheet with your own sales data. Enter the titles and labels first, then enter the numbers and formulas. Save the workbook as Write Brothers on your Student Disk.
4. Make enhancements to the worksheet. Adjust the column widths as necessary. Format labels and values, and change attributes and alignment.
5. Add a column that calculates a 10% increase in sales. Use an absolute cell reference in this calculation.
6. Before printing, preview the file so you know what the worksheet will look like. Adjust any items as needed, check spelling, and print a copy. Save your work before closing the file.
7. Submit your worksheet plan, preliminary sketches, and the final printout.

4. As the manager of your company's computer lab, you've been asked to assemble data on currently available software for use in a business environment. Using the World Wide Web, you can retrieve information about current software and create an attractive worksheet for distribution to department managers.
To complete this independent challenge:

1. Open a new workbook and save it on your Student Disk as Software Comparison.
2. Log on to the Internet and use your browser to go to http://www.course.com. From there, click the link Student On Line Companions, then click the Microsoft Office 97 Professional Edition—Illustrated: A First Course page, then click the Excel link for Unit C.
3. Use each of the following sites to compile your data.
   Microsoft Corporation [www.microsoft.com], and Lotus Corporation [www.lotus.com].
4. Retrieve information on word processors, spreadsheets, presentation graphics, and database programs manufactured by both companies. The software must be Windows 95 compatible.
5. Create a worksheet that includes the information in step 4 above, as well as a retail price for each component, and whether all the programs can be purchased as a suite.
6. Use formatting attributes to make this data look attractive.
7. Use conditional formatting so that individual programs that cost over $100 display in red.
8. Save, print, and hand in a print out of your work.

Visual Workshop

Create the following worksheet using the skills you learned in this unit. Open the file XL C-5 on your Student Disk, and save it as January Invoices. Create a conditional format in the Cost ea. column where entries greater than 50 are displayed in red. (Hint: The only additional font used in this exercise is Times New Roman. It is 22 points in row 1, and 14 points in row 3.)

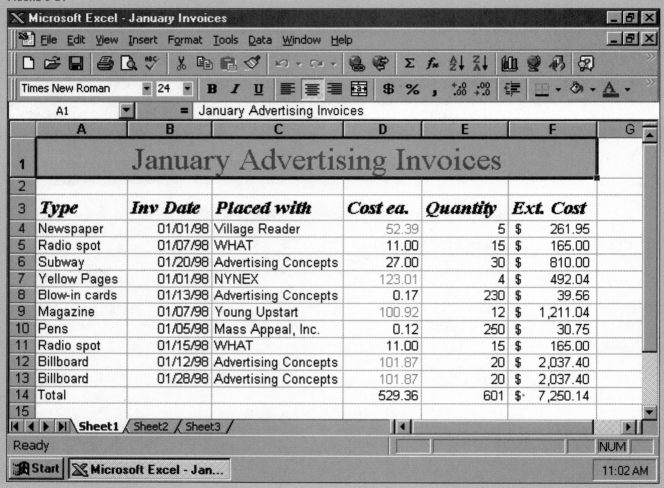

FIGURE C-24

Microsoft Excel - January Invoices

File Edit View Insert Format Tools Data Window Help

Times New Roman 24

A1 = January Advertising Invoices

	A	B	C	D	E	F
1	January Advertising Invoices					
2						
3	*Type*	*Inv Date*	*Placed with*	*Cost ea.*	*Quantity*	*Ext. Cost*
4	Newspaper	01/01/98	Village Reader	52.39	5	$ 261.95
5	Radio spot	01/07/98	WHAT	11.00	15	$ 165.00
6	Subway	01/20/98	Advertising Concepts	27.00	30	$ 810.00
7	Yellow Pages	01/01/98	NYNEX	123.01	4	$ 492.04
8	Blow-in cards	01/13/98	Advertising Concepts	0.17	230	$ 39.56
9	Magazine	01/07/98	Young Upstart	100.92	12	$ 1,211.04
10	Pens	01/05/98	Mass Appeal, Inc.	0.12	250	$ 30.75
11	Radio spot	01/15/98	WHAT	11.00	15	$ 165.00
12	Billboard	01/12/98	Advertising Concepts	101.87	20	$ 2,037.40
13	Billboard	01/28/98	Advertising Concepts	101.87	20	$ 2,037.40
14	Total			529.36	601	$ 7,250.14
15						

Sheet1 / Sheet2 / Sheet3

Ready NUM

Start | Microsoft Excel - Jan... 11:02 AM

Working with Charts

Objectives

- Plan and design a chart
- Create a chart
- Move and resize a chart and its objects
- Edit a chart
- Change the appearance of a chart
- Enhance a chart
- Add text annotations and arrows to a chart
- Preview and print a chart

Worksheets provide an effective way to organize information, but they are not always the best format for presenting data to others. Information in a selected range or worksheet can be easily converted to the visual format of a chart. Charts quickly communicate the relationships of data in a worksheet. In this unit, you will learn how to create a chart, edit a chart and change the chart type, add text annotations and arrows to a chart, then preview and print it. Evan Brillstein needs to create a chart showing the six-month sales history of Nomad Ltd for the annual meeting. He wants to illustrate the impact of an advertising campaign that started in June.

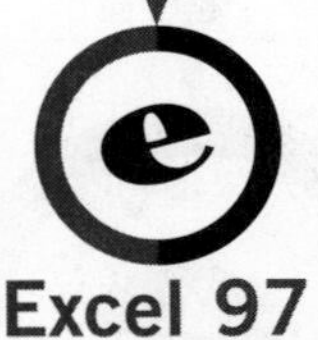

Excel 97

Planning and Designing a Chart

Before creating a chart, you need to plan what you want your chart to show and how you want it to look. Evan wants to create a chart to be used at the annual meeting. The chart will show the spring and summer sales throughout the Nomad Ltd regions. In early June, the Marketing Department launched a national advertising campaign. The results of the campaign were increased sales for the summer months. Evan wants his chart to illustrate this dramatic sales increase. Evan uses the worksheet shown in Figure D-1 and the following guidelines to plan the chart:

CourseHelp

The camera icon indicates there is a CourseHelp for this lesson. Click the Start button, point to Programs, then click Excel 97 Illustrated. Choose the CourseHelp that corresponds to this lesson.

1. **Determine the purpose of the chart, and identify the data relationships you want to communicate visually**
   You want to create a chart that shows sales throughout Nomad's regions in the spring and summer months (March through August). In particular, you want to highlight the increase in sales that occurred in the summer months as a result of the advertising campaign.

2. **Determine the results you want to see, and decide which chart type is most appropriate to use; Table D-1 describes several different types of charts**
   Because you want to compare related data (sales in each of the regions) over a time period (the months March through August), you decide to use a column chart.

3. **Identify the worksheet data you want the chart to illustrate**
   You are using data from the worksheet titled "Nomad Ltd Regions, Spring and Summer Sales," as shown in Figure D-1. This worksheet contains the sales data for the five regions from March through August.

4. **Sketch the chart, then use your sketch to decide where the chart elements should be placed**
   You sketch your chart as shown in Figure D-2. You put the months on the horizontal axis (the **X-axis**) and the monthly sales figures on the vertical axis (the **Y-axis**). The **tick marks** on the Y-axis create a scale of measure for each value. Each value in a cell you select for your chart is a **data point**. In any chart, each data point is visually represented by a **data marker**, which in this case is a column. A collection of related data points is a **data series**. In this chart, there are five data series (Midwest, Northeast, Northwest, South, and Southwest), so you have included a **legend** to identify them.

FIGURE D-1: Worksheet containing sales data

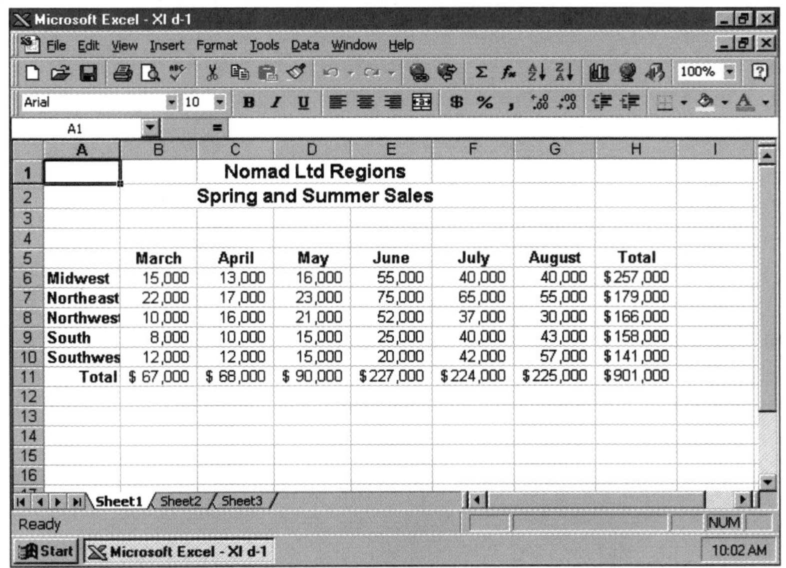

	A	B	C	D	E	F	G	H
1			Nomad Ltd Regions					
2			Spring and Summer Sales					
3								
4								
5		March	April	May	June	July	August	Total
6	Midwest	15,000	13,000	16,000	55,000	40,000	40,000	$257,000
7	Northeast	22,000	17,000	23,000	75,000	65,000	55,000	$179,000
8	Northwest	10,000	16,000	21,000	52,000	37,000	30,000	$166,000
9	South	8,000	10,000	15,000	25,000	40,000	43,000	$158,000
10	Southwes	12,000	12,000	15,000	20,000	42,000	57,000	$141,000
11	Total	$ 67,000	$ 68,000	$ 90,000	$227,000	$224,000	$225,000	$901,000

FIGURE D-2: Sketch of the column chart

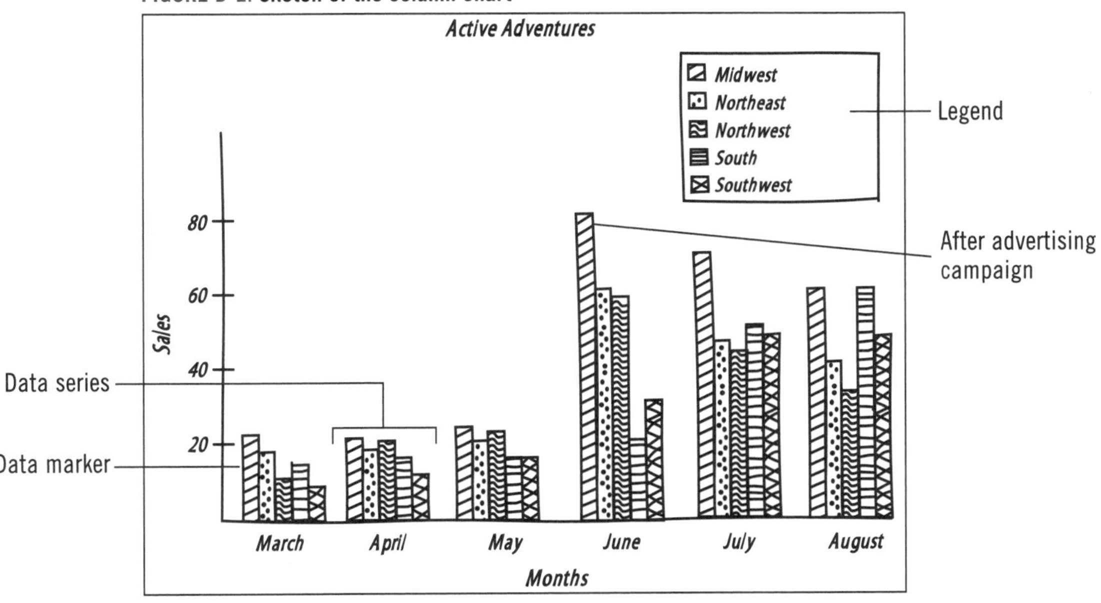

TABLE D-1: Commonly used chart types

type	button	description
Area		Shows how volume changes over time
Bar		Compares distinct, unrelated objects over time using a horizontal format; sometimes referred to as a horizontal bar chart in other spreadsheet programs
Column		Compares distinct, unrelated objects over time using a vertical format; the Excel default; sometimes referred to as a bar chart in other spreadsheet programs
Line		Compares trends over even time intervals; similar to an area chart
Pie		Compares sizes of pieces as part of a whole; can have slices pulled away from the pie, or "exploded"
XY (scatter)		Compares trends over uneven time or measurement intervals; used in scientific and engineering disciplines for trend spotting and extrapolation
Combination	none	Combines a column and line chart to compare data requiring different scales of measure

Excel 97

Creating a Chart

To create a chart in Excel, you first select the range containing the data you want to chart. Once you've selected a range, you can use Excel's Chart Wizard to lead you through the chart creation process. Using the worksheet containing the spring and summer sales data for the five regions, Evan will create a chart that shows the monthly sales of each region from March through August.

1. **Open the workbook XL D-1 from your Student Disk, then save it as Nomad Regions**
   First, you need to select the cells you want to chart. You want to include the monthly sales figures for each of the regions, but not the totals. You also want to include the month and region labels.
2. **Select the range A5:G10, then click the Chart Wizard button on the Standard toolbar**
   When you click the Chart Wizard opens. The first Chart Wizard dialog box lets you choose the type of chart you want to create. See Figure D-3. You can see a preview of the chart by clicking the Press and hold to view sample button.
3. **Click Next to accept the default chart type of column**
   The second dialog box lets you choose the data being charted and whether the series are in rows or columns. Currently, the rows are selected as the data series. You could switch this by clicking the Columns radio button located under the Data range. Since you selected the data before clicking the Chart Wizard button, the correct range A5:G10 displays in the Data range text box. Satisfied with the selections, you accept the default choices.
4. **Click Next**
   The third Chart Wizard dialog box shows a sample chart using the data you selected. Notice that the regions (the rows in the selected range) are plotted according to the months (the columns in the selected range), and that the months were added as labels for each data series. Notice also that there is a legend showing each region and its corresponding color on the chart. Here, you can choose to keep the legend, add a chart title, and add axis titles. You add a title.
5. **Click the Chart title text box, then type Nomad Ltd Regional Sales**
   After a moment, the title appears in the Sample Chart box. See Figure D-4.
6. **Click Next**
   In the last Chart Wizard dialog box, you determine the location of the chart. A chart can be displayed on the same sheet as the data, or a separate sheet in the workbook. You decide to display the chart on the current sheet.
7. **Click Finish**
   The column chart appears, as shown in Figure D-5. Your chart might look slightly different. Just as you had hoped, the chart shows the dramatic increase in sales between May and June. The **selection handles**, the small squares at the corners and sides of the chart borders, indicate that the chart is selected. Anytime a chart is selected (as it is now), the Chart toolbar appears. It might be floating, as shown in Figure D-5, or it might be fixed at the top or bottom of the worksheet window.

QuickTip

When selecting a large, unnamed range, select the upper left-most cell in the range, press and hold **[Shift]**, then click the lower right-most cell in the range.

Trouble?

If you want to delete a chart, select it then press **[Delete]**.

FIGURE D-3: **First Chart Wizard dialog box**

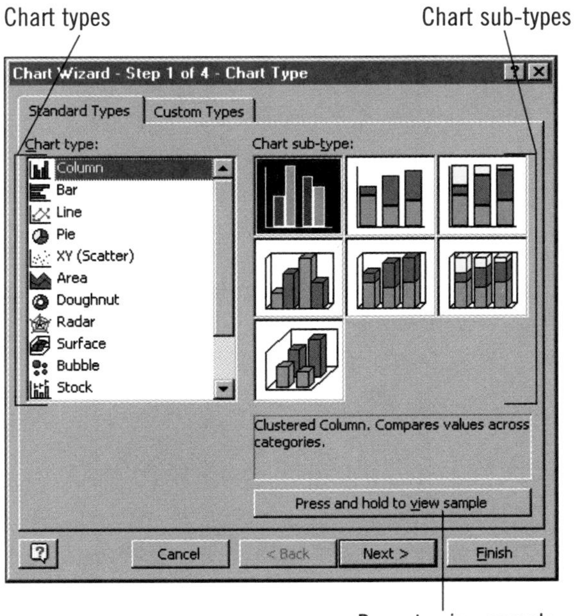

FIGURE D-4: **Third Chart Wizard dialog box**

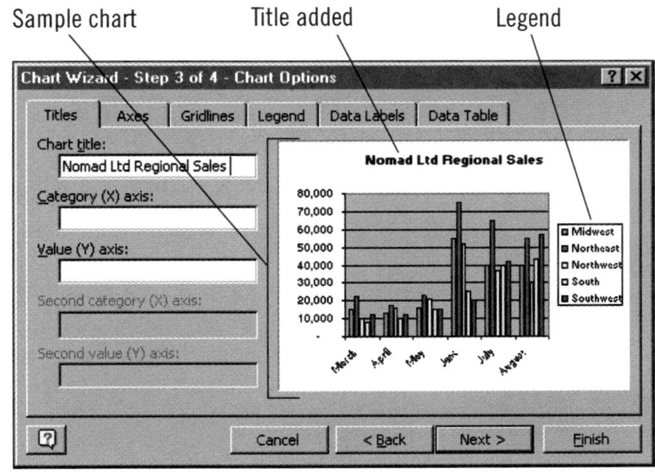

FIGURE D-5: **Worksheet with column chart**

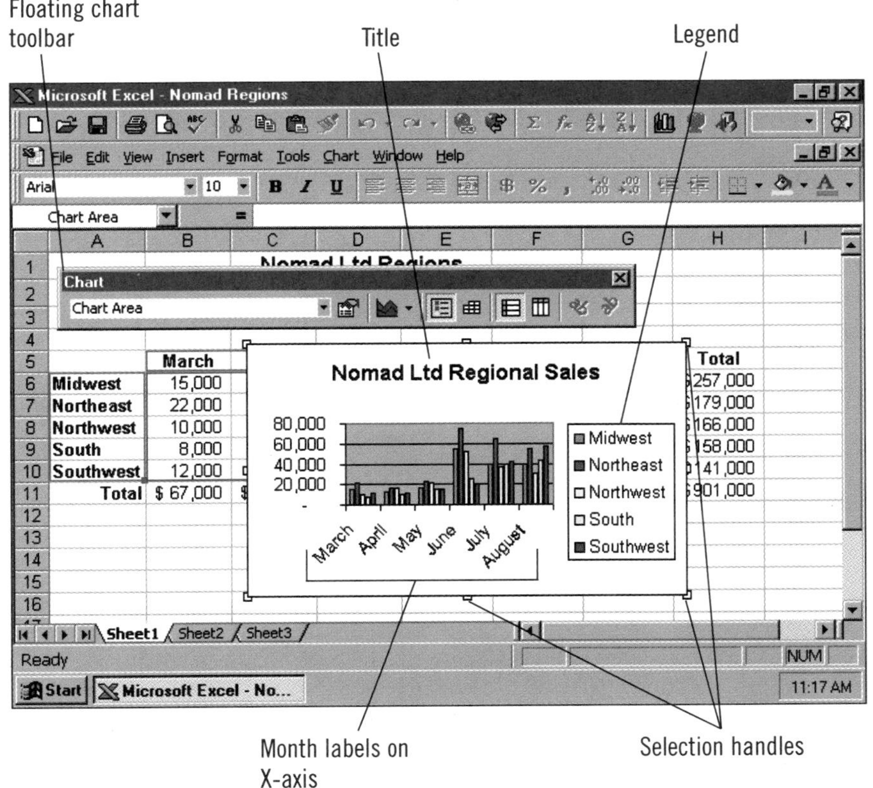

Excel 97

Excel 97

Moving and Resizing a Chart and its Objects

Charts are graphics, or drawn **objects**, and have no specific cell or range address. You can move charts anywhere on a worksheet without affecting formulas or data in the worksheet. You can even put them on another sheet. You can also easily resize a chart to improve its appearance by dragging the selection handles. Drawn objects such as charts can contain other objects that you can move and resize. To move an object, select it then drag it or cut and copy it to a new location. To resize an object, use the selection handles. Evan wants to increase the size of the chart and position it below the worksheet data. He also wants to change the position of the legend.

Steps

1. Make sure the chart is still selected. Scroll the worksheet until **row 28** is visible, then position the pointer over the white space around the chart
   The pointer shape indicates that you can move the chart or use a selection handle to resize it.

Trouble?

If the Chart toolbar is in the way of the legend, move it out of your way first.

2. Press and hold the mouse button and drag the chart until the lower edge of the chart is in **row 28** and the left edge of the chart is in **column A**, then release the mouse button
   A dotted outline of the chart perimeter appears as the chart is being moved, the pointer changes to ✥, and the chart moves to the new location.
3. Position the pointer over one of the selection handles on the right border until it changes to ↔, then drag the right edge of the chart to the **middle of column I**
   The chart is widened. See Figure D-6.
4. Position the pointer over the top middle selection handle until it changes to ↕, then drag it to the **top of row 12**
   Now, you move the legend up so that it is slightly lower than the chart title.
5. Click the **legend** to select it, then drag it to the upper-right corner of the chart until it is slightly lower than the chart title
   Selection handles appear around the legend when you click it, and a dotted outline of the legend perimeter appears as you drag.
6. Press **[Esc]** to deselect the legend. The legend is now repositioned. See Figure D-7.
7. Save your work

FIGURE D-6: Worksheet with reposition and resized chart

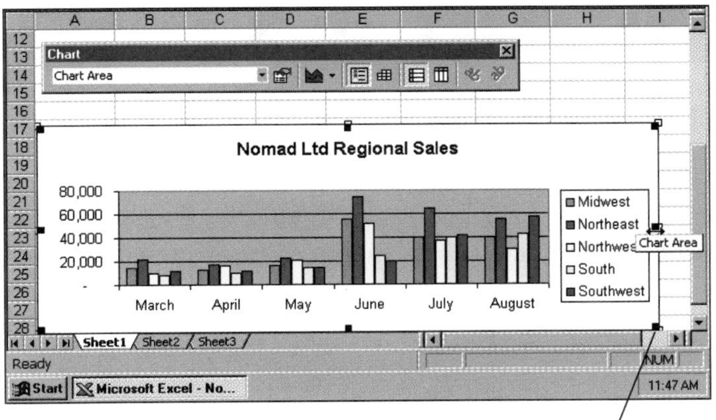

Widened to column I

FIGURE D-7: Worksheet with repositioned legend

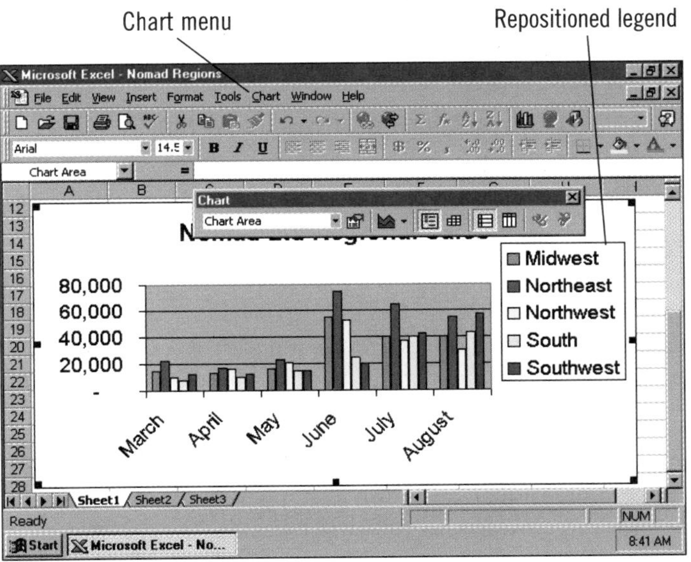

Excel 97

Viewing multiple worksheets

A workbook can be organized with a chart on one sheet and the data on another sheet. With this organization, you can still see the data next to the chart by opening multiple windows of the same workbook. This allows you to see portions of multiple sheets at the same time. Click Window on the menu bar, then click New Window. A new window containing the current workbook opens. To see the windows next to each other, click Window on the menu bar, click Arrange, then choose one of the options in the Arrange Windows dialog box. You can open one worksheet in one window and a different worksheet in the second window. See Figure D-8. To close one window without closing the worksheet, double-click the control menu box on the window you want to close.

FIGURE D-8: Workbook with two windows open

Individual title bars with control menu boxes

Active sheet tabs

Excel 97

Editing a Chart

Once you've created a chart, it's easy to modify it. You can change data values in the worksheet, and the chart will automatically be updated to reflect the new data. You can also easily change chart types using the buttons on the Chart toolbar. Table D-2 shows and describes the Chart toolbar buttons. Evan looks over his worksheet and realizes he entered the wrong data for the Northwest region in July and August. After he corrects this data, he wants to find out what percentage of total sales the month of June represents. He will convert the column chart to a pie chart to find this out.

Steps

1. **Scroll the worksheet so that you can see both the chart and row 8, containing the Northwest region's sales figures, at the same time**
   As you enter the correct values, watch the columns for July and August in the chart change.
2. **Click cell F8, type 49000 to correct the July sales figure, press [→], type 45000 in cell G8, then press [Enter]**
   The Northwest columns for July and August reflect the increased sales figures. See Figure D-9.
3. **Select the chart by clicking anywhere within the chart border, then click the Chart Type list arrow on the Chart toolbar**
   The chart type buttons appear, as shown in Figure D-10.
4. **Click the 2-D Pie Chart button**
   The column chart changes to a pie chart showing total sales by month (the columns in the selected range). See Figure D-11. (You may need to scroll up to see the chart.) You look at the pie chart, takes some notes, and then decide to convert it back to a column chart. You now want to see if the large increase in sales would be better presented with a three-dimensional column chart.
5. **Click , then click the 3-D Column Chart button to change the chart type**
   A three-dimensional column chart appears. You note that the three-dimensional column format is too crowded, so you switch back to the two-dimensional format.
6. **Click , then click the 2-D Column Chart button to change the chart type**

Time To
✔ Save

TABLE D-2: Chart Type buttons

button	description	button	description
	Displays 2-D area chart		Displays 3-D area chart
	Displays 2-D bar chart		Displays 3-D bar chart
	Displays 2-D column chart		Displays 3-D column chart
	Displays 2-D line chart		Displays 3-D line chart
	Displays 2-D pie chart		Displays 3-D pie chart
	Displays 2-D scatter chart		Displays 3-D surface chart
	Displays 2-D doughnut chart		Displays 3-D cylinder chart
	Displays radar chart		Displays 3-D cone chart

FIGURE D-9: Worksheet with new data entered for the Northwest region

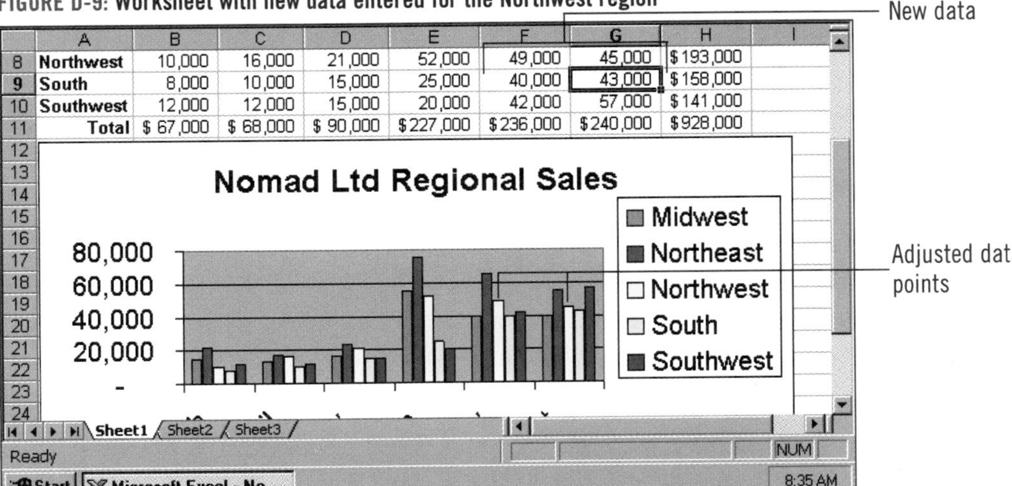

	A	B	C	D	E	F	G	H
8	Northwest	10,000	16,000	21,000	52,000	49,000	45,000	$193,000
9	South	8,000	10,000	15,000	25,000	40,000	43,000	$158,000
10	Southwest	12,000	12,000	15,000	20,000	42,000	57,000	$141,000
11	Total	$ 67,000	$ 68,000	$ 90,000	$227,000	$236,000	$240,000	$928,000

FIGURE D-10: Chart Type list box

FIGURE D-11: Pie chart

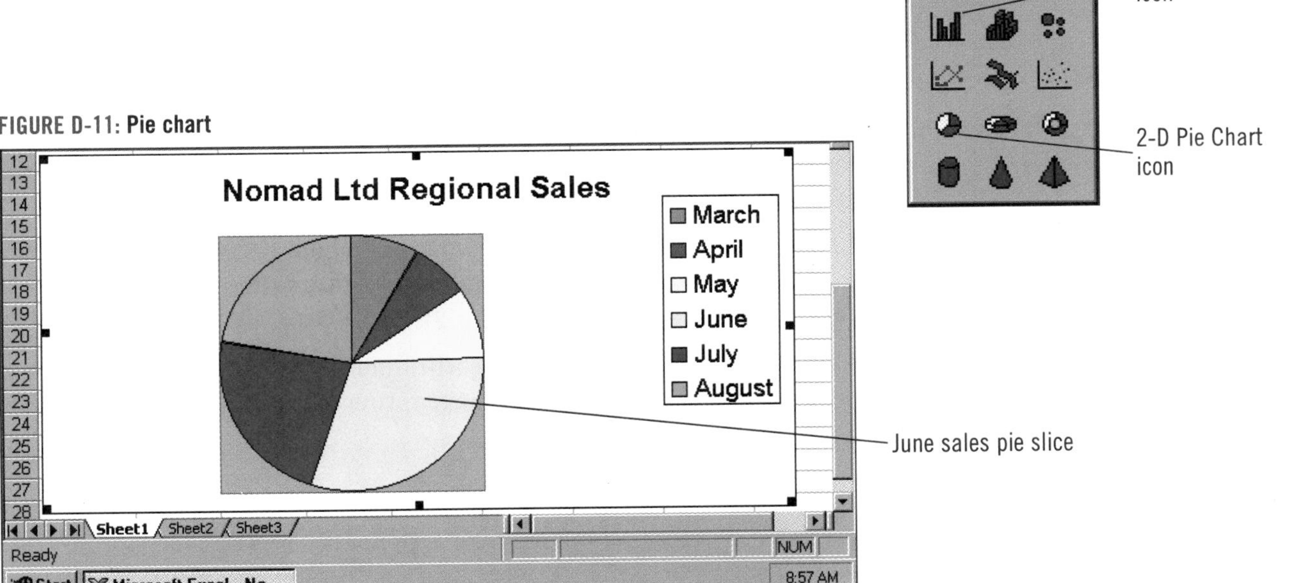

Rotating a chart

In a three-dimensional chart, columns or bars can sometimes be obscured by other data series within the same chart. You can rotate the chart until a better view is obtained. Double-click the chart, click the tip of one of its axes, then drag the handles until a more pleasing view of the data series appears. See Figure D-12.

FIGURE D-12: 3-D chart rotated with improved view of data series

Excel 97

Excel 97

Changing the Appearance of a Chart

After you've created a chart using the Chart Wizard, you can modify its appearance by changing the colors of data series and adding or eliminating a legend and gridlines using the Chart toolbar and the Chart menu. **Gridlines** are the horizontal lines in the chart that enable the eye to follow the value on an axis. The corresponding Chart toolbar buttons are listed in Table D-3. Evan wants to make some changes in the appearance of his chart. He wants to see if the chart looks better without gridlines, and he wants to change the color of a data series.

Steps

1. **Make sure the chart is still selected**
   You want to see how the chart looks without gridlines. Gridlines currently appear on the chart.
2. **Click Chart on the menu bar, then click Chart Options**
3. **Click the Gridlines tab in the Chart Options dialog box, then click the Major Gridlines checkbox for the Value (Y) Axis to remove the check and deselect this option**
   The gridlines disappear from the sample chart in the dialog box, as shown in Figure D-13. You decide that the gridlines are necessary to the chart's readability.
4. **Click the Major Gridlines checkbox for the Value (Y) Axis, then click OK**
   The gridlines reappear. You are not happy with the color of the columns for the South data series and would like the columns to stand out more.
5. **With the chart selected, double-click any column in the South data series**
   Handles appear on all the columns in the South data series, and the Format Data Series dialog box opens, as shown in Figure D-14. Make sure the Patterns tab is the front-most tab.
6. **Click the dark green box (in the third row, fourth from the left), then click OK**
   All the columns in the series are dark green. Compare your finished chart to Figure D-15. You are pleased with the change.
7. **Save your work**

QuickTip

Experiment with different formats for your charts until you get just the right look.

TABLE D-3: Chart enhancement buttons

button	use	button	use
	Displays formatting dialog box for the selected chart element		Charts data by row
	Selects chart type		Charts data by column
	Adds/Deletes legend		Angles selected text downward
	Creates a data table within the chart		Angles selected text upward

FIGURE D-13: **Chart Options dialog box**

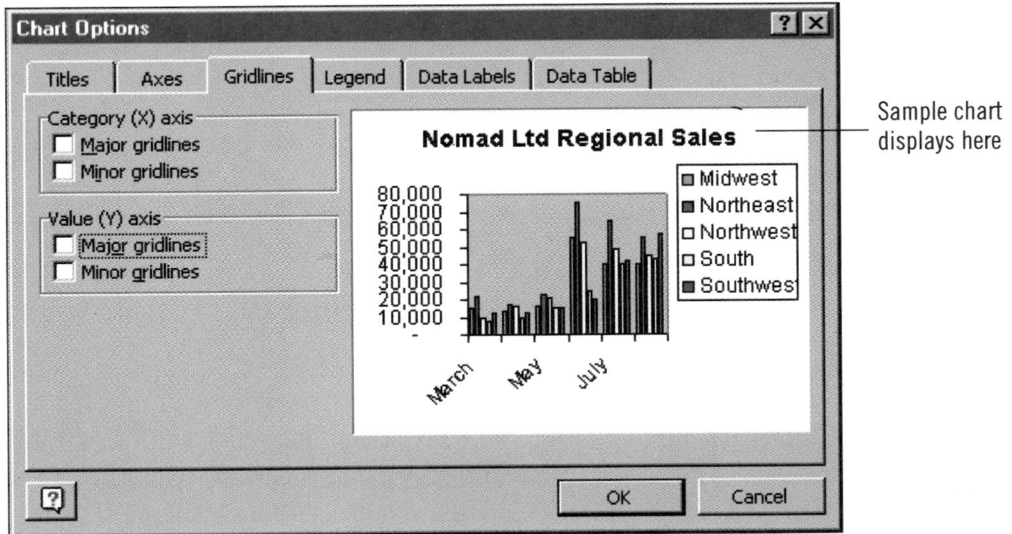

FIGURE D-14: **Format Data Series dialog box**

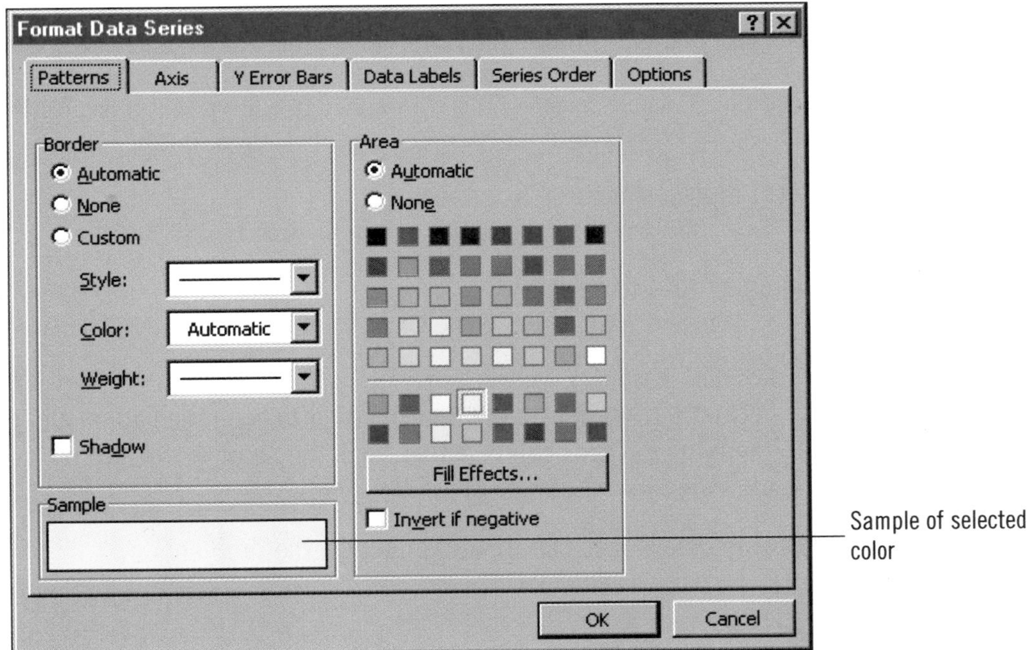

FIGURE D-15: **Chart with formatted data series**

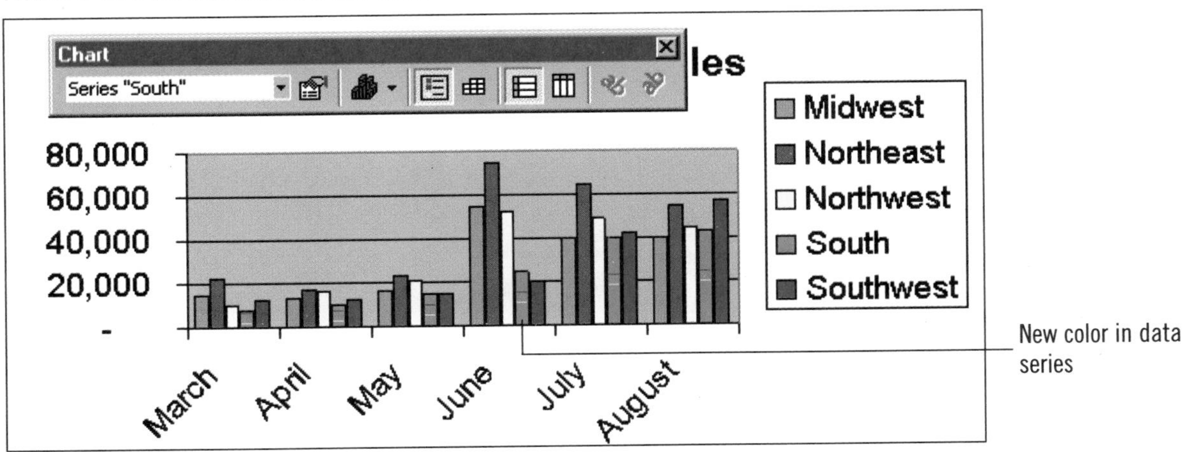

Excel 97

Excel 97

Enhancing a Chart

There are many ways to enhance a chart to make it easier to read and understand. You can create titles for the X-axis and Y-axis, add graphics, or add background color. You can even format the text you use in a chart. Evan wants to improve the appearance of his chart by creating titles for the X-axis and Y-axis. He also decides to add a drop shadow to the title.

Steps

1. **Make sure the chart is selected**
   You want to add descriptive text to the X-axis.

2. **Click Chart on the menu bar, click Chart Options, click the Titles tab in the Chart Options dialog box, then type Months in the Category (X) Axis text box**
   The word "Months" appears below the month labels in the sample chart, as shown in Figure D-16. You now add text to the Y-axis.

3. **Click the Value (Y) Axis text box, type Sales, then click OK**
   A selected text box containing "Sales" appears to the left of the Y-axis. Once the Chart Options dialog box is closed, you can move the axis title to a new position, by clicking on an edge of the selection and dragging it. If you wanted to edit the axis title, position the pointer over the selected text box until it becomes I and click, then edit the text.

4. **Press [Esc] to deselect the Y-axis label**
   Next you decide to draw a rectangle with a drop shadow around the title.

5. **Click the chart title to select it**
   If necessary, you may have to move the Chart toolbar. You use the Format button on the Chart toolbar to create a drop shadow.

6. **Click the Format button on the Chart toolbar to open the Format Chart Title dialog box, make sure the Patterns tab is active, click the Shadow checkbox, then click OK**
   A drop shadow appears around the title.

7. **Press [Esc] to deselect the chart title and view the drop shadow**
   Compare your chart to Figure D-17.

8. **Save your work**

QuickTip

The Format button opens a dialog box with the appropriate formatting options for the selected chart element.

FIGURE D-16: Sample chart with X-axis text

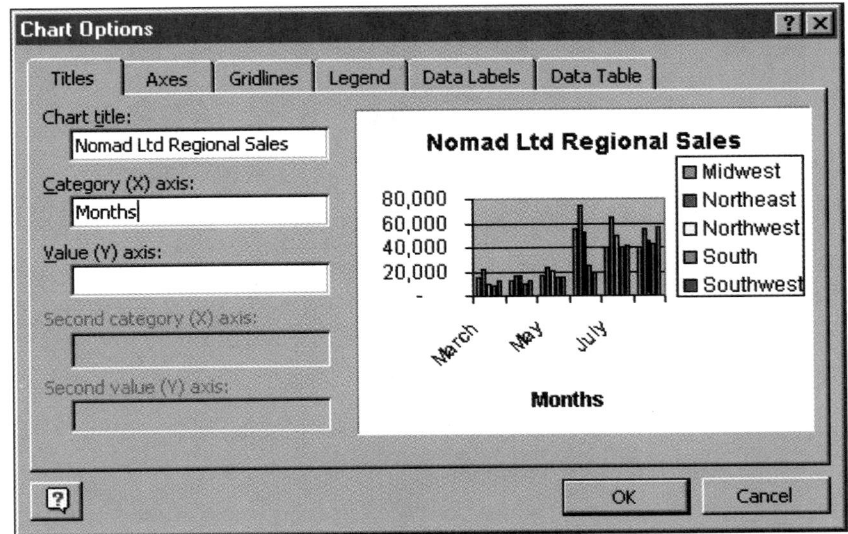

FIGURE D-17: Enhanced chart

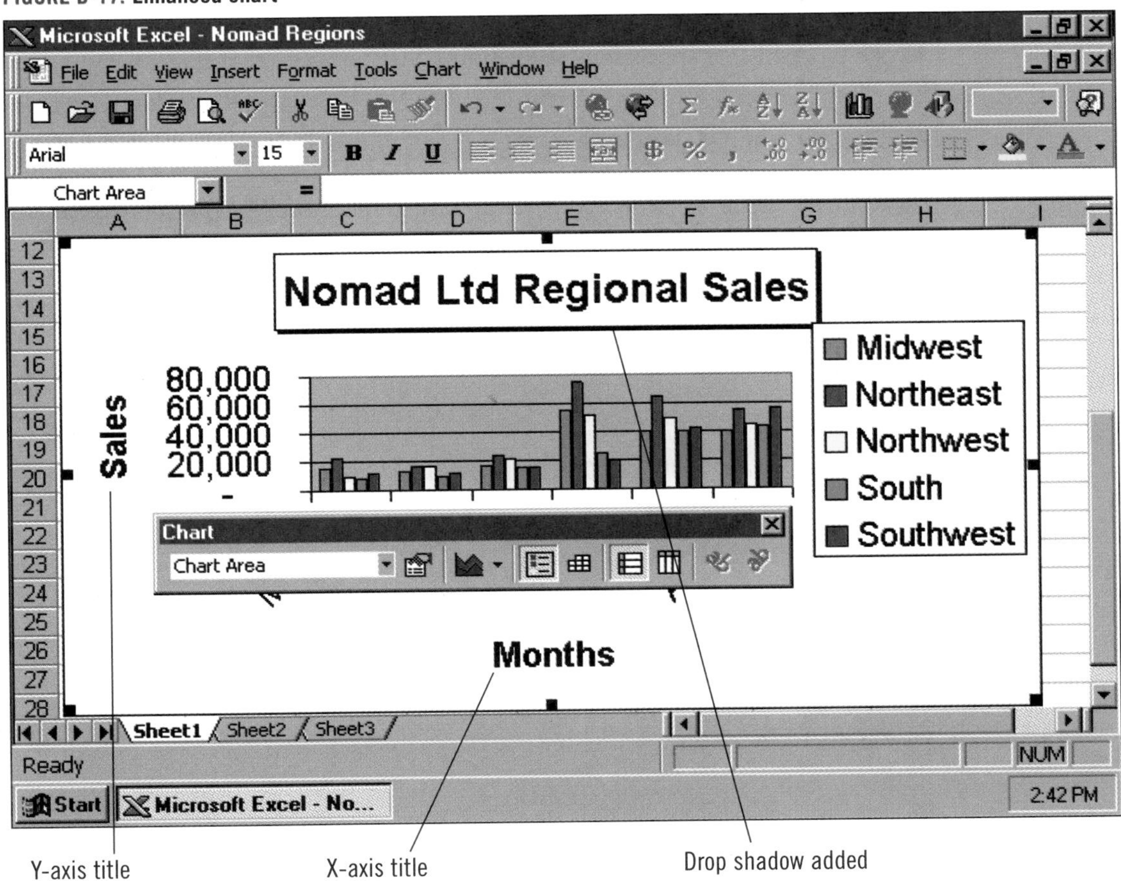

Changing text font and alignment in charts

The font and the alignment of axis text can be modified to make it more readable or to better fit within the plot area. With a chart selected, double-click the text to be modified. The Format Axis dialog box appears. Click the Font or the Alignment tab, make the desired changes, then click OK.

Excel 97

Adding Text Annotations and Arrows to a Chart

You can add arrows and text annotations to highlight information in your charts. Text annotations are labels that you add to a chart to draw attention to a certain part of it. Evan wants to add a text annotation and an arrow to highlight the June sales increase.

Steps

1. **Make sure the chart is selected**
   You want to call attention to the June sales increase by drawing an arrow that points to the top of the June data series with the annotation, "After advertising campaign." To enter the text for an annotation, you simply start typing.
2. **Type After advertising campaign then click the Enter button on the formula bar**
   As you type, the text appears in the formula bar. After you confirm the entry, the text appears in a floating selected text box within the chart window.
3. **Point to an edge of the text box, then press and hold the left mouse button**
   The pointer should be ✥. If the pointer changes to I or ↔, release the mouse button, click outside the text box area to deselect it, then select the text box and repeat Step 3.
4. **Drag the text box above the chart, as shown in Figure D-18, then release the mouse button**
   You are ready to add an arrow.
5. **Click the Drawing button on the Standard toolbar**
   The Drawing toolbar appears.
6. **Click the Arrow button on the Drawing toolbar**
   The pointer changes to +.
7. **Position + under the word "advertising" in the text box, click the left mouse button, drag the line to the June sales, then release the mouse button**
   An arrowhead appears pointing to the June sales. Compare your finished chart to Figure D-19.
8. **Click the Drawing button to close the Drawing toolbar**
9. **Save your work**

QuickTip

You can also insert text and an arrow in the data section of a worksheet by clicking the Text Box button on the Drawing toolbar, drawing a text box, typing the text, and then adding the arrow.

FIGURE D-18: Repositioning text annotation

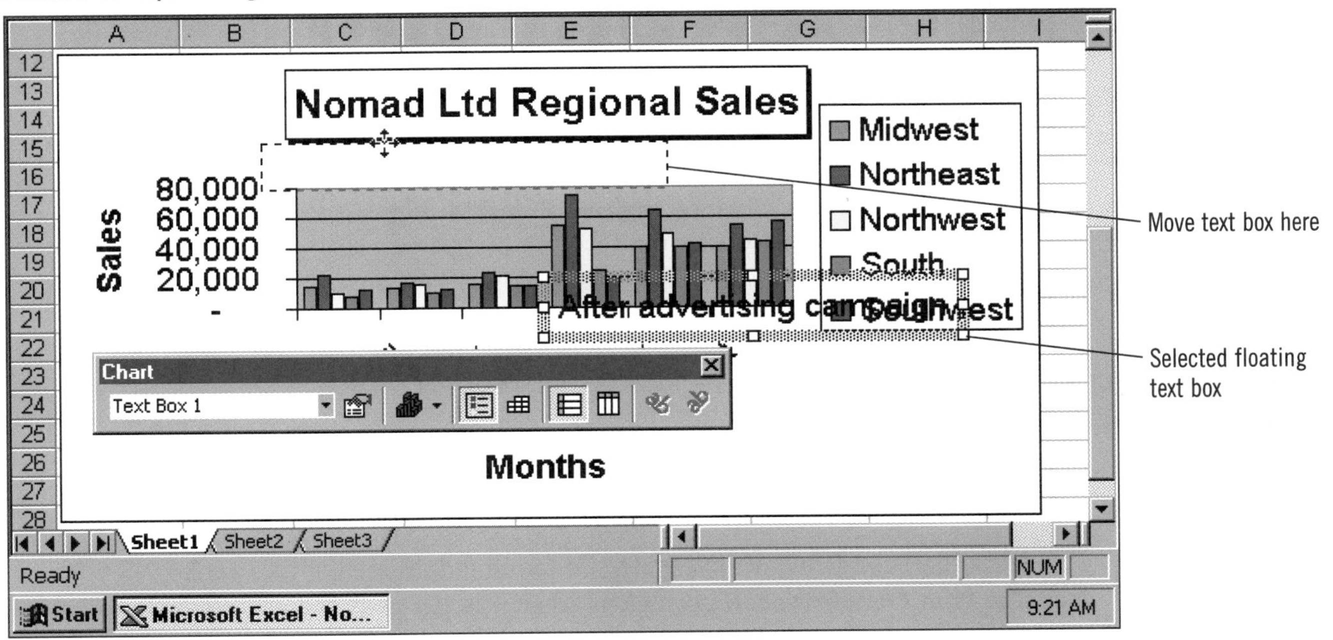

FIGURE D-19: Completed chart with text annotation and arrow

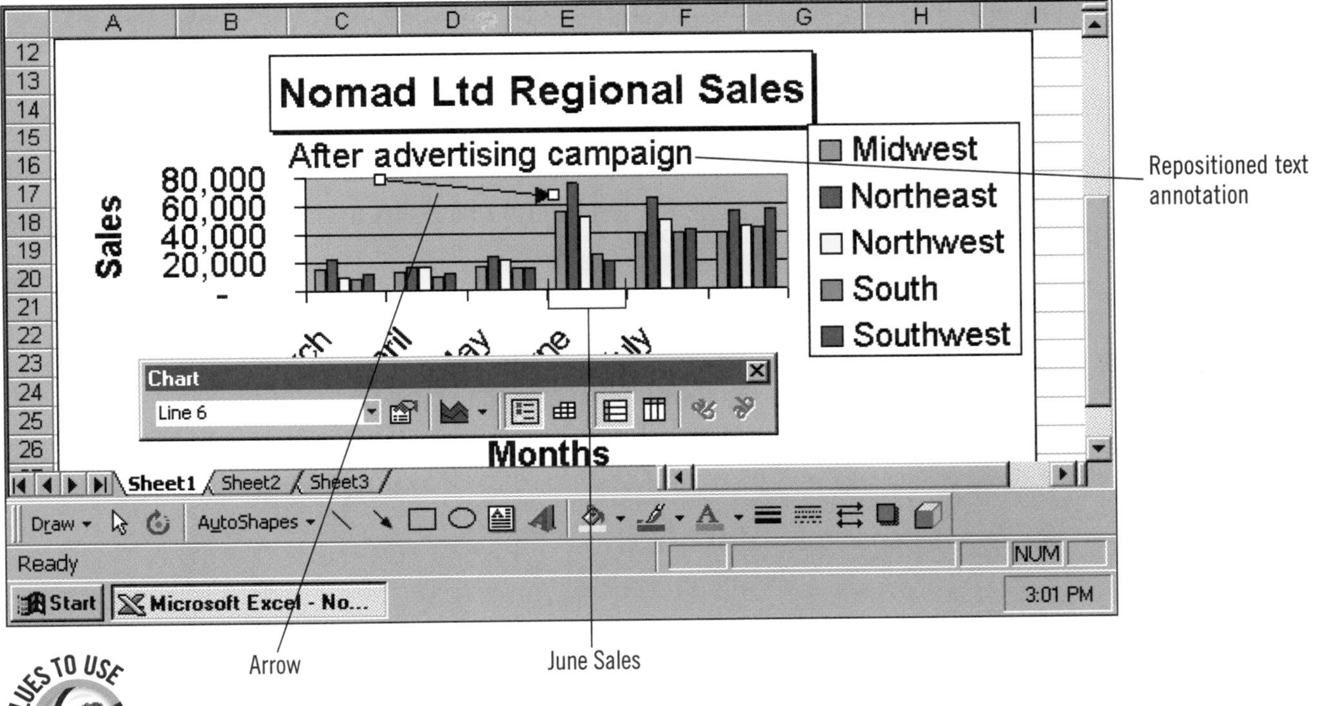

CLUES TO USE

Pulling out a pie slice

Just as an arrow can call attention to a data series, you can emphasize a pie slice by exploding it, or pulling it away from, the pie chart. Once the chart is in Edit mode, click the pie to select it, click the desired slice to select only that slice, then drag the slice away from the pie, as shown in Figure D-20.

FIGURE D-20: Exploded pie slice

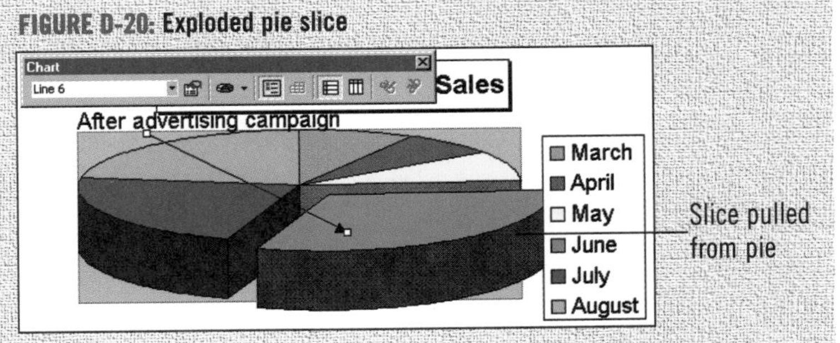

Excel 97

Previewing and Printing a Chart

After you complete a chart to your satisfaction, you will need to print it. You can print a chart by itself, or as part of the worksheet. Evan is satisfied with the chart and wants to print it for the annual meeting. He will print the worksheet and the chart together, so that the shareholders can see the actual sales numbers for each tour type.

Steps

1. Press **[Esc]** twice to deselect the arrow and the chart
   If you wanted to print only the chart without the data, you would leave the chart selected.
2. Click the **Print Preview button** on the Standard toolbar
   The Print Preview window opens. You decide that the chart and data would look better if they were printed in **landscape** orientation—that is, with the page turned sideways. To change the orientation of the page, you must alter the page setup.
3. Click the **Setup button** to display the Page Setup dialog box, then click the **Page tab**
4. Click the **Landscape radio button** in the Orientation section
   See Figure D-21.
   Because each page has a left default margin of 0.75", the chart and data will print too far over to the left of the page. You change this using the Margins tab.
5. Click the **Margins tab**, click the **Horizontal checkbox** in the Center on Page section, then click **OK**
   The print preview of the worksheet appears again. The data and chart are centered on the page that has a landscape orientation, and no gridlines appear. See Figure D-22. You are satisfied with the way it looks and print it.
6. Click **Print** to display the Print dialog box, then click **OK**
   Your printed report should look like the image displayed in the Print Preview window.
7. Save your work
8. Close the workbook and exit Excel

FIGURE D-21: **Page tab of the Page Setup dialog box**

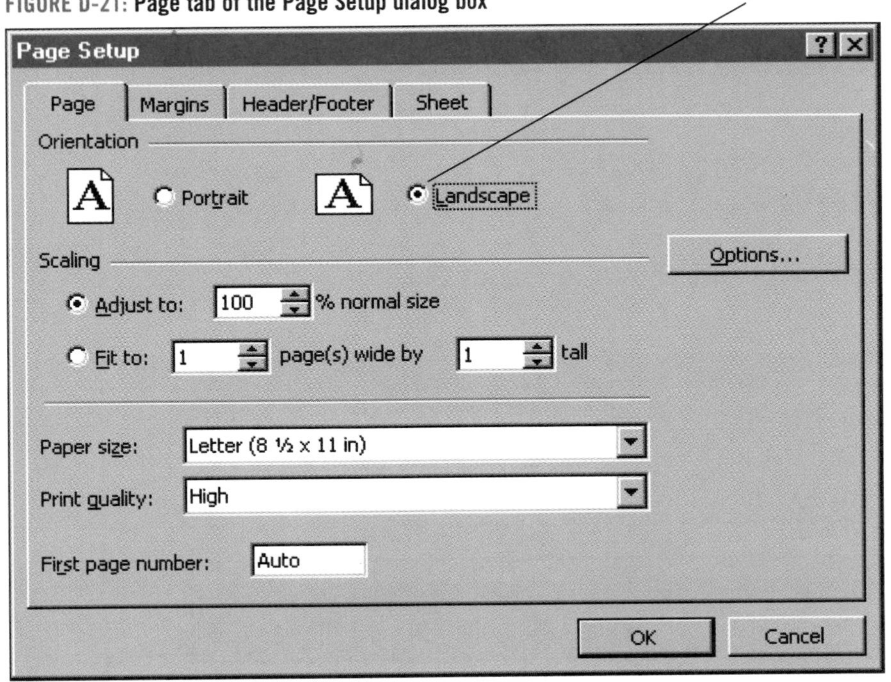

FIGURE D-22: **Chart and data ready to print**

Orientation changed to landscape

Centered on page

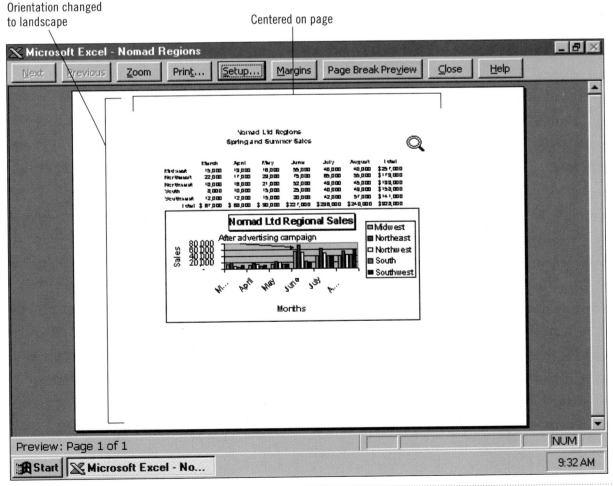

Practice

► Concepts Review

Label each of the elements of the Excel chart shown in Figure D-23.

FIGURE D-23

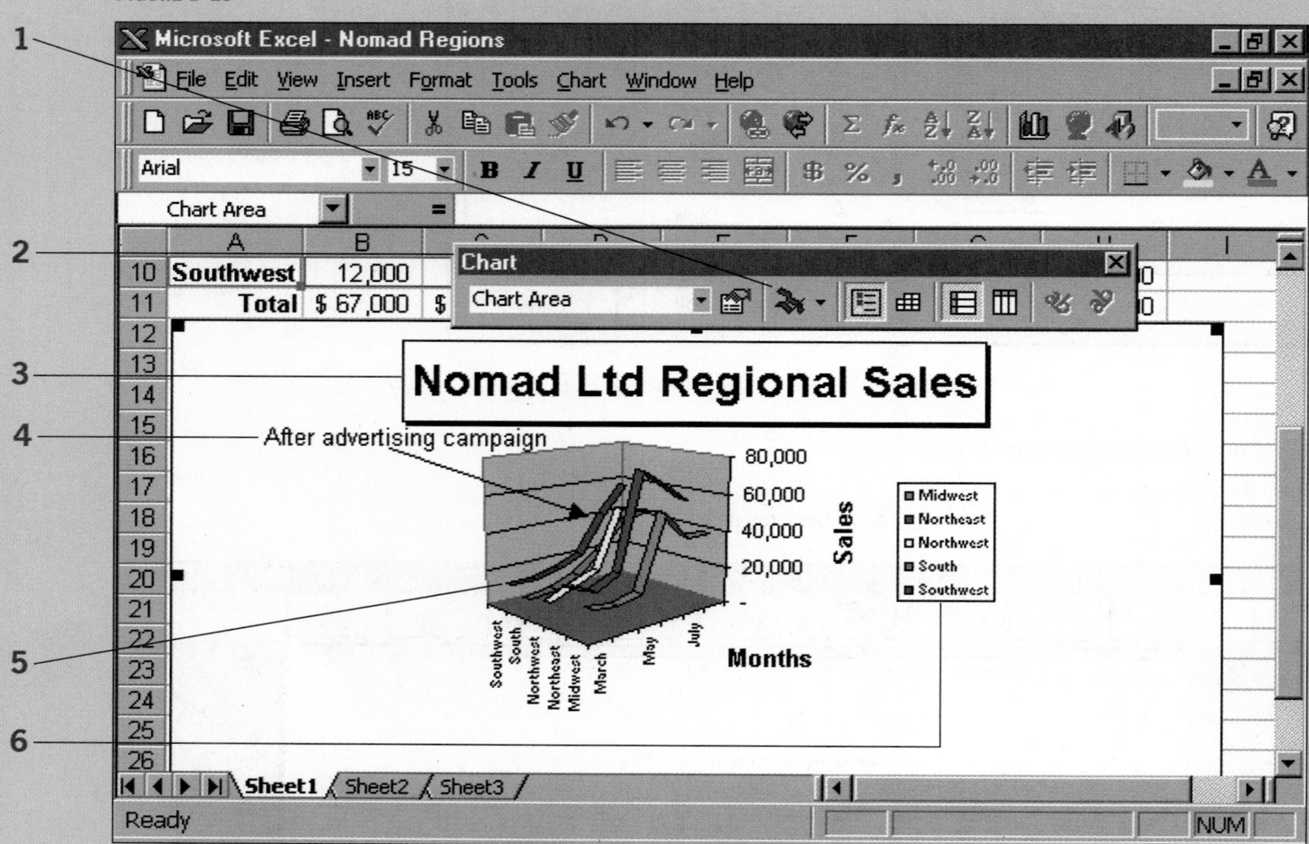

Match each of the statements with its chart type.

7. **Column**
8. **Area**
9. **Pie**
10. **Combination**
11. **Line**

a. Shows how volume changes over time
b. Compares data as parts of a whole
c. Displays a column and line chart using different scales of measurement
d. Compares trends over even time intervals
e. Compares data over time—the Excel default

Select the best answer from the list of choices.

12. The box that identifies patterns used for each data series is a

a. Data point b. Plot c. Legend d. Range

13. What is the term for a row or column on a chart?

a. Range address b. Axis title c. Chart orientation d. Data series

Skills Review

1. Create a worksheet and plan a chart.

a. Start Excel, open a new workbook, then save it as Software Used to your Student Disk.
b. Enter the information from Table D-4 in your worksheet in range A1:E6. Resize columns and rows.
c. Save your work.
d. Sketch a chart for a two-dimensional column chart that shows software distribution by department.

TABLE D-4

	Excel	Word	WordPerfect	PageMaker
Accounting	10	1	9	0
Marketing	2	9	0	6
Engineering	12	5	7	1
Personnel	2	2	2	1
Production	6	3	4	0

2. Create a chart.

a. Select the range you want to chart.
b. Click the Chart Wizard button.
c. Complete the Chart Wizard dialog boxes and build a two-dimensional column chart on the same sheet as the data, having a different color bar for each department and with the title "Software Distribution by Department."
d. Save your work.

3. Move and resize a chart and its objects.

a. Make sure the chart is still selected.
b. Move the chart beneath the data.
c. Drag the chart's selection handles so it fills the range A7:G22.
d. Click the legend to select it.
e. Make the legend longer by about ½".
f. Change the placement of the legend to the bottom right corner of the chart area.
g. Save your work.

4. Edit a chart.

a. Change the value in cell B3 to 6.
b. Click the chart to select it.
c. Click the Chart Type list arrow on the Chart toolbar.
d. Click the 3-D Column Chart button in the list.
e. Rotate the chart to move the data.
f. Save your work.

5. **Change the appearance of a chart.**
   a. Change the chart type to 2-D column chart.
   b. Make sure the chart is still selected.
   c. Turn off the displayed gridlines.
   d. Change the X- and Y-axis font to Times New Roman.
   e. Turn the gridlines back on.
   f. Save your work.

6. **Enhance a chart.**
   a. Make sure the chart is still selected, then click Chart on the menu bar, click Chart Options, then click the Titles tab.
   b. Click the Category (X) axis text box and type "Department."
   c. Click the Value (Y) axis text box, type "Types of Software," and then click OK.
   d. Change the size of the X and Y axes font and the legend font to 8 pt.
   e. Save your work.

7. **Adding a text annotation and arrows to a chart.**
   a. Select the chart.
   b. Create the text annotation "Need More Computers."
   c. Drag the text annotation about one inch above any of the Personnel bars.
   d. Change the font size of the annotation text to 8 pt.
   e. Click the Arrow button on the Drawing toolbar.
   f. Click below the text annotation, drag down any one of the Personnel bars, then release the mouse button.
   g. Open a second window so you can display the data in the new window and the chart in the original window.
   h. Close the second window.
   i. Save your work.

8. **Preview and print a chart.**
   a. Deselect the chart, then click the Print Preview button on the Standard toolbar.
   b. Center the data and chart on the page and change the paper orientation to landscape.
   c. Click Print in the Print Preview window.
   d. Save your work, close the workbook, then exit Excel.

Independent Challenges

1. You are the operations manager for the Springfield Recycling Center. The Marketing Department wants you to create charts for a brochure to advertise a new curbside recycling program. The data provided contains percentages of collected recycled goods. You need to create charts that show:

- How much of each type of recycled material Springfield collected in 1995 and what percentage each type represents. The center collects paper, plastics, and glass from business and residential customers.
- The yearly increases in the total amounts of recycled materials the center has collected since its inception three years ago. Springfield has experienced a 30% annual increase in collections.

To complete this independent challenge:

1. Prepare a worksheet plan that states your goal and identifies the formulas for any calculations.
2. Sketch a sample worksheet on a piece of paper describing how you will create the charts. Which type of chart is best suited for the information you need to display? What kind of chart enhancements will be necessary? Will a 3-D effect make your chart easier to understand?
3. Open the workbook XL D-2 on your Student Disk, then save it as Recycling Center.
4. Add a column that calculates the 30% increase in annual collections based on the percentages given.
5. Create at least six different charts to show the distribution of the different types of recycled goods, as well as the distribution by customer type. Use the Chart Wizard to switch the way data is plotted (columns vs. rows and vice versa) and come up with additional charts.
6. After creating the charts, make the appropriate enhancements. Include chart titles, legends, and axes titles.
7. Before printing, preview the file so you know what the charts will look like. Adjust any items as needed.
8. Save your work. Print the charts, then print the entire worksheet. Close the file.
9. Submit your worksheet plan, preliminary sketches, and the final worksheet printouts.

2. One of your responsibilities at the Nuts and Bolts hardware store is to re-create the company's records using Excel. Another is to convince the current staff that Excel can make daily operations easier and more efficient. You've decided to create charts using the previous year's operating expenses. These charts will be used at the next monthly Accounting Department meeting.

Open the workbook XL D-3 on your Student Disk, and save it as Expense Charts.

To complete this independent challenge:

1. Decide which data in the worksheet should be charted. Sketch two sample charts. What type of charts are best suited for the information you need to display? What kind of chart enhancements will be necessary?
2. Create at least six different charts that show the distribution of expenses, either by quarter or expense type.
3. Add annotated text and arrows highlighting data.
4. In one chart, change the colors of the data series, and in another chart, use black-and-white patterns only.
5. Before printing, preview the file so you know what the charts will look like. Adjust any items as needed.
6. Print the charts. Save your work.
7. Submit your sketches and the final worksheet printouts.

3. The Chamber of Commerce is delighted with the way you've organized their membership roster using Excel. The Board of Directors wants to ask the city for additional advertising funds and has asked you to prepare charts that can be used in their presentation.

Open the workbook XL D-4 on your Student Disk, and save it as Chamber Charts. This file contains raw advertising data for the month of January.

To complete this independent challenge:

1. Calculate the annual advertising expenses based on the January summary data.
2. Use the raw data for January shown in the range A16:B24 to create charts.
3. Decide what types of charts would be best suited for this type of data. Sketch two sample charts. What kind of chart enhancements will be necessary?
4. Create at least four different charts that show the distribution of advertising expenses. Show January expenses and projected values in at least two of the charts.
5. Add annotated text and arrows highlighting important data. Change the colors of the data series if you wish.
6. Before printing, preview the file so you know what the charts will look like. Adjust any items as needed.
7. Print the charts. Save your work.
8. Submit your sketches and the final worksheet printouts.

4. Financial information has a greater impact on others if displayed in a chart. Using the World Wide Web you can find out current activity of stocks and create informative charts. Your company has asked you to chart current trading indexes by category.

To complete this independent challenge:

1. Open a new workbook and save it on your Student Disk as Trading Indexes.
2. Log on to the Internet and use your browser to go to http://www.course.com. From there, click the link Student On Line Companions, then click the Microsoft Office 97 Professional Edition - Illustrated: A First Course page, then click the Excel link for Unit D.
3. Use the following site to compile your data, NASDAQ [www.nasdaq.com].
4. Click the Index Activity button on the NASDAQ home page.
5. Locate Index Value data by category and retrieve this information.
6. Create a chart of the Index Values, by category.
7. Save, print, and hand in a print out of your work.

► Visual Workshop

Modify a worksheet using the skills you learned in this unit, using Figure D-24 for reference. Open the file XL D-5 on your Student Disk, and save it as Quarterly Advertising Budget. Create the chart, then change the data to reflect Figure D-24. Preview and print your results, and submit your printout.

FIGURE D-24

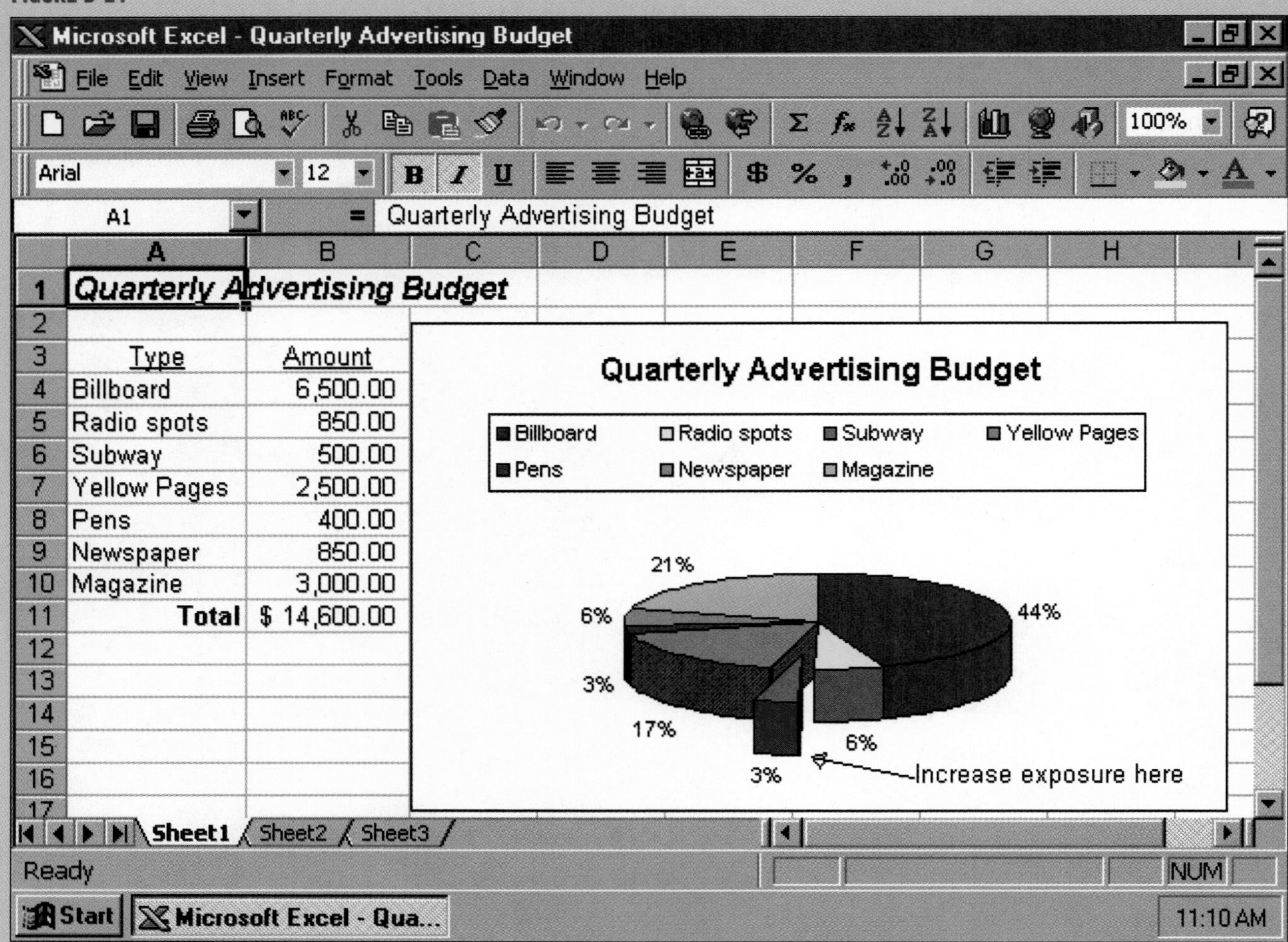

Managing Workbooks

Objectives

- Freeze columns and rows
- Insert and delete sheets
- Reference worksheet data
- Hide and protect worksheet areas
- Specify headers and footers
- Save custom views of a worksheet
- Control page breaks and page numbering
- Set margins and alignment

In this unit, you will learn several Excel features to help you manage and print workbook data. Nomad Ltd has increased the number of its hourly workers by 50% over the past year. Evan Brillstein's manager has designed a timecard summary worksheet to track salary costs for hourly workers. She turned the management of this worksheet over to Evan. In doing so, she has alerted him that she will need several reports generated from the worksheet data.

Excel 97

Freezing Columns and Rows

As rows and columns fill up with data, you might need to scroll through the worksheet to add, delete, modify, and view information. Looking at information without row or column labels can be confusing. In Excel, you can temporarily freeze columns and rows, which enables you to view separate areas of your worksheets at the same time. **Panes** are the columns and rows that **freeze**, or remain in place, while you scroll through your worksheet. The freeze feature is especially useful when you're dealing with large worksheets. Sometimes, though, even freezing is not sufficient. In those cases, you can create as many as four areas, or panes, on the screen at one time and move freely within each of them. Evan has been asked to verify the hourly pay rate, total hours worked, and total pay for two janitors at Nomad Ltd, Wilbur Collins and Orson Wilks. Because the worksheet is becoming more difficult to read as its size increases, Evan decides to freeze the column and row labels. To gather the requested information, Evan needs to view simultaneously a person's last name, total number of hours, hourly pay rate, and total pay. To do this, he will freeze columns A, B, and C and rows 1 through 5.

Steps

1. **Open the workbook titled XL F-1, save it as Timecard Summary, then scroll through the Monday worksheet to view the data**

2. **Return to cell A1, then click cell D6**
   Position the pointer in cell A1 to reorient the worksheet, then move to cell D6 because you want to freeze columns A, B, and C. By doing so, you can still view the last name when you scroll to the right. Because you want to be able to scroll down the worksheet and read the column headings, you also freeze the labels in rows 1 through 5. When instructed to do so, Excel freezes the columns to the left and the rows above the cell pointer.

Trouble?

If you do not see a thin vertical line in the worksheet area between columns C and D and a thin horizontal black line between rows 5 and 6, click Window on the menu bar, click Unfreeze Panes, then repeat Steps 2 and 3.

3. **Click Window on the menu bar, then click Freeze Panes**
   Everything to the left and above the active cell is frozen. A thin line appears along the column border to the left of the active cell, and another line appears along the row above the active cell indicating that columns A through C and rows 1 through 5 are frozen.

4. **Scroll to the right until columns A through C and L through P are visible**
   Because columns A, B, and C are frozen, they remain on the screen; columns D through K are temporarily hidden from view. Notice that the information you are looking for in row 12 (last name, total hours, hourly pay rate, and total pay for Wilbur Collins) is readily available. You jot down Wilbur's data but still need to verify Orson Wilks's information.

5. **Scroll down until row 23 is visible**
   Notice that in addition to columns A through C, rows 1 through 5 remain on the screen as well. See Figure F-1. Evan jots down the information for Orson Wilks. Even though a pane is frozen, you can click in the frozen area of the worksheet and edit the contents of the cells there, if necessary.

QuickTip

When you open an existing workbook, the cell pointer is in the cell it was in when you last saved the workbook. Press [Ctrl][Home] to return to cell A1 prior to saving and closing a workbook.

6. **Press [Ctrl][Home]**
   Because the panes are frozen, the cell pointer moves to cell D6, not A1. Now that you have gathered the requested information, you are ready to unfreeze the panes.

7. **Click Window on the menu bar, then click Unfreeze Panes**
   The panes are unfrozen. You are satisfied with your ability to navigate and view the worksheet and are ready to save the workbook.

8. **Return to cell A1, then save the workbook**

FIGURE F-1: Scrolled worksheet with frozen rows and columns

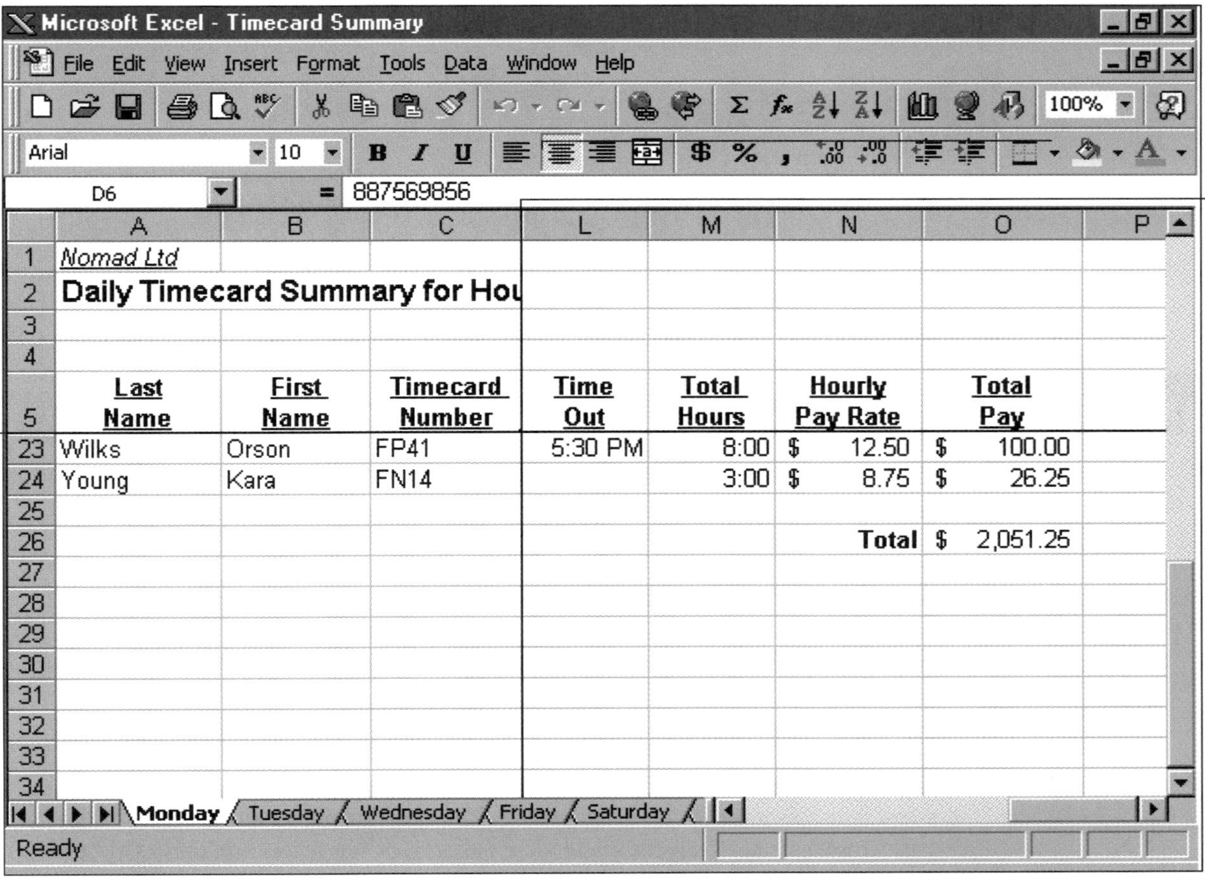

Microsoft Excel - Timecard Summary

File Edit View Insert Format Tools Data Window Help

Arial 10 100%

D6 = 887569856

	A	B	C	L	M	N	O	P
1	*Nomad Ltd*							
2	**Daily Timecard Summary for Hou**							
3								
4								
5	**Last Name**	**First Name**	**Timecard Number**	**Time Out**	**Total Hours**	**Hourly Pay Rate**	**Total Pay**	
23	Wilks	Orson	FP41	5:30 PM	8:00	$ 12.50	$ 100.00	
24	Young	Kara	FN14		3:00	$ 8.75	$ 26.25	
25								
26						**Total**	$ 2,051.25	
27								
28								
29								
30								
31								
32								
33								
34								

Monday / Tuesday / Wednesday / Friday / Saturday

Ready

Break in row numbers due to frozen rows 1–5

Break in column letters due to frozen columns A–C

Excel 97

CLUES TO USE

Splitting the worksheet into multiple panes

Excel provides a way to split the worksheet area into vertical and/or horizontal panes so that you can click inside any one pane and scroll to locate desired information in that pane without any of the other panes moving. See Figure F-2. To split a worksheet area into multiple panes, drag the split box (the small box at the top of the vertical scroll bar or at the right end of the horizontal scroll bar) in the direction you want the split to appear. To remove the split, move the mouse over the split until the pointer changes to ≑, then double-click.

FIGURE F-2: Worksheet split into two horizontal panes

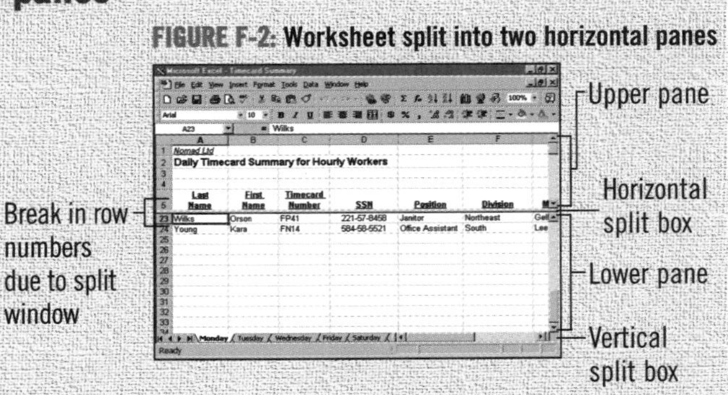

Excel 97

Inserting and Deleting Sheets

You can insert and delete worksheets in a workbook as needed. For example, because new workbooks open with only three sheets available (Sheet1, Sheet2, and Sheet3), you need to insert at least one more sheet if you want to have four quarterly worksheets in an annual financial budget workbook. As for other Excel features, you can do this by using commands on the menu bar or pop-up menu. Evan was in a hurry when he added the sheet tabs to the Timecard Summary workbook. He needs to insert a sheet for Thursday and delete the sheet for Sunday because hourly workers do not work on Sunday.

QuickTip

You also can copy the active worksheet by clicking Edit on the menu bar, then clicking Move or Copy Sheet. You choose the sheet the copy will precede, then select the Create a copy check box.

1. **Click the Friday sheet tab, click Insert on the menu bar, then click Worksheet**
   Excel automatically inserts a new sheet tab labeled Sheet1 to the left of the selected sheet. See Figure F-3. Next, rename the inserted sheet to something more meaningful.
2. **Rename the Sheet1 tab Thursday**
   Now the tabs read Monday, Tuesday, Wednesday, Thursday, Friday, and Saturday. The tabs for Sunday and Weekly Summary are not visible, but you still need to delete the Sunday worksheet.
3. **Scroll until the Sunday sheet tab is visible, move the pointer over the Sunday tab, then click the right mouse button**
   A pop-up menu appears. See Figure F-4. The pop-up menu allows you to insert, delete, rename, move, or copy sheets, select all the sheets, or view the code in a workbook.
4. **Click Delete on the pop-up menu**
   A message box warns that the selected sheet will be deleted permanently. You must acknowledge the message before proceeding.
5. **Click OK**
   The Sunday sheet is deleted. Next, to check your work, you view a menu of sheets in the workbook.

QuickTip

You can scroll several tabs at once by pressing [Shift] while clicking one of the middle tab scrolling buttons.

6. **Move the mouse pointer over any tab scrolling button, then right-click**
   When you right-click a tab scrolling button, Excel automatically opens a menu of the sheets in the active workbook. Compare your list with Figure F-5.
7. **Click Monday, return to cell A1, then save the workbook**

FIGURE F-3: **Workbook with inserted sheet**

17	
18	

Monday / Tuesday / Wednesday / **Sheet1** / Friday / Sa

Ready

Inserted sheet

FIGURE F-4: **Sheet pop-up menu**

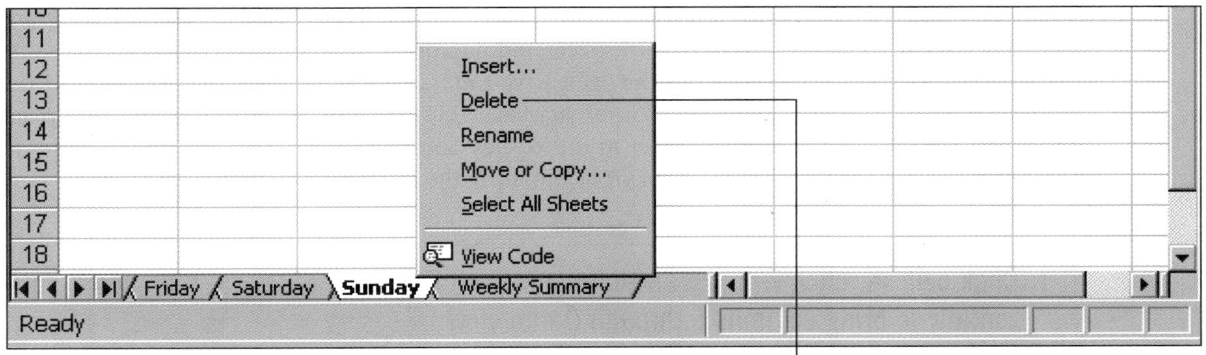

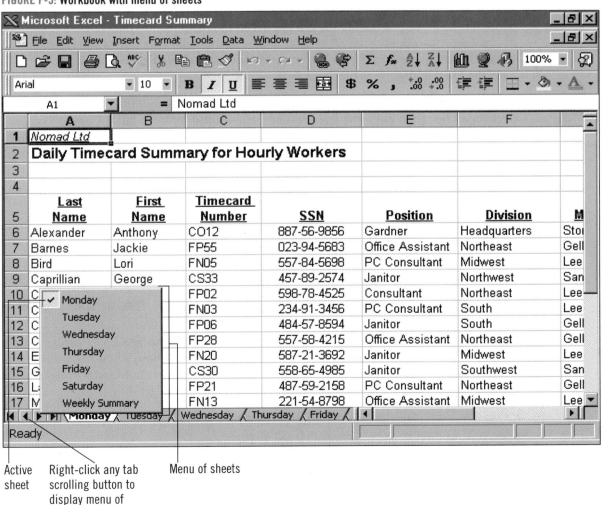

Click to delete selected sheet

FIGURE F-5: **Workbook with menu of sheets**

Microsoft Excel - Timecard Summary

File Edit View Insert Format Tools Data Window Help

Arial 10 100%

A1 = Nomad Ltd

	A	B	C	D	E	F	
1	*Nomad Ltd*						
2	**Daily Timecard Summary for Hourly Workers**						
3							
4							
5	**Last Name**	**First Name**	**Timecard Number**	**SSN**	**Position**	**Division**	**M**
6	Alexander	Anthony	CO12	887-56-9856	Gardner	Headquarters	Stor
7	Barnes	Jackie	FP55	023-94-5683	Office Assistant	Northeast	Gell
8	Bird	Lori	FN05	557-84-5698	PC Consultant	Midwest	Lee
9	Caprillian	George	CS33	457-89-2574	Janitor	Northwest	San
10	C		FP02	598-78-4525	Consultant	Northeast	Lee
11	C		FN03	234-91-3456	PC Consultant	South	Lee
12	C		FP06	484-57-8594	Janitor	South	Gell
13	C		FP28	557-58-4215	Office Assistant	Northeast	Gell
14	E		FN20	587-21-3692	Janitor	Midwest	Lee
15	G		CS30	558-65-4985	Janitor	Southwest	San
16	L		FP21	487-59-2158	PC Consultant	Northeast	Gell
17	M		FN13	221-54-8798	Office Assistant	Midwest	Lee

✓ Monday
Tuesday
Wednesday
Thursday
Friday
Saturday
Weekly Summary

Monday / Tuesday / Wednesday / Thursday / Friday

Ready

Active sheet

Right-click any tab scrolling button to display menu of sheets

Menu of sheets

Excel 97

Excel 97

Referencing Worksheet Data

You can reference data within a worksheet, between sheets, and between workbooks. For example, you can reference data within a worksheet if you want to reference a calculated total elsewhere in the sheet. Retyping the calculated result in another cell is not recommended because the data values on which the calculated total depend might change. Referencing data between sheets might be necessary if you have quarterly worksheets and an annual summary worksheet in the same workbook. Although Evan does not have timecard data for the remaining days of the week, he wants to try out the Weekly Summary sheet. He does this by creating a reference from the total pay data in the Monday sheet to the Weekly Summary sheet. First, he freezes panes to improve the view of the worksheets prior to initiating the reference between them.

Steps

1. **Click cell D6, click Window on the menu bar, click Freeze Panes, then scroll horizontally to bring columns L through O into view**
   Next, you right-click a tab scrolling button to access the pop-up menu for moving between sheets.

2. **Right-click a tab scrolling button, then click Weekly Summary**
   Because the Weekly Summary sheet will contain the reference, the cell pointer must reside there when the reference is initiated. A simple **reference** within the same sheet or between sheets is made by positioning the cell pointer in the cell to contain the reference, typing = (equal sign), positioning the cell pointer in the cell containing the contents to be referenced, and then completing the entry. You complete the entry either by pressing [Enter] or clicking the Enter button on the formula bar.

Trouble?

If you have difficulty referencing cells between sheets, press [Esc] and begin again.

3. **While in the Weekly Summary sheet, click cell C6, type =, activate the Monday sheet, click cell O6, then click the Enter button on the formula bar**
   The formula bar reads =Monday!O6. See Figure F-6. *Monday* references the Monday sheet. The ! (exclamation point) is an **external reference indicator** meaning that the cell referenced is outside the active sheet; O6 is the actual cell reference in the external sheet. The result $41.00 appears in cell C6 of the Weekly Summary sheet showing the reference to the value displayed in cell O6 of the Monday sheet. You are ready to copy the formula reference down the column.

4. **While in the Weekly Summary sheet, copy cell C6 into cells C7:C24**
   Excel copies the contents of cell C6 with its relative reference down the column. Test the reference for Anthony Alexander in cell C6 by correcting the time he clocked out for the day.

5. **Make the Monday sheet active, edit cell L6 to read 3:30 PM, then activate the Weekly Summary sheet**
   Cell C6 now shows $20.50. By changing Anthony's time-out to two hours earlier, his pay dropped from $41.00 to $20.50. This makes sense because Anthony's hours went from four to two and his hourly salary is $10.25. Additionally, the reference to Monday's total pay was automatically updated in the Weekly Summary sheet. See Figure F-7.

6. **Preview, then print the Weekly Summary sheet**

7. **Activate the Monday sheet, then unfreeze the panes**
   You are ready to save the workbook.

8. **Save the workbook**

FIGURE F-6: Worksheet showing referenced cell

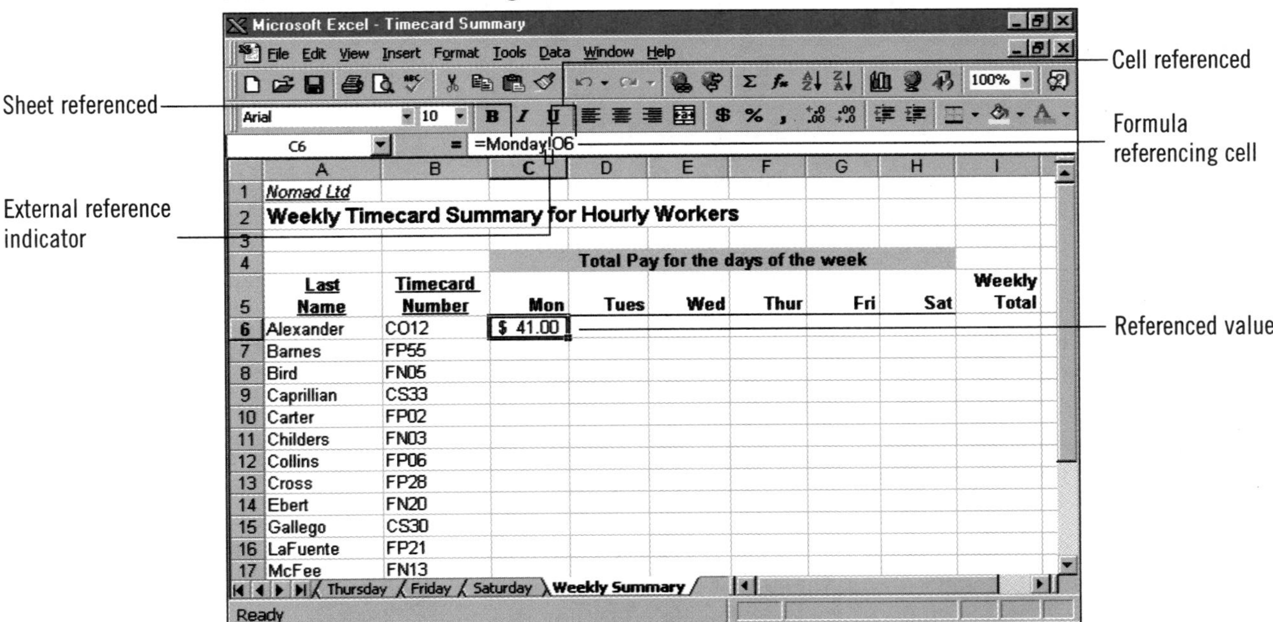

FIGURE F-7: Weekly Summary worksheet with updated reference

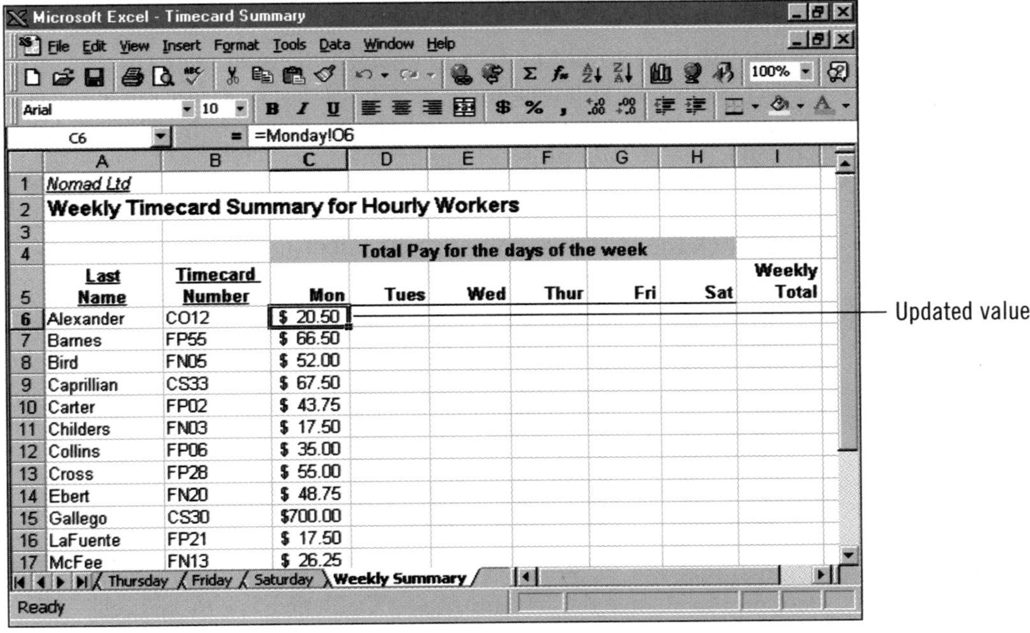

Linking workbooks

Just as you can reference data between cells in a worksheet and between sheets, you can reference data between workbooks dynamically so that any changes made in one workbook are reflected immediately in the other workbook. This dynamic referencing is called **linking**. To link a single cell between workbooks, simply open both workbooks, select the cell to receive the linked data, press = (equal sign), select the cell containing the data to be linked, then press [Enter]. If you are linking more than one cell, you can copy the linked data to the Clipboard, select the upper-left cell to receive the link, click Edit on the menu bar, click Paste Special, then click Paste Link.

Excel 97

Hiding and Protecting Worksheet Areas

Worksheets can contain sensitive information that is not intended to be altered or even viewed by all users. In Excel, you can hide individual formulas, rows, columns, or entire sheets. In addition, you can **protect** selected cells so they cannot be changed while allowing other cells in the worksheet to be altered. See Table F-1 for a list of options you can use to hide and protect a worksheet. Cells that are protected so that their contents cannot be altered are called **locked cells**. You lock and unlock cells by clicking the Locked check box in the Format Cells dialog box. A common worksheet protection strategy is to unlock cells that will be changed, sometimes referred to as the **data entry area**, and to leave the remaining cells locked. Because Evan will assign someone to enter the sensitive timecard information into the worksheet, he plans to hide and protect selected areas of the worksheet.

Steps

1. **Make sure the Monday sheet is active, select range I6:L25; click Format on the menu bar, click Cells, then click the Protection tab**
   You include row 25, even though it does not contain data, in the event that new data is added to the row later. Notice that the Locked box in the Protection tab is checked, as shown in Figure F-8. By default, the Locked check box is selected, which indicates that all the cells in a new workbook start out locked.
2. **Click the Locked check box to deselect it, then click OK**
   Excel stores time as a fraction of a 24-hour day. In the formula for total pay, hours must be multiplied by 24. This concept might be confusing to the data entry person, so you hide the formulas before you protect the worksheet.
3. **Select range O6:O25; click Format on the menu bar, click Cells, click the Protection tab, click the Hidden check box to select it, then click OK**
   The screen data remains the same (unhidden and unlocked) until you set the protection in the next step.
4. **Click Tools on the menu bar, point to Protection, then click Protect Sheet**
   The Protect Sheet dialog box opens. You choose not to use a password.
5. **Click OK**
   You are ready to put the new worksheet protection status to the test.
6. **Click cell O6**
   Notice that the formula bar is empty because of the hidden formula setting. Now you attempt to change the cell contents of O6, which is a locked cell.
7. **In cell O6, type T to confirm that locked cells cannot be changed, then click OK**
   When you attempt to change a locked cell, a message box reminds you of the protected cell's read-only status. See Figure F-9. Next, you attempt to make an entry in the Time In column to make sure it is unlocked.
8. **Click cell I6, type 9, and notice that Excel allows you to begin the entry; press [Esc] to cancel the entry, then save the workbook**
   Evan is satisfied that the Time In and Time Out data can be changed as needed.

QuickTip

To turn off worksheet protection, click Tools on the menu bar, point to Protection, then click Unprotect Sheet. If prompted for a password, type the password, then click OK. Keep in mind that passwords are case sensitive.

FIGURE F-8: Protection tab in Format Cells dialog box

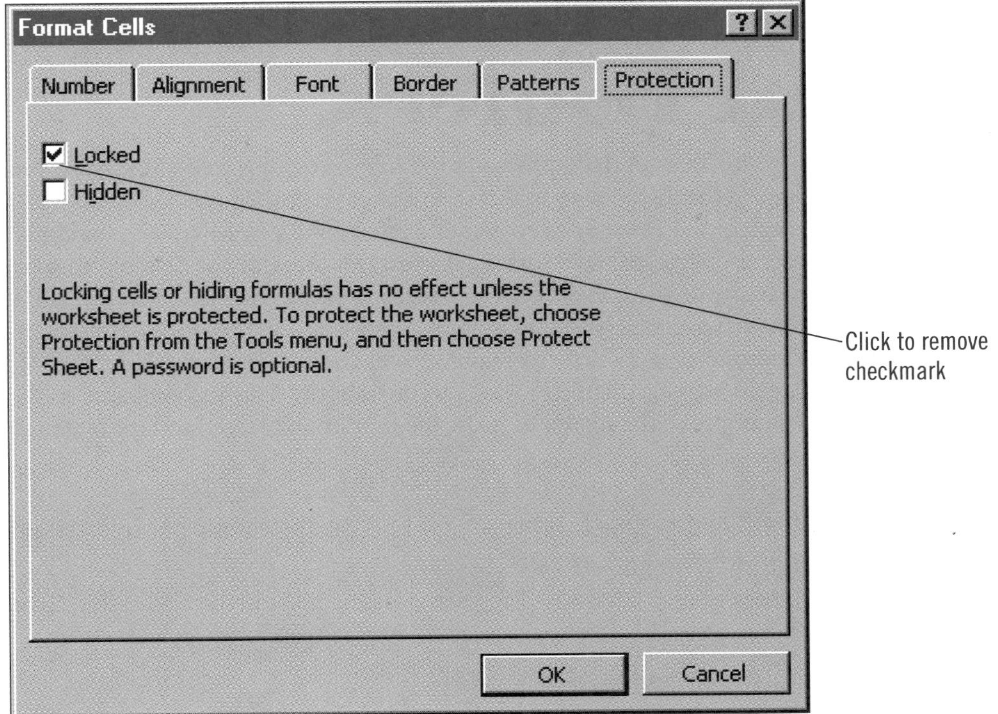

FIGURE F-9: Message box reminder of protected cell's read-only status

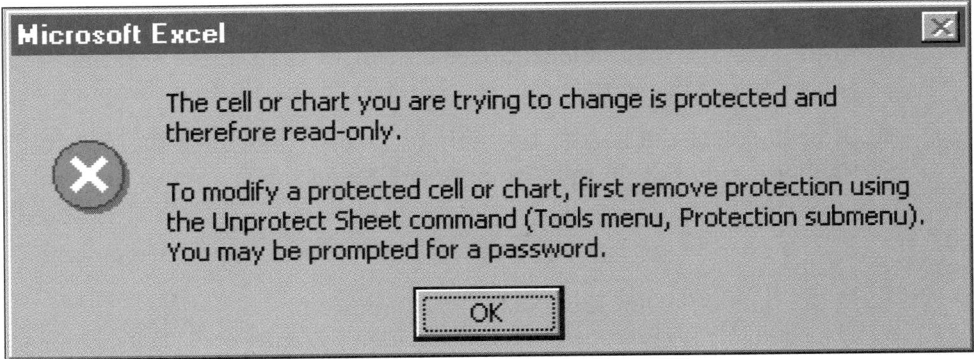

Excel 97

TABLE F-1: Options for hiding and protecting worksheet elements

task	menu commands
Hide/Unhide a column	Format, Column, Hide, or Unhide
Hide/Unhide a formula	Format, Cells, Protection tab, select/deselect Hidden check box
Hide/Unhide a row	Format, Row, Hide, or Unhide
Hide/Unhide a sheet	Format, Sheet, Hide, or Unhide
Protect workbook	Tools, Protection, Protect Workbook, assign optional password
Protect worksheet	Tools, Protection, Protect Sheet, assign optional password
Unlock/Relock cells	Format, Cells, Protection tab, deselect/select Locked check box

***Note:** Some of the hide and protect options do not take effect until protection is enabled.*

Excel 97

Specifying Headers and Footers

A **header** is information that appears at the top of each printed page, and a **footer** is information that appears at the bottom of each printed page. You do not see headers and footers on the screen, except in the Print Preview window. By default, in Microsoft Excel 97 the header and footer are set to "none" in new worksheets. You can override the default of no headers and footers by creating your own. Excel provides a group of buttons that you can use to print specific information in your headers and footers. See Table F-2 for a description of these buttons. Evan remembers that his manager will use the Timecard Summary sheet as part of a report to upper management. He wants to include the date and filename in the footer, and he thinks it will improve the report to make the header text larger and more descriptive.

1. With the Monday sheet active, click **File** on the menu bar, click **Page Setup**, then click the **Header/Footer tab**
   The Header/Footer tab of the Page Setup dialog box opens. Notice that Excel automatically sets the header and footer to none. First, you customize the header.
2. Click **Custom Header**
   The Header dialog box opens, as shown in Figure F-10. By entering your header information in the Center section box, Excel automatically centers this information on the printout.
3. Click the **Center section box**, then type **Monday – 8/4**
   In the case of a long header, header text might wrap to the next line in the box but will appear on one line in the printout. Next, you change the font size and style.
4. Drag to select the header text **Monday – 8/4**, then click the **Font button** in the Header dialog box; in the Size box click **12**, in the Font style box click **Bold**, click **OK**, then click **OK** to return to the Header/Footer tab
   The new header appears in the Header box. You are ready to customize the footer.
5. In the Header/Footer tab, click **Custom Footer**
   The Footer dialog box opens. The information you enter in the Left section box is left-aligned on the printout. The text you enter in the Right section box is right-aligned on the printout.
6. Click the **Right section box**, type **Workbook:** and press **[Spacebar]**, then click the **File Name button** in the Footer dialog box to insert the filename code **&[File]**, then click **OK**
   You return to the Page Setup dialog box, and the revised footer appears in the Footer box. See Figure F-11.
7. Preview, print, then save the worksheet
   Evan is ready to submit the report to his manager.

QuickTip
You can easily turn off the header and/or footer in a worksheet by clicking the header or footer list arrow on the Header/Footer tab, scrolling to the top of the list, then choosing (none).

FIGURE F-10: Header dialog box

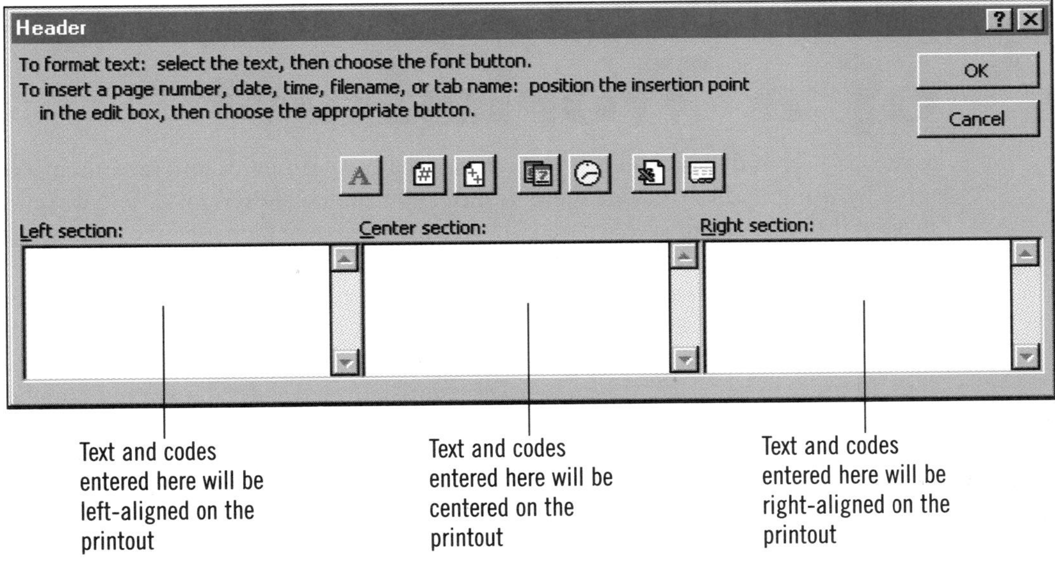

FIGURE F-11: Header/Footer tab with revised header and footer information

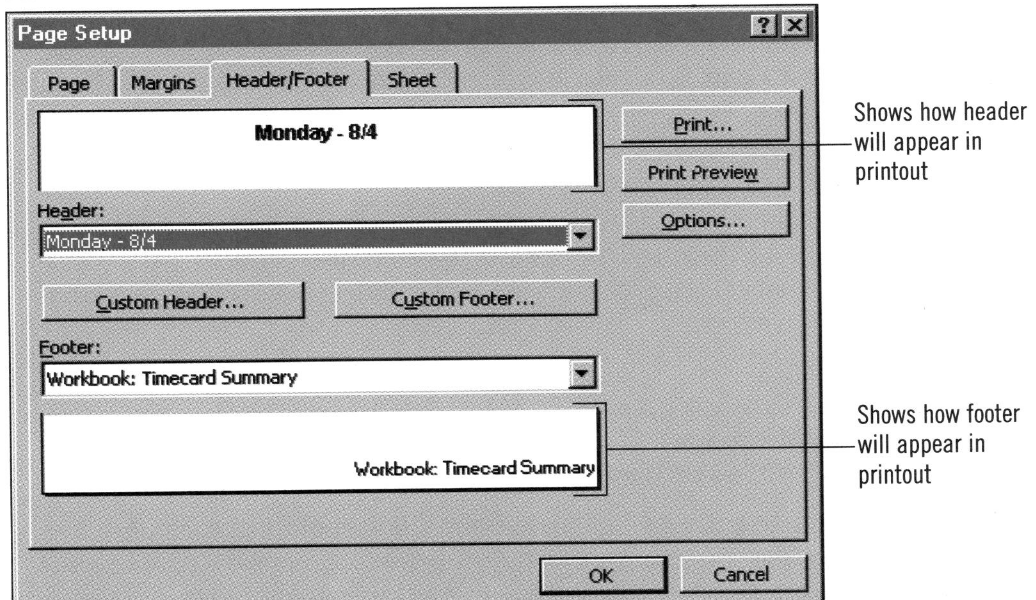

TABLE F-2: Buttons for customizing headers and footers

button	button name	code	result
	Font	None	Displays the Font dialog box in which you choose attributes for the header or footer
	Page Number	&[Page]	Inserts current page number
	Total Pages	&[Pages]	Inserts total number of printed pages
	Date	&[Date]	Inserts the current date as it is stored in your computer
	Time	&[Time]	Inserts the current time as it is stored in your computer
	File Name	&[File]	Inserts the name of the workbook file
	Sheet Name	&[Tab]	Inserts the name of the worksheet

Excel 97

Saving Custom Views of a Worksheet

A **view** is a set of display and/or print settings that you can name and save, then access at a later time. By using Excel's Custom Views feature, you can create several different views of a worksheet without having to save separate sheets under separate filenames. For example, if you often switch between portrait and landscape orientations when printing different parts of a worksheet, you can create two views with the appropriate print settings for each view. You define the display and/or print settings first, then name the view. Because Evan will be generating several reports from this data, he will save the current print and display settings as a custom view. In order to better view the data to be printed, Evan decides to use the Zoom box to display the entire worksheet on one screen. The Zoom box has a default setting of 100% magnification and appears on the Standard toolbar.

Steps

QuickTip

With **Report Manager add-in**, you can group worksheets and their views to be printed in sequence as one large report.

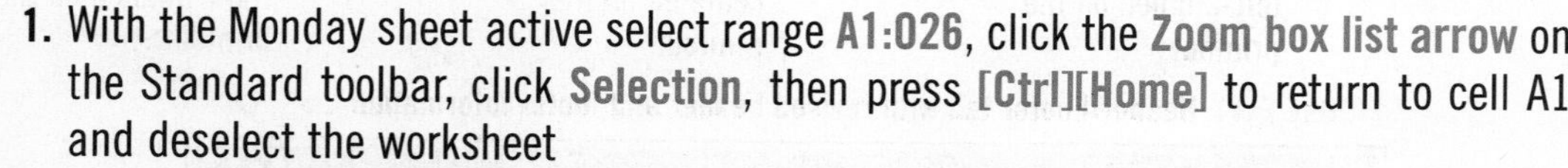

1. **With the Monday sheet active select range A1:O26, click the Zoom box list arrow on the Standard toolbar, click Selection, then press [Ctrl][Home] to return to cell A1 and deselect the worksheet**
   Excel automatically adjusts the display magnification so that the data selected fit on one screen. See Figure F-12. After selecting the **Zoom box**, you also can pick a magnification percentage from the list or type the desired percentage. Now that you have set up the desired view of the data, you are ready to save the current print and display settings as a custom view.
2. **Click View, then click Custom Views**
   The Custom Views dialog box opens. Any previously defined views for the active worksheet appear in the Views box. In this case, Evan's manager had created a custom view named Generic containing default print and display settings. See Figure F-13. Next, you choose Add to create a new view.
3. **Click Add**
   The Add View dialog box opens, as shown in Figure F-14. Here, you enter a name for the view and decide whether to include print settings and hidden rows, columns and filter settings. Leave these two options checked.
4. **In the Name box, type Complete Daily Worksheet, then click OK**
   After creating a custom view of the worksheet, you return to the worksheet area. You are ready to test the two custom views. First, you turn off worksheet protection in case the views require a change to the worksheet.
5. **Click Tools on the menu bar, point to Protection, then click Unprotect Sheet**
   With the worksheet protection turned off, you are ready to show your custom views.
6. **Click View on the menu bar, then click Custom Views**
   The Custom Views dialog box opens, listing both the Complete Daily Worksheet and Generic views.
7. **Click Generic in the Views list box, click Show, then preview the worksheet**
   The Generic custom view returns the worksheet to Excel's default print and display settings. Now, you are ready to test the new custom view.
8. **Click View on the menu bar, click Custom Views, click Complete Daily Worksheet in the Views list box, click Show, then save the workbook**
   Evan is satisfied with the custom view of the worksheet he created.

QuickTip

To delete views from the active worksheet, select the view in the Views list box, then click Delete.

Trouble?

If you receive the message, "Some view settings could not be applied," repeat Step 5 to ensure worksheet protection is turned off.

FIGURE F-12: Worksheet at 48% magnification

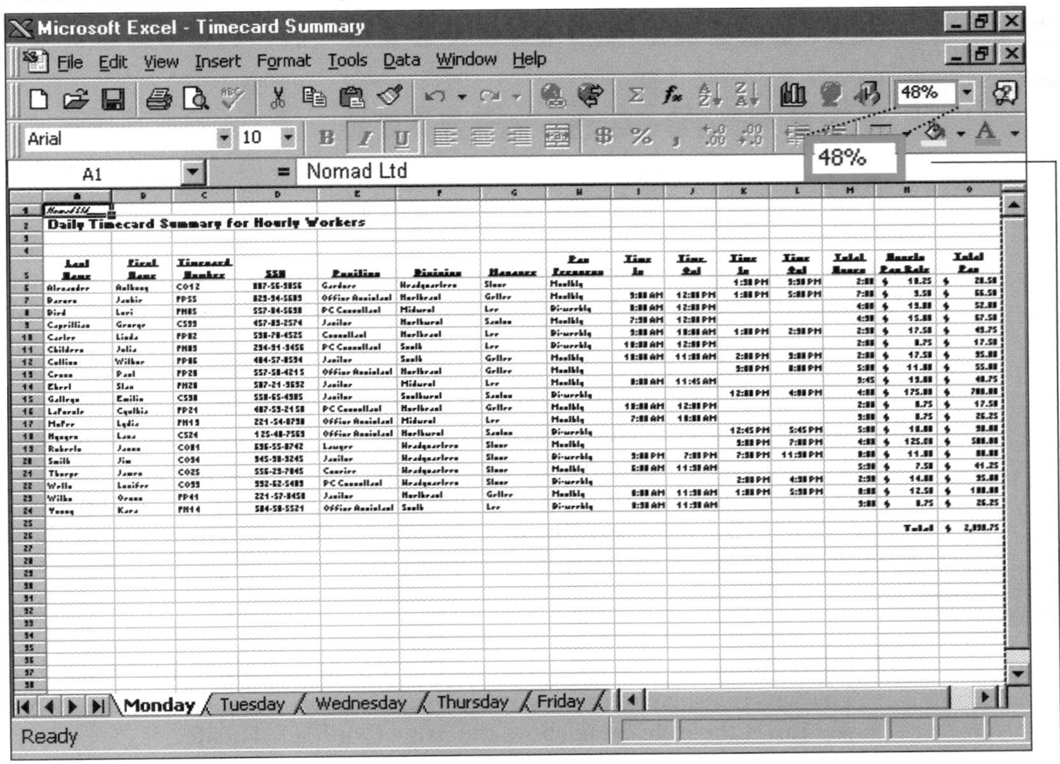

FIGURE F-13: Custom Views dialog box

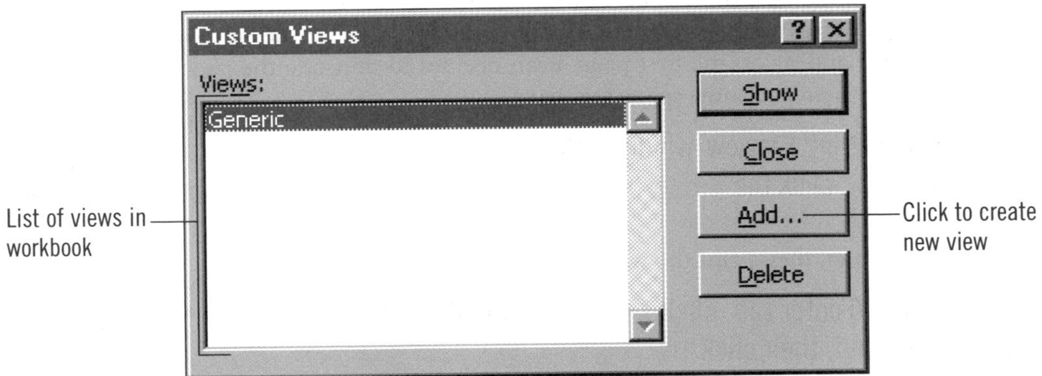

FIGURE F-14: Add View dialog box

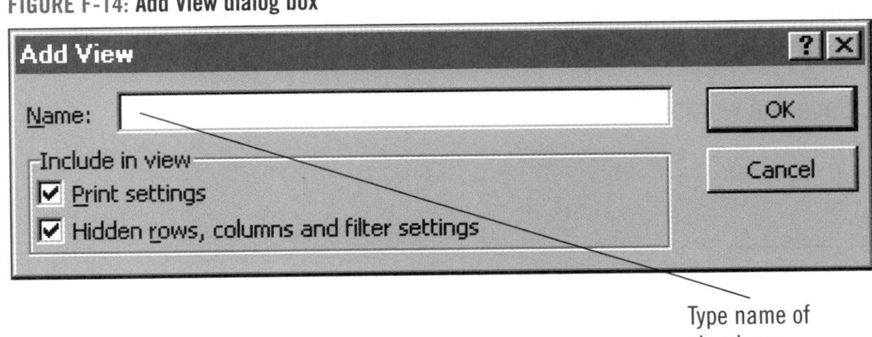

Excel 97

Controlling Page Breaks and Page Numbering

The vertical and horizontal dashed lines in your worksheets indicate page breaks. Excel automatically inserts a page break when your worksheet data doesn't fit on one page. These page breaks are **dynamic**, which means they adjust automatically when you insert or delete rows and columns and when you change column widths or row heights. Everything to the left of the first vertical dashed line and above the first horizontal dashed line is printed on the first page. You can override the automatic breaks by choosing the Page Break command on the Insert menu. Table F-3 describes the different types of page breaks you can use. Evan's manager wants another report displaying no more than half the hourly workers on each page. To accomplish this, Evan must insert a manual page break. He begins by returning the screen display to 100% magnification.

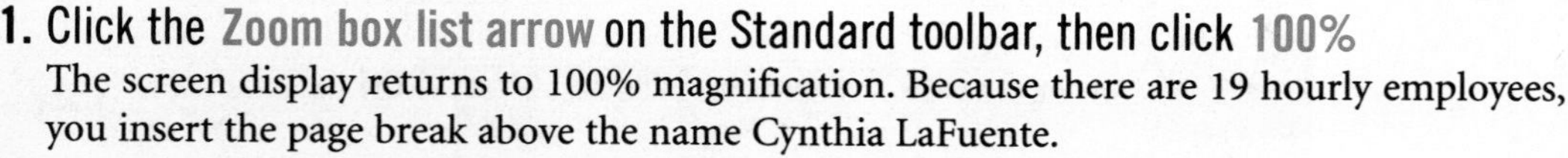

Steps

Trouble?
If you don't see the page breaks inserted by Excel, click Tools on the menu bar, click Options, then click the View tab. Make sure the Page breaks check box is selected.

QuickTip
To remove a manual page break, select any cell directly below or to the right of the page break, click Insert on the menu bar, then click Remove Page Break.

1. **Click the Zoom box list arrow on the Standard toolbar, then click 100%**
   The screen display returns to 100% magnification. Because there are 19 hourly employees, you insert the page break above the name Cynthia LaFuente.
2. **Click cell A16, click Insert on the menu bar, then click Page Break**
   A dashed line appears between rows 15 and 16 indicating a horizontal page break. See Figure F-15. Next, you preview the worksheet.
3. **Preview the worksheet, then click Zoom**
   Notice that the status bar reads "Page 1 of 2" and that the data for the employees up through Emilio Gallego appear on the first page. Evan decides to reinstate the page number in the footer because the report now spans two pages.
4. **While in the Print Preview window, click Setup, click the Header/Footer tab, click Custom Footer, click the Center section box, click the Page Number button, then click OK**
   Check your footer, then print the worksheet.
5. **In the Header/Footer tab, click OK, check to make sure both pages show page numbers, click Print, then click OK**
   Next, you save a custom view with the current display and print settings.
6. **Click View on the menu bar, click Custom Views, click Add, type Half N Half, then click OK**
7. **Save the workbook**

TABLE F-3: Page break options

type of page break	where to position cell pointer
Both horizontal and vertical page breaks	Select the cell below and to the right of the gridline where you want the breaks to occur
Only a horizontal page break	Select the cell in column A that is directly below the gridline where you want the page to break
Only a vertical page break	Select a cell in row 1 that is to the right of the gridline where you want the page to break

FIGURE F-15: Worksheet with horizontal page break

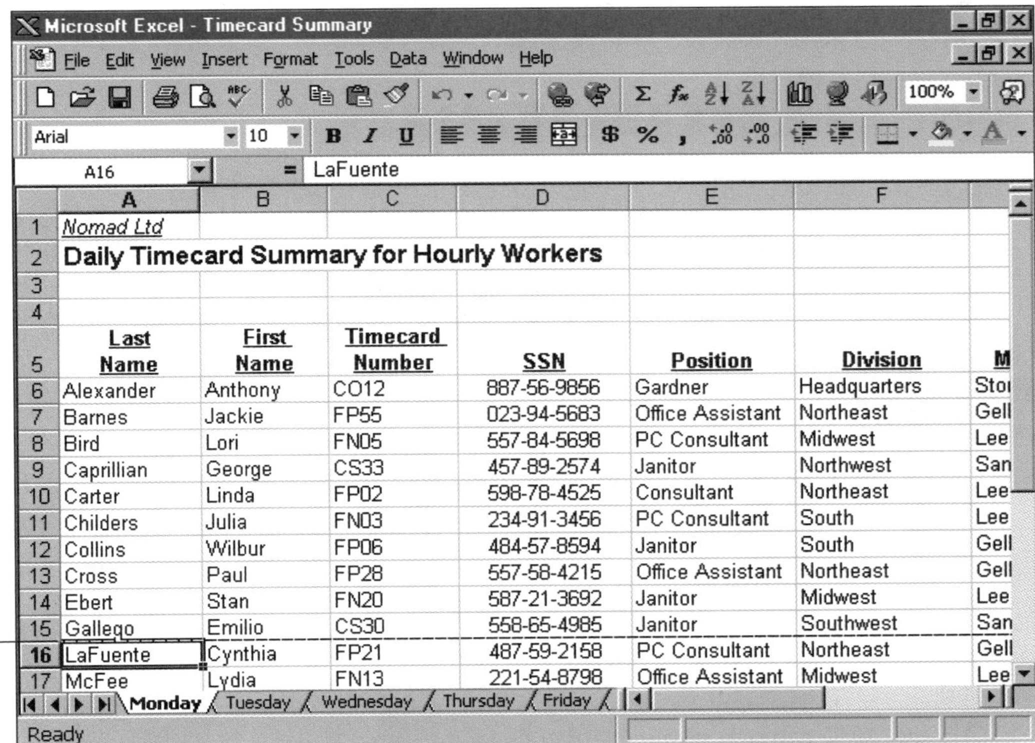

	A	B	C	D	E	F	
1	Nomad Ltd						
2	Daily Timecard Summary for Hourly Workers						
3							
4							
5	Last Name	First Name	Timecard Number	SSN	Position	Division	M
6	Alexander	Anthony	CO12	887-56-9856	Gardner	Headquarters	Sto
7	Barnes	Jackie	FP55	023-94-5683	Office Assistant	Northeast	Gell
8	Bird	Lori	FN05	557-84-5698	PC Consultant	Midwest	Lee
9	Caprillian	George	CS33	457-89-2574	Janitor	Northwest	San
10	Carter	Linda	FP02	598-78-4525	Consultant	Northeast	Lee
11	Childers	Julia	FN03	234-91-3456	PC Consultant	South	Lee
12	Collins	Wilbur	FP06	484-57-8594	Janitor	South	Gell
13	Cross	Paul	FP28	557-58-4215	Office Assistant	Northeast	Gell
14	Ebert	Stan	FN20	587-21-3692	Janitor	Midwest	Lee
15	Gallego	Emilio	CS30	558-65-4985	Janitor	Southwest	San
16	LaFuente	Cynthia	FP21	487-59-2158	PC Consultant	Northeast	Gell
17	McFee	Lydia	FN13	221-54-8798	Office Assistant	Midwest	Lee

Dashed line indicates horizontal break after row 15

CLUES TO USE

Using Page Break Preview

By clicking View on the menu bar, then clicking Page Break Preview, or clicking Page Break Preview in the Print Preview window, you can view and change page breaks manually. Simply drag the dashed page break lines to the desired location. See Figure F-16.

FIGURE F-16: Page Break Preview window

5	Last Name	First Name	Timecard Number	SSN	Position	Division	Manager	Pay Frequenc	Time In	Time Out	Time In	Time Out
6	Alexander	Anthony	CO12	887-56-9856	Gardner	Headquarters	Stone	Monthly			1:30 PM	3:30 F
7	Barnes	Jackie	FP55	023-94-5683	Office Assistant	Northeast	Geller	Monthly	9:00 AM	######	1:00 PM	5:00 F
8	Bird	Lori	FN05	557-84-5698	PC Consultant	Midwest	Lee	Bi-weekly	8:00 AM	######		
9	Caprillian	George	CS33	457-89-2574	Janitor	Northwest	Santos	Monthly	7:30 AM	######		
10	Carter	Linda	FP02	598-78-4525	Consultant	Northeast	Lee	Bi-weekly	9:00 AM	######	1:00 PM	2:30 F
11	Childers	Julia	FN03	234-91-3456	PC Consultant	South	Lee	Bi-weekly	######	######		
12	Collins	Wilbur	FP06	484-57-8594	Janitor	South	Geller	Monthly	######	######	2:00 PM	3:00 F
13	Cross	Paul	FP28	557-58-4215	Office Assistant	Northeast	Geller	Monthly			3:00 PM	8:00 F
14	Ebert	Stan	FN20	587-21-3692	Janitor	Midwest	Lee	Monthly	8:00 AM	######		
15	Galleqo	Emilio	CS30	558-65-4985	Janitor	Southwest	Santos	Bi-weekly			######	4:00 F
16	LaFuente	Cynthia	FP21	487-59-2158	PC Consultant	Northeast	Geller	Monthly	######	######		
17	McFee	Lydia	FN13	221-54-8798	Office Assistant	Midwest	Lee	Monthly	7:00 AM	######		
18	Nquyen	Lana	CS24	125-48-7569	Office Assistant	Northwest	Santos	Bi-weekly			######	5:45 F
19	Roberts	Jason	CO01	696-55-8742	Lawyer	Headquarters	Stone	Monthly			3:00 PM	7:00 F
20	Smith	Jim	CO34	345-98-3245	Janitor	Headquarters	Stone	Bi-weekly	3:00 PM	7:00 PM	7:30 PM	####1
21	Thorpe	James	CO25	556-23-7845	Courier	Headquarters	Stone	Monthly	6:00 AM	######		
22	Wells	Lucifer	CO99	332-62-5489	PC Consultant	Headquarters	Stone	Bi-weekly			2:00 PM	4:30 F
23	Wilks	Orson	FP41	221-57-8458	Janitor	Northeast	Geller	Monthly	8:00 AM	######	1:00 PM	5:30 F
24	Younq	Kara	FN14	584-58-5521	Office Assistant	South	Lee	Bi-weekly	8:30 AM	######		
25												
26												

Page 1

Page 2

Cell pointer in cell A16

Dashed page break line

Excel 97

Setting Margins and Alignment

You can set top, bottom, left, and right margins for a worksheet printout and determine the distance you want headers and footers to print from the edge of a page. Also, you can align data on a page by centering it horizontally and/or vertically between the margins. Evan has been asked to print selected information from the Timecard Summary. His manager wants an additional report showing last name, first name, timecard number, social security number, position, and division. First, Evan returns to the Generic custom view of the worksheet.

Steps

1. Click **View** on the menu bar, click **Custom Views**, click **Generic**, then click **Show**
   Excel's default print and display settings return. Notice the vertical dashed line indicating an automatic page break after column F. Now you indicate that you want to print only a selected range.

QuickTip

You can group multiple worksheets to print by selecting nonadjacent worksheets using [Ctrl] or by selecting adjacent worksheets using [Shift] before issuing the print command.

2. Select range **A1:F24**, click **File** on the menu bar, click **Print**, under Print what click **Selection**, then click **Preview**
   The Print Preview window displays only the selected cells. Next, center the data horizontally and start printing farther down the page.
3. From the Print Preview window, click **Setup**, click the **Margins tab**, double-click the **Top text box** to select the 1, then type **3**
   Notice that the top margin line darkens in the Preview section of the dialog box. The Preview section reflects your activity in the Margins tab. Next, change the header so it prints 1.5" from the top edge of the page.
4. Double-click the **Header text box**, then type **1.5**
   Finally, center the report horizontally on the page.
5. In the Center on page section, click the **Horizontally check box** to select it
   You have completed the changes in the Margins tab. See Figure F-17. Because all the data fits nicely on one page, you decide to set the footer to "none".
6. Click the **Header/Footer tab**, click the **Footer list arrow**, scroll to the top of the list, then click **(none)**
   Check the report to ensure that it begins farther down from the top of the page, is centered horizontally, and does not include a page number. Because the report is complete, preview and print the worksheet.

QuickTip

You can adjust page margins, header and footer margins, and column widths manually. When you click the Margins button in the Print Preview window, horizontal and vertical guides appear on the worksheet. Drag these margin guides to adjust the format of the sheet.

7. Click **OK** to preview the worksheet, then print the worksheet
   Compare your screen with Figure F-18. Because Evan will be switching between reports, he first prints this latest report, and then creates a custom view called Employee Info.
8. Click **View** on the menu bar, click **Custom Views**, click **Add**, type **Employee Info**, then click **OK**
9. Save the workbook

FIGURE F-17: **Margins tab with changed settings**

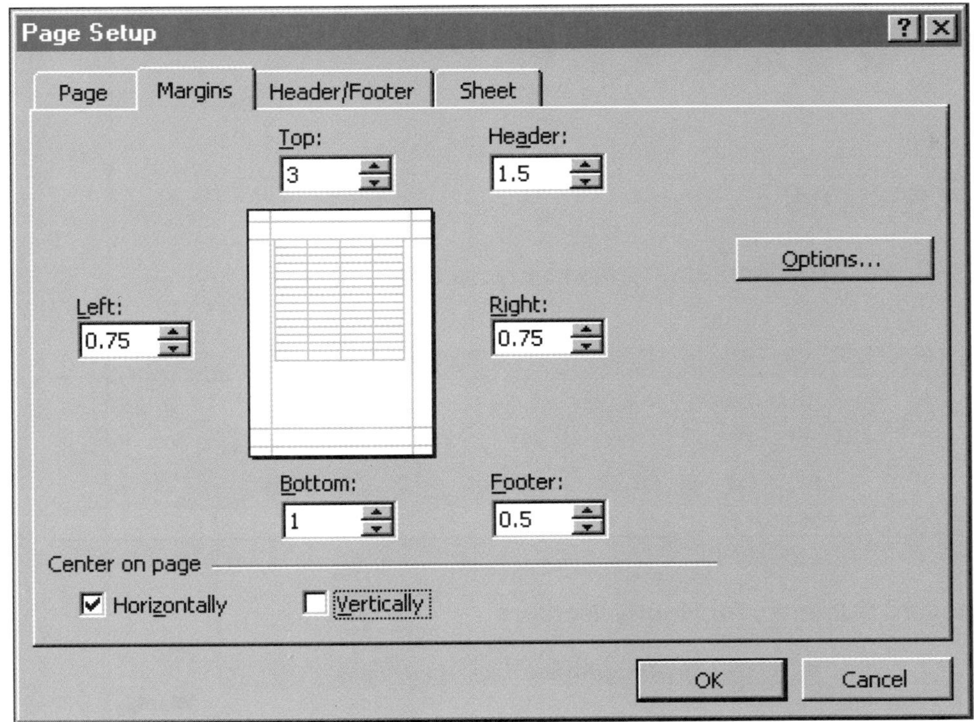

FIGURE F-18: **Print Preview window showing employee information**

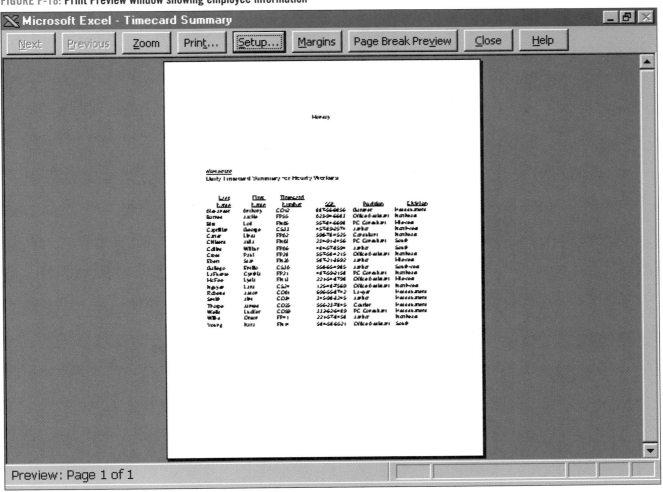

Microsoft Excel - Timecard Summary

Next | Previous | Zoom | Print... | Setup... | Margins | Page Break Preview | Close | Help

Preview: Page 1 of 1

Practice

▶ Concepts Review

Label each of the elements of the Excel screen shown in Figure F-19.

FIGURE F-19

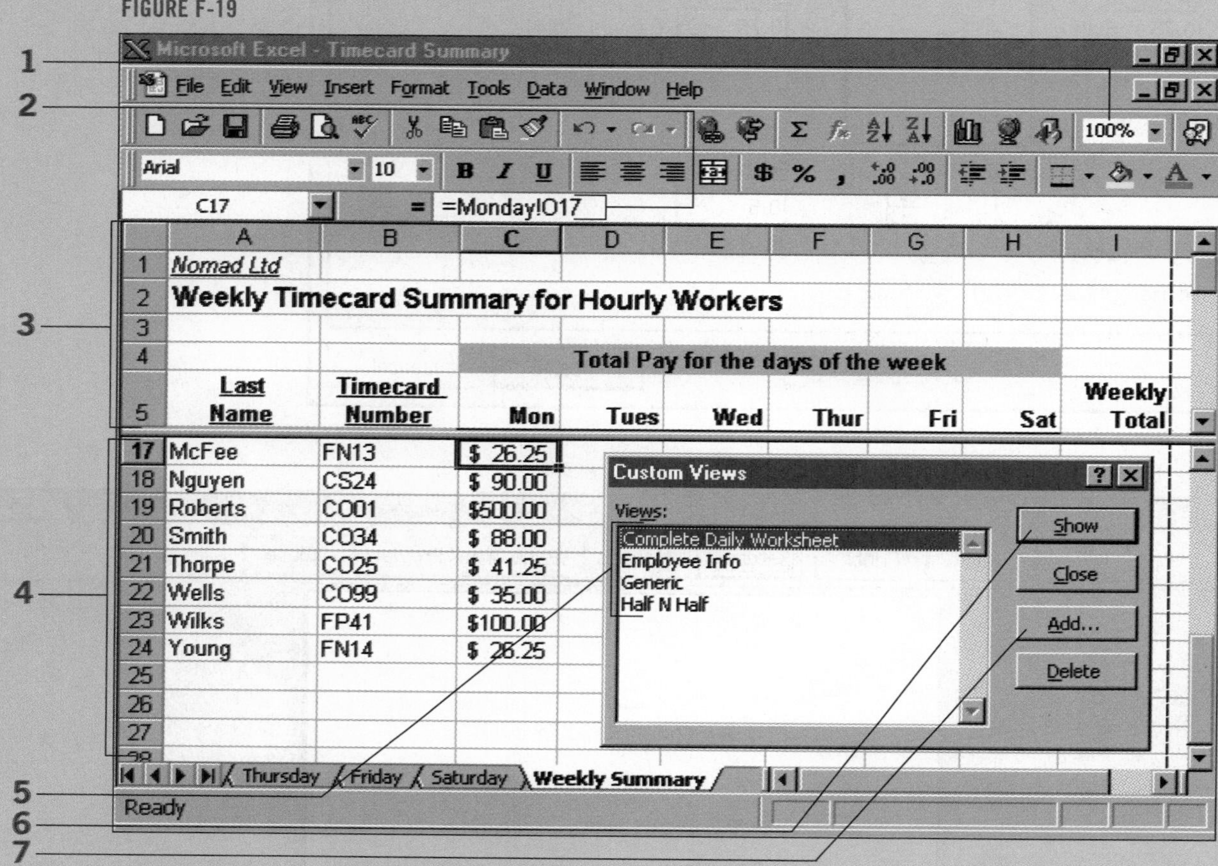

Match each of the terms with the statement that describes its function.

8. Inserts a code to print the total number of pages
9. Indicates how far down the page to start printing worksheet data
10. Indicates a page break
11. Inserts a code to print the sheet tab name in a header or footer
12. Indicates a selection to be printed

a. Dashed line
b. [icon]
c. Top margin
d. [icon]
e. Print what

Select the best answer from the list of choices.

13. You can save frequently used display and print settings by using the _________ feature.
   a. Report Manager **b.** View menu **c.** Custom Views **d.** Save command

14. You freeze areas of the worksheet to_________.
   a. Freeze data and unlock formulas.
   b. Lock open windows in place.
   c. Freeze all data in place so that you can see it.
   d. Lock column and row headings in place while you scroll through the worksheet.

15. To protect a worksheet, you must first unlock those cells that _________, and then issue the Protect Sheet command.
   a. never change
   b. the user will be allowed to change
   c. have hidden formulas
   d. are locked

► Skills Review

1. Freeze columns and rows.
   a. Open the workbook titled XL F-2, then save it as "Quarterly Household Budget".
   b. Freeze columns A through B and rows 1 through 4 for improved viewing. (*Hint:* Click cell C4 prior to issuing the Freeze Panes command.)
   c. Scroll until columns A through B and F through H are visible.
   d. Press [Ctrl][Home] to return to cell C4.
   e. Unfreeze the panes.

2. Insert and delete sheets.
   a. With the 1997 sheet active, use the sheet pop-up menu to insert a new Sheet1.
   b. Activate Sheet1.
   c. Delete Sheet1.

3. Reference worksheet data.
   a. In the 1997 sheet, click cell C22.
   b. Type =, click cell G7, then press [Enter].
   c. In cell C23, type =, click cell G18, then press [Enter].
   d. To link data between the two worksheets, first activate the 1998 worksheet.
   e. Click cell C4.
   f. Type =.
   g. Activate the 1997 worksheet.
   h. Click cell F4, then press [Enter].
   i. In the 1998 worksheet, copy the contents of cell C4 into cells C5:C6.
   j. Preview, then print the 1998 worksheet.
   k. Save the workbook.

4. Hide and protect worksheet areas.
- **a.** In the 1997 worksheet, select row 16.
- **b.** Issue the Hide Row command.
- **c.** To unlock the expense data so you can make changes, first select range C10:F17.
- **d.** Using the Protection tab of the Format Cells dialog box, turn off the locked status.
- **e.** Using the Tools, Protection menu options, protect the sheet.
- **f.** To make sure the other cells are locked, click cell D4.
- **g.** Type 3.
- **h.** Confirm the message box warning.
- **i.** To change the first-quarter mortgage expense to $3,400, click cell C10, then type 3400.
- **j.** Save the workbook.

5. Specify headers and footers.
- **a.** Activate the 1997 worksheet. Using the File, Page Setup menu options, customize the Center Section of the Header to read "Lowe Family".
- **b.** Further customize the header by changing it to appear in 12 pt bold type.
- **c.** Set the footer to (none).
- **d.** Preview, then print the 1997 worksheet.
- **e.** Save the workbook.

6. Save custom views of a worksheet.
- **a.** In the 1997 worksheet, select the range A1:H23.
- **b.** Using the Zoom box, set the magnification so that the entire selection appears on the screen.
- **c.** Using the View, Custom Views menu options, add a new view called "Entire Budget".
- **d.** Save the workbook.

7. Control page breaks and page numbering.
- **a.** Click cell A9.
- **b.** Using the Insert, Page Break menu options, insert a page break.
- **c.** Customize the footer to include a page number.
- **d.** Preview and print the worksheet.
- **e.** Save the workbook.

8. Set margins and alignment.
- **a.** Activate the Generic custom view.
- **b.** Select range A1:C20.
- **c.** Using the Print menu option, under Print what, click Selection.
- **d.** Preview the worksheet.
- **e.** From the Print Preview window, click Setup; using the Margins tab, change the left margin to 2", and center the worksheet vertically on the page.
- **f.** Preview, then print the worksheet.
- **g.** Save the workbook.

Independent Challenges

1. You own PC Assist, a software training company. You have added several new entries to the August check register and are ready to enter September's check activity. Because the sheet for August will include much of the same information you need for September, you decide to copy it. Then you will edit the new sheet to fit your needs for September check activity. You will use sheet referencing to enter the beginning balance and beginning check number. Using your own data, you will complete five checks for the September register.

To complete this independent challenge:

1. Open the workbook entitled XL F-3, then save it as "Update to Check Register".
2. Delete Sheet2 and Sheet3, then create a worksheet for September by copying the August sheet.
3. With the September sheet active, delete the data in range A6:E24.
4. To update the balance at the beginning of the month, use sheet referencing from the last balance entry in the August sheet.
5. Generate the first check number. (*Hint:* Use a formula that references the last check number in August and adds one.)
6. Enter data for five checks.
7. Add a footer that includes your name left-aligned on the printout and the system date right-aligned on the printout. Add a header that displays the sheet name centered on the printout.
8. Save the workbook. Preview the September worksheet, then print it in landscape orientation on a single page.
9. Submit your printout.

2. You are a new employee for a computer software manufacturer. Your responsibility is to track the sales of different product lines and determine which computer operating system generates the most software sales each month. Although sales figures vary from month to month, the format in which data is entered does not. Use Table F-4 as a guide to create a worksheet tracking sales across personal computer (PC) platforms. Use your own data for the number of software packages sold in the DOS, Windows, and Macintosh columns. Create a summary report with all the sales summary information, then create three detailed reports for each software category: Games Software, Business Software, and Utilities Products.

To complete this independent challenge:

1. Create a new workbook, then save it as "Software Sales Summary".
2. Enter row and column labels, your own data, and formulas for the totals.

TABLE F-4

	DOS	Windows	Macintosh	Total
Games Software				
Space Wars 99				
Safari				
Flight School				
Total				
Business Software				
Word Processing				
Spreadsheet				
Presentation				
Graphics				
Page Layout				
Total				
Utilities Products				
Antivirus				
File recovery				
Total				

3. Create a summary report that includes the entire worksheet. Customize the header to include your name and the date. Set the footer to (none). Center the page both horizontally and vertically. Save the workbook. Preview and print the report.
4. Create three detailed report pages. Insert page breaks so that each software category is printed on a separate page. Number the report pages consecutively as follows: Games Software, page 1; Business Software, page 2; Utilities Products, page 3. Include your name and the date in the header of each page and the page number in the footer of each page. Save the workbook. Preview and print the report.
5. Submit your printouts.

3. You are a college student with two roommates. Each month you receive your long-distance telephone bill. Because no one wants to figure out who owes what, you split the bill three ways. You are sure that one of your roommates makes two-thirds of the long-distance calls. In order to make the situation more equitable, you decide to create a spreadsheet to track the long-distance phone calls each month. By doing so, you hope to determine who is responsible for each call. Create a spreadsheet with a separate area for each roommate. Track the following information for each month's long-distance calls: date of call, time of call, (AM or PM), call minutes, location called, state called, area code, phone number, and call charge. Total the charges for each roommate. Print a summary report of all three roommates' charges, and print a report for each roommate totaling his or her charges for the month.

To complete this independent challenge:

1. Create a new workbook, then save it as "Monthly Long Distance" to the appropriate folder on your Student Disk.
2. Enter column headings and row labels to track each call.
3. Use your own data, entering at least three long-distance calls for each roommate.
4. Create a report that prints all the call information for the month. Use the filename as the header. Format the header to make it stand out from the rest of the text. Enter your name and the date in the footer.
5. Create a report page for each roommate. Insert appropriate page breaks to print out a report for each roommate. Use the roommate's name as the header, formatted in 14-point italic type. Enter your name and the date in the footer. Center the reports on the page both horizontally and vertically. Save the workbook.
6. Preview, print, then submit the reports.

4. The World Wide Web can be used as a research tool to locate information on just about every topic imaginable, including careers. You have decided to conduct a job search using the Web. Currently, you are taking classes on computer programming, specializing in the C++ language and the Internet tool called Java. You plan to perform a search for jobs requiring these skills tracking the following information: position title, company name, city and state where company is located, whether experience is required, and salary. Your goal is to locate and list in a worksheet at least five jobs requiring C++ knowledge, and, in a separate worksheet, at least five jobs requiring Java knowledge.

To complete this independent challenge:

1. Open the workbook titled XL F-4, then save it as "Job Research – PC Programming".
2. Log on to the Internet and use your Web browser to go to http://www.course.com. From there, click Student Online Companions, click the link for this textbook, then click the Excel link for Unit F.
3. Use any combination of the following sites to search for and compile your data: Online Career Center, America's Job Bank, or The Monster Board.
4. Fill in information on at least five positions in each of the two above-mentioned worksheets.
5. Name the two sheets based on their content and copy sheets where appropriate.
6. Using your own judgment, customize the header, footer, margins, and alignment of each sheet.
7. Save the workbook, print both worksheets, then submit your printouts.

▶ Visual Workshop

Create the worksheet shown in Figure F-20. Save the workbook as "Generations of PCs". Preview, print, then submit the worksheet.

FIGURE F-20

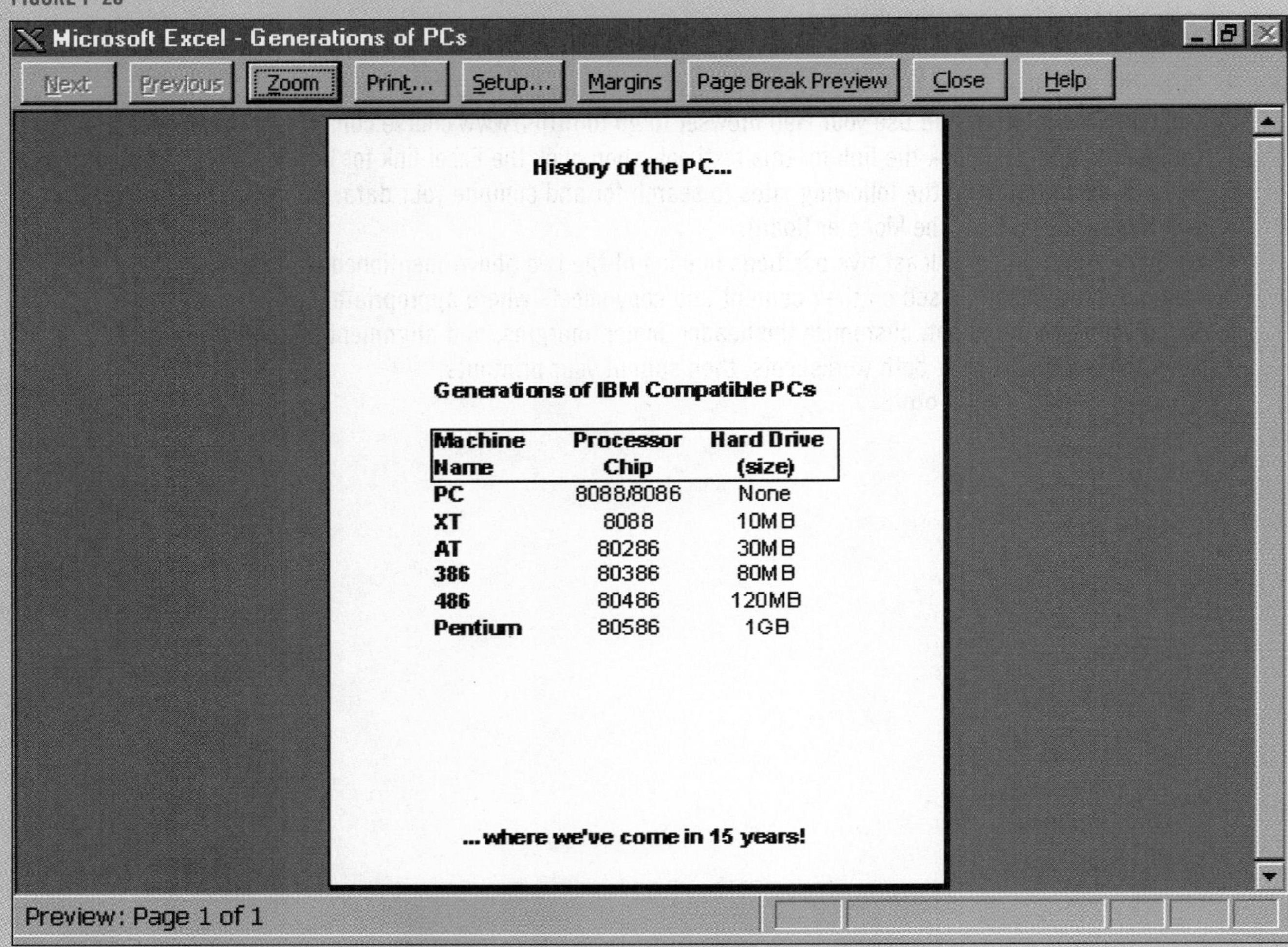

Excel 97

Glossary

Alignment The horizontal placement of cell contents; for example, left, center, or right.

Argument A value, range of cells, or text used in a macro or function. An argument is enclosed in parentheses; for example, =SUM(A1..B1).

Attribute A styling feature such as bold, italics, and underlining that can be applied to cell contents.

AutoFill A feature that automatically enters a list into a range of cells.

AutoSum A feature that automatically calculates worksheet totals accessed by a button on the Standard toolbar.

Border Edges of a selected area of a worksheet. Lines and color can be applied to borders.

Cell The intersection of a column and row.

Cell address Unique location identified by intersecting column and row coordinates.

Cell pointer A highlighted rectangle around a cell that indicates the active cell.

Cell reference The address or name of a specific cell; cell references can be used in formulas and are relative or absolute.

Check box A square box in a dialog box that can be clicked to turn an option on or off.

Clear A command on the Edit menu used to erase a cell's contents, formatting, or both.

Clipboard A temporary storage area for cut or copied items that are available for pasting.

Close A command that puts a file away but keeps Excel open so that you can continue to work on other workbooks.

Copy A command that copies the selected information and places it on the Clipboard.

Custom view A set of display and/or print settings that you can name and save, then access at a later time.

Cut A command that removes the contents from a selected area of a worksheet and places them on the Clipboard.

Data entry area The cells in a protected (locked) worksheet that must be unlocked because you need to change them.

Data label Descriptive text that appears above a data marker in a chart.

Data series The information, usually numbers or values, that Excel plots on a chart.

Dialog box A window that displays when you choose a command whose name is followed by an ellipsis (...). A dialog box allows you to make selections that determine how the command affects the selected area.

Edit A change made to the contents of a cell or worksheet.

External reference indicator An ! (exclamation point) within a formula indicating that the cell referenced is outside the active sheet.

Fill handle Small square in the lower-right corner of the active cell used to copy cell contents.

Font The typeface used to display information in cells.

Footer Information that appears at the bottom of each printed page; for example, the page number and the date.

Format The appearance of text and numbers, including color, font, attributes, and worksheet defaults. See also Number format.

Formula A set of instructions that you enter in a cell to perform numeric calculations (adding, multiplying, averaging, etc.); for example, =A1+B1.

Formula bar The area below the menu bar and above the Excel workspace where you enter and edit data in a worksheet cell. The formula bar becomes active when you start typing or editing cell data. The formula bar includes an Enter button and a Cancel button.

Freeze Lock-in specified columns and/or rows to assist in scrolling through large worksheets.

Function A special predefined formula that provides a shortcut for commonly used calculations; for example, AVERAGE. Also, in the Visual Basic for Applications programming language, a predefined procedure that returns a value.

Header Information that appears at the top of each printed page; for example the report name and the date.

Insertion point Blinking I-beam that appears in the formula bar during entry and editing.

Label Descriptive text or other information that identify the rows and columns of a worksheet. Labels are not included in calculations.

Landscape orientation Printing on a page whose dimensions are 11" (horizontally) by 8½" (vertically).

Launch To start a software program so you can use it.

Locked cells Cells that are protected so that their contents cannot be altered.

Menu A group of related commands located under a single word on the menu bar. For example, basic commands (New, Open, Save, Close, and Print) are grouped on the File menu.

Menu bar The area under the title bar on a window. The menu bar provides access to most of the application's commands.

Name A name assigned to a selected cell or range in a worksheet. See also Range name.

Name box The leftmost area in the formula bar that shows the cell reference or name of the active cell. For example, A1 refers to cell A1 of the active worksheet. You can also get a list of names in a workbook using the name list arrow.

Number format A format applied to values to express numeric concepts, such as currency, date, and percent.

Object Every element of a program, including a cell, a range, a worksheet, and a workbook.

Operators Perform mathematical functions.

Option button A circle in a dialog box that can be clicked when only one option can be chosen.

Order of precedence The order in which Excel calculates parts of a formula: (1) exponents, (2) multiplication and division, and (3) addition and subtraction.

Page Break Preview Allows you to view and change page breaks manually in the Print Preview window.

Pane A column or row that always remains visible.

Paste A command that moves information on the Clipboard to a new location. Excel pastes the formulas rather than the result, unless the Paste Special command is used.

Paste Special A command that enables you to paste formulas as values, styles, or cell contents.

Plot area The main area of a chart, containing the plotted and formatted chart data and chart axes.

Point A unit of measure used for fonts and row height. One inch equals 72 points.

Precedence The order in which Excel calculates parts of a formula: (1) exponents, (2) multiplication and division, and (3) addition and subtraction.

Print Preview window A window that displays a reduced view of area to be printed.

Protect An option that lets you prevent cells in a worksheet from being changed.

Range A selected group of adjacent cells.

Range format A format applied to a selected range in a worksheet.

Range name A name applied to a selected range in a worksheet.

Reference Populate cell data using existing cell content. You do this by typing = (equal sign) and then selecting the desired cell(s).

Relative cell reference Used to indicate a relative position in the worksheet. This allows you to copy and move formulas from one area to another of the same dimensions. Excel automatically changes the column and row numbers to reflect the new position.

Row height The vertical dimension of a cell.

Save A command used to save incremental changes to a workbook.

Save As A command used to create a duplicate of the current workbook.

Scroll bars Bars that display on the right and bottom borders of the worksheet window that give you access to information not currently visible in the current worksheet as well as others in the workbook.

Sheet A term used for worksheet.

Sheet tab A description at the bottom of each worksheet that identifies it in a workbook. In an open workbook, move to a worksheet by clicking its sheet tab. See also Tab.

Standard chart type A kind of Excel chart (available on the Standard Types tab of the first Chart Wizard dialog box) to which you need to add formatting and other options. Useful when you need to control exactly which elements appear in your chart.

Status bar The bar near the bottom of the screen that provides information about the tasks Excel is performing or about any current selections.

Tab A description at the bottom of each worksheet that identifies it in a workbook. In an open workbook, move to a worksheet by clicking its tab.

Toggle A button that can be clicked to turn an option on. Clicking again turns the option off.

Toolbar An area within the Excel screen that contains buttons that you can click to perform frequently used Excel tasks.

Values Numbers, formulas, or functions used in calculations.

View A set of display and/or print settings that you can name and save, then access at a later time. See also Custom view.

Window A framed area of a screen. Each worksheet occupies a window.

Wizard A series of dialog boxes that lists and describes all Excel functions and assists the user in function creation.

Workbook A collection of related worksheets contained within a single file.

Worksheet An electronic spreadsheet containing 256 columns by 65,536 rows.

x-axis The horizontal axis in a two- or three-dimensional chart on which categories are plotted.

y-axis The vertical axis in a two- or three-dimensional chart on which values are plotted.

Zoom Enables you to focus on a larger or smaller part of the worksheet in print preview.

Zoom box Option on the Standard toolbar that allows you to change the screen magnification percentage.

Index

Index

Index